Hilarious High Jinks
&
DANGEROUS ASSIGNMENTS

Lee E. Echols, Yuma County Sheriff, 1961.

Hilarious High Jinks
& DANGEROUS ASSIGNMENTS

By Lee E. Echols

A Publication of
The National Rifle Association
of America

BOOK SERVICE

Copyright © 1990 by the National Rifle Association of America

All rights reserved including the right to reproduce
this book or portions thereof. Published 1990.
For information, address the National Rifle Association,
1600 Rhode Island Avenue, N.W., Washington, D.C. 20036

ISBN 0-935998-60-8
Library of Congress Catalog Number 90-082503
Printed in the United States

Jacket Cover Design and Art by Harry L. Jaecks

Published by the
National Rifle Association of America
1600 Rhode Island Avenue, N.W.
Washington, D.C. 20036

George Martin, Executive Director, NRA Publications
Frank A. Engelhardt, Book Service Manager
Lourdes Fleckenstein, Assistant Manager, Book Service
Michael A. Fay, Manufacturing Director
Harry L. Jaecks, Art Director

To my wife, Helen, who has gone through hell and medium-high water with me for over 61 years and who, through it all, has retained her laughter and tolerance for my inofficious and egregious escapades.

CONTENTS

	Foreword	ix
	Acknowledgements	xi
I	The Old Treasury Pistol Team	1
II	Top Investigator Guilfoyle	9
III	Two Stone-Deaf Investigators	19
IV	The Case Of The Newman Brothers	25
V	The Great Ketchup Deception	29
VI	The Future Mrs. Echols	35
VII	A Slick Humbug Artist	39
VIII	The 62 Pound Bar Of Gold And Silver	47
IX	The Mafia, Narcotics And The Border	53
X	A Good Opium Bust	69
XI	More Pistol Tournaments	79
XII	Naval Indoctrination School	85
XIII	Guns Of The Navy And Graduation	93
XIV	Mare Island Police Department	99
XV	Almost Off To War	107
XVI	The Korean Espionage Operation	115
XVII	The Korean Project Rolls On...And Abruptly Ends	121
XVIII	Humbugable "Howlin' Mad" Smith	129
XIX	From Naval Intelligence To The NRA	137
XX	Salvos In Guatemala	145
XXI	Back With Customs	155
XXII	Bolivia, The First Latin American Assignment	165
XXIII	We Lose Our Donna And Gain A New Daughter	173
XXIV	The World's Biggest Snake	175

CONTENTS

XXV	Nixon Comes Calling In Bolivia	183
XXVI	The Pan American Games	189
XXVII	Echols For Sheriff	195
XXVIII	Crime and Politics In Yuma	207
XXIX	Santo Domingo And The Big Revolution	217
XXX	Help From The 82nd Airborne And The U.S. Marines	231
XXXI	Win, Lose Or Draw	241
XXXII	A Mighty Rough Assignment In Uruguay	245
XXXIII	The Deadly Tupamaro Terrorists	249
XXXIV	Retirement? Hardly!	259

FOREWORD

If I were assigned to go into any of the world's politically dangerous places — places beset and bedevilled with terrorists, Communists and assorted evil people — and my assignment included doing a good job on them while having a hilariously good time at it, I'd want to go side by side with Lee Echols. We always called him "Leffus." Don't ask me why. I don't know, but I suggest that's just the name, somewhere away back, a couple of bourbons, or more, inspired.

This book tells the story of events not often found, even in a life dedicated to law enforcement, and never found in the life of the pedestrian multitudes who do a good job but who never really enjoy it. Exciting, yes, to those who are excitable. Sad, yes, to those given to reflections on the past. But interesting to everyone with any sense of enjoyment in waving one's job in one hand, his life in the other and going for broke.

It is a story told, in hearty good humor, of a man, Echols, whose qualifications for the life he lived were bold, robust and numerous. In an environment where life itself often depended on a man's personal arms, Echols was superior to them all. He was the holder of four world pistol shooting records and, in 1941, was the winner of the magnificent Custer Trophy awarded in the National Pistol Matches at Camp Perry, Ohio, for the U.S. Individual National Championship with the military .45 automatic. Furthermore, he led the famous U.S. Treasury Department Pistol Team during years in which it won all the team matches at the U.S. National Championships.

It is the kind of story that might have been written by the reckless, the buccaneers and the smugglers of all ages, but Echols and his small band of *compadres* were their superiors at their own game and, moreover, were on the side of the law — as the greatest of such men have almost always been.

Tough as hell would have them, but real. And happy. No psychological hang-ups. No distorted personalities seen so often on television today. They enjoyed the fight and between assignments were happy family men and sportsmen. They were the kind of men who built the kind of civilization lesser breeds enjoy today in this country.

Harlon B. Carter

ACKNOWLEDGEMENTS

Chapter Five: The Great Ketchup Deception. Excerpt from the author's earlier book, *Dead Aim*.

Chapter Eighteen: Humbugable "Howlin' Mad" Smith. Reprinted by permission of *Leatherneck* magazine.

Chapter Twenty-Nine: Santo Domingo And The Big Revolution. Reprinted by permission of *Eagle* magazine.

Chapter Thirty: Help From The 82nd Airborne And The U.S. Marines. Reprinted by permission of *Eagle* magazine.

Chapter Thirty-Two: A Mighty Rough Assignment In Uruguay. Reprinted by permission of *Eagle* magazine.

Chapter Thirty-Three: The Deadly Tupamaro Terrorists. Reprinted by permission of *Eagle* magazine.

CHAPTER ONE

THE OLD TREASURY PISTOL TEAM

The date was September 7, 1941, and the place was the pistol range of the National Matches at Camp Perry, Ohio. More than 300 of the top pistol shooters in the United States were preparing to contest one another for the famous U.S. National Pistol Championship called "The Custer Trophy Match." It was put on by the U.S. Army and the shooters were limited to Colt semi-automatic pistols in "as is" condition. That is, fixed sights, issue grips and no fancy gunsmithing on the interior. Regular hard-ball Army issue .45 caliber ammunition was to be fired and, compared to the reloads the top shooters were using in those days, when one of them went off, it raised the shooter about three inches off the ground and sounded like one of General John Hood's field pieces going off at the Battle of Atlanta.

I was standing on the line with 99 other shooters in the first relay and the autumn weather had cooled things off to where I had taken on about three big dollops of Stumphole whiskey to sort of amortize the bone-chilling conditions coming right off Lake Erie, which was less than a mile away.

Just as we were to begin the 10-shot, slow-fire at 50 yards, Colonel Endicott, who was running the match, announced over the loudspeaker that he had been called to Washington for a conference. He was to leave immediately and he wished to congratulate the winner prior to the firing.

With a little help from the Stumphole whiskey, which I had consumed along with my inherent proclivity for being a smart aleck, I yelled, "Thanks a lot, Colonel!" waving my arm at him.

This brought quite a bit of laughter along the firing line, usually conducive to good scores, and the match opened.

I fired a miserable 89 slow-fire, which at least made me believe that I didn't have a chance of winning the match. The pressure left me like the swallows leaving Capistrano in late summer. The time and rapid-fire was shot at 25 yards and I fired a fairly good timed fire score of 96. However, still figuring I didn't have a chance of winning the match, I felt very little pressure with my rapid-fire, in which five shots are fired twice in 10 seconds each. I was completely amazed when my score showed up as a 98 and I won the National Individual Pistol Championship by one point over my Treasury Department teammate, Arnvid Anderson, who shot a score of 283. This was the second best score ever fired over the course at that time.

Our Treasury Department Team was formed in 1938 with the Coast Guard overseeing the tryouts throughout the United States. All the top shooters in the eight gun-carrying agencies of the Treasury Department were called to Washington for a couple of weeks to determine who would form the first and second teams. All this was done under the Secretary of the Treasury, Henry Morgenthau. Our first team wound up with four Customs men and one Alcohol and Tobacco tax agent. The Customs shooters were Arnvid Anderson from Warroad, Minnesota, Pete Chapman from Seattle, Mel Rogers, a New Mexican transplanted to the Canadian border and myself. The Alcohol tax agent was Arnold Meloche from Phoenix, Arizona.

We fired all over the Western Hemisphere against the best shooters of that era and, when World War II came along and we disbanded, we held every world team record and most of us held several individual world records.

In those days, before the advent of the advanced marksmanship programs set up after World War II, we could usually beat any of the service teams. Our two most formidable opponents were the Detroit Police Team, headed by Harry Reeves, and the Los Angeles Police Team, whose best shooter in those days was Emmett Jones.

Occasionally a Marine team was put together that made us wish we'd taken up golf, but this didn't happen too often.

Our forays would usually start in early March when most of the hard-hitters would converge on Coral Gables, Florida, for the Flamingo Open. This four-day match was ramrodded by an efficient, highly congenial lawyer named Clem Theed and the fun times would commence a day or two prior to the tournament. I don't believe there was ever a group of contestants in any sport who had more fun than the pistol shooters prior to World War II, and the Treasury Department Team fell in right away with this style of living.

When we gathered for the Flamingo Open in 1938, our team arrived a couple of days before the matches began and I had all of them but Mel Rogers up in my room for a gab fest and a few random drinks of George Dickel whiskey. Pet Chapman was the last to arrive and I asked him about Mel Rogers.

"I met him downstairs in the lobby a few minutes ago," Chapman said. "He met a woman shooter from New Jersey and told her of his new bull-barreled High Standard .22 pistol. She indicated an interest in seeing it and he took her up to his room to show it to her."

This was all the information I needed. I put a handkerchief over the mouthpiece of my phone to change the sound of my voice and called Mel's room. When he answered, I let him have the full treatment.

"This is the assistant manager of the hotel," I boomed. "Do you have a woman up there in your room?"

"Why...yes...I do," he replied, with a surprised tone in his voice.

"Well, get her right out of there!" I shouted at him. "I'll give

3

you five minutes to have her out of that room or I'll have the house detective up there to arrest you both!"

"Now, you look here!" Mel expostulated. "We're not doing anything up here! I'm showing her my gun!"

"Well," I told him, "you just put it right back in your britches, zipper it up, and get her out of there!"

"Why, damn it!" Mel squalled. "I've never been in a hotel before with such narrow-minded employees! I'll get her out, all right! And I'll come with her. I'll pack my suitcase and come down and check out and move into the hotel across the street where I don't think I'll be insulted like this!"

"All right," I told him, "you just do that. We can get along fine in this hotel without a nasty playboy like you taking charge of things. And by the way," I went on, "on your way downstairs, stop off at room 357 and have a drink with Lee Echols and the rest of the Treasury Team."

The bellowing, bawling roar which came over the telephone filled my room and even started the window curtains billowing. Mel and the very modest little lady from New Jersey lost no time joining us.

Our Treasury Team formed such a bond of friendship that everywhere we went our hilarious good times seemed to permeate the air and affect the people around us. We had a ukulele player and a harmonica player (me) and all of us were singers, though almost always in different keys at once. And after firing some of the damnedest scores ever fired at that time, we'd go out at night to the barbecues and dances and have fun in every direction.

From Coral Gables we crossed the Tamiami Trail to Tampa where the renowned "Smitty" Brown was putting on the Midwinter International Pistol Tournament.

Smitty got hold of a big gibbon ape, or an orangutan, or some such anthropoid monstrosity and he taught him to hold a pistol and fire at a target. Smitty would fill the revolver with blanks and the monkey was so scared that he would empty it in about a second and a half. He'd throw the gun at the targets, run back off the firing line and climb a tall palm tree, where it took Smitty two or three hours to coax him down.

In the summertime, we'd shoot in San Diego and Los Angeles, then Chicago and on to Cincinnati to the Indian Hill Rangers Matches. From there we'd go to Detroit for the pre-Perry matches and then on to Camp Perry for the National Matches in August.

I was living in Puerto Rico when the Treasury Team was first formed. In 1936, I was Officer-in-Charge of a fifteen man Customs Patrol Unit in Calexico, California, where my father was Chief of Police. About that time an old buddy of mine, Aaron Quick, with whom I had worked for several years, wheedled me into coming down to San Juan as his assistant and help him form a 60-man patrol unit. By 1938, however, I had managed to get an appointment as a Customs special agent in New York City. This was an extremely difficult operation to put over. At that time there were only 150 of these agents in the world and it was probably the choice Government service. About 50 of them were working in the New York area. I managed to spend about half my time investigating narcotics smuggling cases and the other half traveling and shooting with the Treasury Pistol Team. It was a mighty fine way of spending part of my youth!

In the fall of 1938, I was sent to Savannah, Georgia, for a big pistol tournament. We didn't have our first team, but we had several mighty good shooters from the East Coast and as far west as El Paso, so we did a fair job in the team matches.

Meantime, I had been reading in the ammunition ads of the AMERICAN RIFLEMAN magazine about an Air Force shooter named Charlie Densford. He had been making some helatious scores around the country and when he flew to Savannah in a fighter plane, I hastened to get acquainted with him. He was a captain at that time and we seemed to hit it off together quite well right from the start. The captain of the Savannah Vice Squad invited us to accompany his boys on their

HILARIOUS HIGH JINKS

rounds of the town so we could actually see how the old southern city operated.

We found it to be a city of tranquility and lush magnolia scents. There is an old saying that Savannah is like a mint julep. It should be sampled at a leisurely pace. However, on the night Charlie Densford and I covered Savannah with the vice squad, there was nothing leisurely about it.

To quote George Goebel, "A man going through such a historical old bar as the Pirate's House might get 'over-served'," and we certainly did! We didn't get back to our hotel until very late or very early, depending on which way you looked at it.

When we were getting into our clothes for the match in the morning, Charlie said, "Have you ever read what William Makepiece Thackeray wrote about this town in 1855 after a holiday here? He said, 'No tearing, northern bustle, no ceaseless hotel racket, no crowds.' Well, he must not have visited the part of Savannah we did!"

The first match was the center-fire, slow-fire match, 20 shots at 50 yards, and both of us were as steady as though shooting from a machine rest. The great Detroit shooter, Harry Reeves, won it with a mighty high score. Charlie was second, right on his tail, and I was third, one point behind Densford.

Then the timed-fire match came up with center-fire guns. This was another 20-shot match, shooting in strings of five shots each at 25 yards in 20 seconds. On my first three strings I went clean and finally dropped one nine in my last string for a total of 199, breaking the world record set a couple of years earlier by Charlie Askins.

Next came the rapid-fire match, four strings of five shots each, also at 25 yards, in 10 seconds each. Densford took a big breath just before the match began.

"I'm getting better all the time," he said. "Maybe that all-night deal with the vice squad is the answer!"

He got up on the line and broke the world record with a score of 198.

We went from there to a big match in Tampa, Florida. "Let's try it again," Charlie said, and we went to a little Cuban town just outside of Tampa and spent most of the night carousing with the natives. As we both spoke Spanish, we had a wonderful time. We got back in time to get ready for the onslaught, and it almost turned out to be one. Both of us fired such terrible scores that it almost made us hang up our pistols in disgrace. I could hardly hold my own on the pistol range, let alone keep sight of the little black and white target, and Charlie Densford told me that his arm was wilder than a March hare. We gave up on the night-before-carousing after that. It only worked one time.

Charlie and I got together every once in awhile in later years. He retired as a Colonel and had a ranch near Pipe Creek, Texas. We reminisced on our meeting in Savannah and the unbelievable scores we fired the next day after an all-night imbroglio. Charlie died in 1986 and is buried at West Point.

CHAPTER TWO

TOP INVESTIGATOR GUILFOYLE

Most of the U.S. Customs investigators in New York in 1938 were assigned to the job of ferreting out the big traffickers in narcotics. I had worked practically nothing else on the Mexican border after the repeal of Prohibition, so they assigned me to that group. Others worked undervaluation, drawback, personnel investigations and false invoicing. One man worked nothing but the smuggling of all things other than narcotics. The entire bunch were the saltiest, finest Irishmen, Italians, Poles and Jews I had ever worked with or known. Chief of the Narcotics Investigative group was a big Irishman named George Collins and, besides being an excellent administrator and investigator, he was a trickster of the deepest dye.

His assistant was another Irishman, a little, baldheaded guy named Danny Guilfoyle. Danny was a top investigator and although he could dictate a syllabus report to the U.S. Attorney in faultless English, his spoken word was right out of the Red Hook section of Brooklyn. He would come up with such dandies as, "Dat boid's as crooked as Poil Street! Slap a subpoena on him. We'll t'row him in da damn can!"

I had only been in New York a couple of weeks when Danny accosted me. "Up here in N'Yawk," he said, looking as profound as a tree frog full of mango worms, "we got a black list of all the known international narcotics traffickers. We give 'dis list to the State Department and whenever one of 'em goes overseas, 'dey tell us bout it.

"Now, here's a couple of brisk lads goin' to Cherbourg dis mornin' on de *Berengaria*."

He handed me a piece of paper on which was written "Guglielmo Marselisi" and "Joseph Gagliano."

"Dey're two of Luciano's top boys and dey've gotta be goin' to Europe for heroin. Now you git down dere to Pier 90, yuh damn Oklahoma alfalfa eater, and see what yez can loin about dese boids."

I felt that Danny was beginning to like me after hearing these descriptive words of scorn from him and I got to Pier 90 as quickly as possible.

I learned from the purser of the *Berengaria* that our boys were on board, all right. I also learned from him that they'd given him $100,000 to keep in the ship's safe until they reached Cherbourg. And finally, they were having a champagne party on deck with some of their cohorts who had come to see them off.

I identified myself to their room steward and, for a five dollar bill, he let me into their room. I found three steamer trunks and a couple of suitcases and, remembering that in many large narcotics transactions baggage changes hands several times before the actual smuggler brings it into the United States, I scratched my initials on a brass corner of each of the steamer trunks with my pocket knife.

I then grabbed a cab and went back to the office at the corner of Church and Vesey Streets, downtown.

Danny was waiting for me. "Wot's dem damn boids up to?" he wanted to know.

I told him about the $100,000 in the safe and also that I had put my initials on all three of the steamer trunks.

"Good boy!" he said. "We'll shoot a cable to our Paris office and dey'll put somebody right in dese boids' hip pockets when dey arrive."

About two weeks later we received a cable from Paris. It stated that surveillance had been put on Marselisi and Gagliano and that they had been tailed to Istanbul, probably the prime illegal drug center in the world at that time.

The cable went on to say that they undoubtedly made a purchase of heroin and had consorted with two known big-time traffickers. They returned to Paris where they had associated themselves with several questionable looking characters, the only one positively identified was one Frank Caruso. The cable ended by saying our suspects left France that day on the *Normandie* and would arrive four days later in New York.

Danny had the reception committee there when they arrived. They were searched from their skin out and their baggage gone over completely. They were clean, but one of their steamer trunks was missing.

The only thing Danny could do then was put Frank Caruso's name on the hot-sheet. About two weeks later, an agent named Jerry Lundy and I were sent out on the quarantine boat to meet a Greek passenger ship. The wife of a small-time gangster whom Jerry thought might be bringing in an illegal load of narcotics was on board. As it turned out, she was clean but about four names below hers on the passenger list we saw the name "Frank Caruso."

"It's a common Italian name, Lee," Jerry said. "It might not be the one we're looking for, but we'll give him a look-see."

When the ship docked, I called Danny Guilfoyle to tell him what we had learned.

"Good boys!" Danny said. "I'll be right up!"

In those days, when the big ships docked in New York, all the baggage would be brought out on the pier by stevedores. The pier would be alphabetically marked off and the baggage would be placed under the initial of the passenger's last name. Jerry and I sauntered over to where the "C" baggage was being assembled and found Frank Caruso had two steamer trunks and a suitcase ready to be opened and inspected. We found that one of the steamer trunks had my initials on it, which I had carved about a month before in the state room. We told the Customs inspector and asked him to give the trunk a particularly close search.

Frank Caruso arrived to open his baggage. He was sneaky looking. He had on the customary wide-shouldered suit, a fuzzy snap-brimmed hat pulled down over his left eye, and he wore a pair of ochre-colored alligator shoes. The inspector had him open the steamer trunk. It was the kind which stands on end, with drawers on one side and space to hang clothes on the other. The inspector had him take all the clothing out of the right side and then all the drawers out of the left side. This revealed nothing illegal and I was about to decide we had a water haul. However, the inspector took a ruler and measured the outside depth of both sides of the trunk, then the inside. The inside measurements were about an inch and a half less than the outside measurements. The trunk lining, however, looked old and worn and was watermarked. There were no signs of tampering.

About this time I saw Danny Guilfoyle coming down the pier. The inspector took out his knife and pushed it through the lining of the trunk to a depth of about a half inch. Then he pulled it downward, making a three-inch slit in the lining. When he did this, heroin spewed out on the pier and Danny Guilfoyle looked at Caruso.

"Frank Caruso," he said quietly, "yer a hairy bastahd! Ain't yuh a hairy bastahd, yuh?"

The compartment on each side of the trunk held a total of 32 pounds of refined, uncut heroin. It was in cellophane bags and had been covered and pressed down with a thin piece of plywood prior to putting on the new lining. Then the lining had been "aged" by pouring coffee over it.

Our Paris agents were able to link Caruso with Marselisi and Gagliano. My initials had been etched on the trunk when it was on the *Berengaria* and in the possession of those two worthies. With our combined testimonies and the available evidence, we were able to convict them, along with Frank Caruso.

Danny was a top investigator and, at the same time, he was the butt of many of the practical jokes around the office. He got so spooky about this that he put a strong Yale lock on his locker to keep the office whimsy boys out of his things.

He was a dresser, all right. In the winter, he would wear a velvet-collared Chesterfield overcoat, either a derby hat or a Homburg, fawn-colored gloves and spats, a suit of the latest cut, black blucher shoes and, invariably, a cane.

When he arrived at work he would go immediately to his locker and take off his gloves, overcoat, hat and spats. Then he would put these items, along with his cane, in his locker and secure the door with the Yale lock. After these ceremonies, he would sit down at his desk and get busy with the myriad of cases he had in his basket.

George Collins, our boss and a prankster of the first order, told of a plan he had to drive Guilfoyle crazy. He had noticed that occasionally Danny would not put his keys back in his pocket when seated at his desk after his morning locker ritual, but would instead lay them on top of his desk as long as he was sitting there and could watch them.

George's plan was for me to buy a package of chewing gum, chew it up and get it rubbery and ready. George would then call Danny to his desk to discuss a case with him. As my desk adjoined Danny's, I would reach over, pick up Danny's keys and make an impression of both sides of the locker key with the big wad of chewing gum.

About three days later, Danny left his keys on his desk. As planned, I chewed all five sticks of gum, while George called him away from his desk. I was able to get the impressions and place the keys back on Danny's desk before George was finished talking to him. A few minutes later I put on my overcoat and hat, went out to the elevator and down to Vesey Street to a locksmith about a block away. I presented the big wad of chewing gum to him and he was able to duplicate

HILARIOUS HIGH JINKS

Danny's key, which I immediately turned over to George.

"Now, here's the way we'll do it, boys," George Collins said after Danny had gone home that evening. "We'll start off real easy. The first day, we'll get one of his gloves out of his locker and lay it on his desk. He'll see that, and wonder if he inadvertently forgot to lock it up. He'll put it back in the locker and then he'll get to thinking about it and decide some of us did it, so he'll start looking for a repeat. We won't touch a damn thing for about a week. Then we'll get his cane out and hang it on the edge of his desk. We'll leave him alone this time for about two weeks and then we'll get his hat out and leave it on his desk."

A few mornings later, Danny came in and went through his rigamarole of meticulously putting his things in his locker and fastening the Yale lock. He was then called into the office of John Roberts, the Supervising Agent, where he remained for 10 to 15 minutes. Plenty of time for George to get into his locker, purloin a glove and lay it on his desk.

When Danny returned, he was deep in thought. We finally saw him casually glance down at his desk and his gimlet eyes focused on his fawn-colored glove lying right in the middle of the desk. He gave a slight paroxysm of his shoulders like a man who was getting an immunization shot from a mean nurse with a dull needle.

He looked away for about a minute and then focused on the glove again, this time for about 30 seconds, without changing his expression. Then he looked up quickly and his eyes covered the room in an endeavor to catch one of us looking at him. George had drilled us well about this possibility, so all of us were busy with our morning chores. He looked at his glove again and then picked it up, examining it closely, apparently to either make sure it was his or to see if it could have crawled out of his locker and made it to the top of his desk on its own accord. Then he slowly shook his head, got up and returned the glove to his locker, and firmly closed the Yale lock.

The following morning Danny deliberately went in to see

the supervising agent after his morning ritual, only to come tearing out in a few minutes and rushing to his cluttered desk, but of course, none of his wearing apparel was there. He did this again the next morning. By the third day he sat for long periods of time with his chin cupped in his hand, trying to figure out whether he had inadvertently left his glove out or if some of us had, by some means of legerdemain, got it out of his locker.

By the end of the week, although he never said anything, he felt sure he had forgotten to put it away, as he would come in whistling some Irish tune and go about his work lightheartedly.

On the eighth day, while Danny was in the men's room, George removed his cane from the locker and hung it on the edge of his desk. Danny came in, sat down, and prepared to go over the morning syllabus reports prior to forwarding them to the U.S. Attorney for prosecutions. He didn't see the cane for about a half hour until he pushed some papers over to that side of his desk, causing the cane to clatter to the floor.

When he reached down to pick it up, I thought he was actually going to scream. This time he looked at all of us like a hunted animal. He jumped up, hurried to his locker, opened it and replaced his can on a hook inside. He returned to his desk and went into his act of deep concentration, going over every second of the morning, trying to determine if it was humanly possible for him to have left his cane hanging on the edge of his desk.

He never said a word to us in an attempt to ferret out the culprit, if there was a culprit, or if not, wondering what was happening to his mind.

George didn't pull the ruse again for three weeks, and then he left one of the fawn-colored spats on Danny's desk.

When Danny saw this he jumped from his desk. His legs were so shaky he turned his chair over and made his way into Roberts' office holding on to things as he went along.

George Collins had told Roberts what we were doing to

HILARIOUS HIGH JINKS

Danny. Roberts was expecting him and later recounted their conversation.

"I wanna week off," Danny said.

"What's the matter, Danny, too much work lately?"

"No, John, it ain't dat. I t'ink I'm losin' me damn mind! T'ings are happenin' to me dat I...I can't quite believe. I wanna go up the country and sit under a tree and try to get t'ings straightened out."

Collins stopped laying things on his desk after that, but never did tell him anything about it, much less that we had a copy of his locker key. In about a month Danny had bought himself a beautiful green velour Homburg hat. He had paid $30 for it, which, during the Great Depression, was a mighty high price for a hat.

George Collins then got us together at Began's Bar after work one evening. "We'll really fix him this time," George promised. "We'll put up a dollar apiece and go to the same store and buy another hat. Danny wears a size six and seven eighths and we're going to buy a hat size seven and five eighths and switch them on him."

We each paid our dollar and I went to see the man who sold Danny the hat. I explained our plan and asked him to run Danny out of the store if he came back trying to trade hats.

"That'll be easy," said the clerk. "Danny had his initials stamped in gold on the sweatband. I'll put them in this big one, too, and when Danny comes charging back here, I'll remind him of the initials and tell him my boss would fire me if I took it back."

I surreptitiously took the big hat to the office and slipped it to George. The next day George had no problem switching hats and, when Danny put on "our" hat to wear out to lunch, it slipped down over his ears and almost settled on his shoulders, just above his Adam's apple. The wily George Collins had even dampened the hat earlier as it was dripping rain outside.

Danny jerked it off, suspecting a trick. He felt the hat's

dampness and then furiously looked inside for his initials. He found them, all right, and then he started roundly cussing the man who sold it to him.

"Probably got wet and stretched," George told him, laconically.

"Holy mackerel, Collins! Dis is a $30 hat! Rain shouldn't effect de damn t'ing!"

Special Agent Eddie Cleveland offered to accompany Danny to the store and help him return the hat or get his money back, since this one had obviously stretched completely out of shape.

When they arrived the clerk was solicitous and sympathetic to Danny's plight, but would have none of this giving him his money back or trading it for a smaller hat.

"If those initials weren't in there, Danny, I could get away with a switch, but my boss would fire me from here to Greenpoint if I took it back.

"Now, here, Danny," he continued. "Here's what you do," and he pulled a roll of lampwick from under the counter. "You put a thick layer of this under the sweatband and it will fit fine again."

Danny didn't like this a bit, but the clerk insisted and he finally agreed. When they put the lampwick in, the hat stood out from Danny's head like the eaves of a Normandy provincial house. It wasn't three days, of course, until George switched hats again, putting the lampwick in Danny's own hat and returning it to his locker.

Later that day Danny got a call from an agent on Pier 57 who had just apprehended an opium smuggler. He ran to his locker for his haberdashery equipment. He put his hat on last and when he did, it sat perched on his head about three inches above his ears. Danny jerked it off, looked to see if his initials were still there, and tried it on again to see if he had been mistaken on the first try. He then pulled all the lampwick out and tore for the elevator, finally wearing the hat that fit him.

This didn't last long, though. About four days later, when it began to drizzle again, George dampened the big hat and

HILARIOUS HIGH JINKS

placed it, without the lampwick, in Danny's locker, removing Danny's good hat.

When Danny put his hat on this time, it fell over his head like a butter tub over a banty chicken.

"Yuh must 'a got it wet again," George drolled.

CHAPTER THREE

TWO STONE-DEAF INVESTIGATORS

In those days, with the help of the U.S. Attorney, we had a deal with one of the federal judges and it went like this. A high-ranking Mafia member would be caught bringing in a big load of narcotics. He would plead guilty. At that point, we had three counts against him, any one of which called for a maximum sentence of 10 years, under the old Harrison Narcotics Act. The U.S. Attorney would advise the judge that although this man was pleading guilty, he had shown no inclination to aid the Government in bringing about the arrest and conviction of his cohorts. With the great amount of narcotics involved, the Government recommended that no leniency be shown the defendant.

The judge would then sentence him to 10 years on each count, to run consecutively. The defendant would usually blanch under this and, after allowing him to reconsider for a few minutes, the judge would say, "However, I will send you to a federal penitentiary for a period of six months. If during that time you can see your way clear to aid the Government in bringing about the arrest and successful prosecution of your partners in this crime, I will reconsider the sentence." A man would rat on his wife with a sentence like that confronting him.

The accused would usually go to the Federal Penitentiary at

HILARIOUS HIGH JINKS

Fort Leavenworth, Kansas, and within a few months, they would invariably say they wanted to see a Customs special agent so they could sing the sad song.

Well, we got word from Fort Leavenworth that one of them was ready and anxious to see a Customs investigator and start informing on his pals, so John Roberts decided that Danny Guilfoyle and I would go to Kansas to hear his story.

Now, Danny had never been out of New York City in his life, other than to go "up de country" as he called it, and that meant 40 miles up the Hudson River. So Danny was quite excited about the trip. He came to the office on the day we were to leave by train, with his well packed suitcase. As we talked with John Roberts about our approach to the "singer" at Leavenworth, the boys in the outer office obligingly exchanged all of Danny's clothing and shaving gear for old, out-of-date telephone books.

I figured Danny would connect the great difference in the weight of his bag when we swung aboard the train, but he was so excited he didn't notice. We went through the Holland Tunnel, into New Jersey, and were on our way.

At that time there was a Major League baseball player named Heinie Manusch. When the train stopped at Trenton, a Western Union boy delivered to Danny a telegram from George Collins. It said, "When you get to rolling through New Jersey try to keep the wheels from saying 'Heinie Manusch to play today'."

This almost drove Danny straight to the loony bin, but I got small comfort from that. It almost made me get off the train before we got to Pittsburgh. As we neared Chicago, I began to dream up another little Jim Dandy to lay on Danny, as I'd finally driven that crazy, rollicking rhythm about Heinie Manusch from my thoughts. In those days it was impossible to go directly through Chicago on a train. You not only had to change trains, but you also had to change depots and they were across town from each other.

I was never able to understand this and apparently it had

others baffled, too, as they used to have signs all over Chicago which read, "A hog can get through Chicago without changing trains, but you can't!"

My scheme, which I intended to try in Chicago, also included my friend, Fred Gardner, who was holding forth as Customs Supervising Agent there. I told Danny that we had a three-hour layover in Chicago.

"Let's go up and see Fred Gardner," I suggested.

"Dat's fine!" Danny replied. "Had t'irty years of correspondence wit' him and never layed me eyes on 'im!"

I told Danny I'd call Fred when we got in to see if he was available and, if so, we'd take a cab and go visit him.

By then, Danny had discovered that all of his clothes and shaving gear had been replaced with telephone books, but he was philosophical about it. "Dat's life," he said and suggested that we take enough time after seeing Gardner to make a few small purchases in Chicago.

When we arrived I called Fred Gardner from a phone booth. His secretary put him on and I told him Danny Guilfoyle and I were on our way to Fort Leavenworth, Kansas, to interview a prisoner and had about three hours before our train left. I said that Danny had wanted to meet him for many years and this would be his chance. Fred said for us to get right over.

"I sort of hesitate to tell you this, Fred," I told him, "but I suppose you already know it. Danny's so deaf you've got to scream at him to get him to understand you. He's extremely touchy about it, too, so I'm going to have to ask you to raise your voice and really beller at him and don't let on you're doing it. This will allow him to hear you quite well, but won't indicate to him that you're being solicitous about it."

"I didn't know about his condition," Gardner said. "I'll be glad to go along with you on this. It'll sure be good to finally meet the fabulous Danny Guilfoyle!"

When I got out of the phone booth, Danny asked, "Did yuh git him, Lee?"

"Yeah, I got him all right, Danny," I told him. "Had one

helatious time making him understand me. Finally got through to him, though. He'll be glad to see you, Danny."

"Why'd yuh have such a time gittin' him to understand yuh?" Danny asked, mildly interested.

"Well, Danny, you know he's almost totally deaf, don't you? Mighty touchy about it, too. Gets madder than a bee-stung bear when it's mentioned around him, too."

"How do yuh handle it, Lee?" Danny wanted to know.

"Well, the only way to keep him happy and well pleased is to just raise your voice almost to the breaking point. You've literally got to squall at him, Danny, so when I introduce you, don't ever let your voice get down a single decibel from the beginning until we leave."

"Okay, I'll humor de ol' bastahd!" Danny said as we hailed a cab for the Post Office building where the supervising agent had his office.

On arrival, the secretary ushered us into Fred Gardner's office. "Fred!" I yelled at him, in a voice that would make a hog caller quit in disgust, "Want you to meet Danny Guilfoyle!"

"Hell's fire, Danny!" Fred bellowed in a bass voice that would have driven buzzards off a gut wagon. "Heard of you all my life! Mighty good to finally meet up with you!" I noticed a huge blue vein pop out on his forehead from the effort.

"Fred!" Danny shouted in a sort of keening shriek and his face was redder than the rear end of a raccoon in persimmon season. "After all these years an' all this correspondence between us, here we are, finally toget'er!"

His eyes were sticking out to where they almost pushed his glasses off. You could have knocked them off with a stick.

I heard running footsteps and Fred Gardner's secretary came barreling into the room.

"Good heavens!" she shouted, "what happened?"

I waved vaguely toward both Gardner and Guilfoyle, "Damn near stone deaf!" I shouted back.

"What a way to make a living!" she mumbled and went back to her chores.

Gardner started talking about a narcotics case they had both been involved in some 10 years before and his voice could have bent corn stalks. Danny nodded in agreement for a few minutes and then cut in. It's a mighty good thing he did, too, as Gardner would have collapsed soon. His eyes had started to cross about a foot in front of his face and drool was running out of both sides of his mouth as he trumpeted and roared at Guilfoyle.

"Good t'ing you phoned us right when yuh did!" Danny shrieked at him, his face almost up to Gardner's. "We was already on de train!"

Danny was at least 30 feet from me but he gave me a feeling I was in a maelstrom, upside down and sinking into a great void in the sea.

"Why don't you stay over a day and we'll all have dinner together!"

The rumbling stridency of Fred Gardner's bombination made it extremely difficult for him to finish a sentence without taking a big breath of air. I saw him grab the edge of his desk to keep from falling.

By this time, Danny was bobbing and weaving like a man in the last stages of Meniere's Syndrome. "Can't do it!" he yelled in his ear-splitting contralto and I thought I could see paint blistering off the walls. "Already got our reservations!"

The secretary came back, but I waved her out of the room. This was too good to allow someone who wasn't in on it to break it up. It was resonant, resonant! Neither of them paid any attention to me at all and each of them tried to outdo the other in clangor, reverberations and pure hell-let-loose.

Finally, Danny looked at me, gasped a few times to catch his breath, and said in a normal tone, "Maybe we can stop off on our way back."

Fred Gardner, still holding onto his desk and breathing like a badly beaten marathon runner, got his voice back down to its usual tone and said, "Hey, that would be great!"

Both of them looked at each other for a full minute, still

breathing hard, and then Danny centered his gaze on me, sitting quietly in a corner with the most innocent expression I could possibly muster. When he spoke again, his voice was so sincere that it quivered with emotion.

"Dat damn, shallow-minded, imbecilic Oakie has done it to me ag'in!" he said, and there was a sort of moan in his voice.

On the trip from Chicago, Danny was mighty huffy at me for the dastardly trick I'd played on him and Fred Gardner. However, the prisoner gave us a statement that put us in a position to send two of his partners in crime to the penitentiary, and Danny's feelings softened somewhat toward me.

The U.S. Attorney confronted the partners with the man's statement. When they read it over, they gladly accepted a plea bargain deal that put them away for five years.

CHAPTER FOUR

THE CASE OF THE NEWMAN BROTHERS

The Customs Service in New York City believed that it had devised a fool-proof system of keeping incoming passengers from working in collusion with a few crooked Customs inspectors in bringing large quantities of narcotics into the United States.

There were no passenger airplanes in those days and all the returning passengers came by ship. Accordingly, every morning the inspectors would line up for roll call. They would each be issued a little booklet of labels to stick on the incoming baggage after they had been inspected. There were 12 different colors of labels and the inspectors never knew what particular color would be used on any given day.

The inspectors would then be told on what pier they would operate and the name of the incoming ship. This would keep them from making any prearranged plans with a passenger. They would proceed to the pier in buses and, when the ship arrived and the passengers disembarked, the deputy collector would sit at a desk on the pier with all the baggage declarations he had received from the purser who had met the ship.

The baggage was brought from the ship to the pier by stevedores using dollies and the pier was alphabetically marked so that the baggage was placed under the initial of the passenger who owned it.

HILARIOUS HIGH JINKS

As soon as the passenger's baggage was on the pier and under his initial, he would get in line. When he got up to the deputy collector the next Customs inspector in the opposite line would accept his declaration from the deputy collector and go with the passenger to examine his baggage. As he finished with a piece of baggage, he would lick one of the labels and stick it on the trunk or suitcase. When Customs had labeled all the baggage, the passenger would summon a stevedore with his dolly, who would proceed with it to the end of the pier facing the street.

There, three Customs guards awaited. The first one would check the baggage to see that each piece had a label and that it was the correct color label for that day. The second one would cancel the label with a rubber stamp and the third guard would check all the labels to see that they were the right color and had been cancelled. Then the stevedore would roll the baggage out on the street where the passenger would obtain transportation and depart with his luggage.

Now, as everyone knows, it is impossible to run a big narcotics operation without using a telephone. In those days, the Supreme Court hadn't yet clobbered us with a decision that would make it extremely difficult for Customs to get permission to tap a telephone used by mobsters whom we suspected of being in the narcotics business.

We began to get information from various sources that a family named Newman had become the top trafficker in New York. We put taps on all their telephones. Several of them were living in expensive apartments in Manhattan and we were able to put "bugs" in the phone and get tapes of their conversations.

By putting several pieces of conversations together, it didn't take long to learn that the 22 year old son of one of the Newmans had taken the Customs inspector's examination and had passed it with high marks. George Collins and Danny Guilfoyle watched this procedure very carefully and soon the Newman lad was given an appointment.

It took us some time to learn that they had finally begun

their operation with the son who, about every other week, would steal one of the different colored labels from the booklet furnished him. And then, through our valuable telephone taps, we finally learned that he had stolen one each of the entire 12-colored label set. They were then ready to go on their big operation.

Early in 1939, one of our telephone taps picked up a very graphic conversation between two of the Newman brothers. We learned they were sending a man around the world and that he was leaving San Francisco for Hong Kong the following week. Collins got this information to our San Francisco agents and they verified that the suspect had a round-trip ticket and boarded a ship with a first stop in Hong Kong. This information was relayed to our agents in Hong Kong and they were awaiting the suspect when he arrived. They reported by cable that he had received a huge steamer trunk there and that it was brought aboard the morning he departed.

The ship proceeded around the world and docked at Bordeaux, France, where our agents in France were waiting. The suspect put all his baggage in bond and it was taken by train to Le Havre where it was loaded on the *Ile de France* for New York. Our agents advised us by cable and we awaited his arrival.

Meantime, one of the Newman brothers went to the office of the Customs collector where he advised that his wife was arriving on the French ship. He would appreciate a boarding pass that would allow him on the pier to greet her. This was a common courtesy and he was given the pass. He purchased a bouquet of flowers and went to the pier the morning of the arrival of the *Ile de France*.

The suspect had his baggage set up in his state room, awaiting the stevedore. He had his name on all the baggage except the huge steamer trunk he had received in Hong Kong. On it, he had tied a label which said, "Colonel John W. Abrams, Colorado Springs, Colorado," and when the stevedore took the baggage down to the pier, he placed the passenger's luggage under his own initial and the big steamer trunk under the initial "A."

The man who had come on the pier to "meet his wife" looked the situation over and saw the inspectors were using a sort of light orange-colored label that day. As he had all 12 labels in his pocket, he went into the men's room, located the right label, threw his bouquet of flowers into the trash barrel and went out on the pier where he quickly located the big trunk under the initial "A." He waited until he thought he wasn't being observed, licked the label, stuck it on the trunk and hailed a stevedore.

The stevedore loaded it on his dolly and pushed it up to the three guards. The first one checked it to see that the right colored label was on it, the second one stamped it with a cancelling stamp and the third saw that it was the right color and had been cancelled. Mr. Newman was then safely out on the streets of New York with 200 kilograms of pure heroin from the Golden Triangle...or at least so he thought. He was met by another of the Newman clan and, as they were struggling to get the heavy piece of baggage into the trunk of a big Cadillac, Danny Guilfoyle, Special Agent John Yale and I walked up to them with our pistols in our hands.

"Yer a bunch of hairy bastahds," Danny told them as we handcuffed them. "Ain't yuh a bunch of hairy bastahds, yuh?"

Meantime, Agents Eddie Cleveland and Johnny Hooe grabbed the actual smuggler on the pier and, over a few months' time, other agents throughout the city began rounding up the rest of the Newman gang, including the young Customs inspector who had stolen the 12 labels.

We got nine members of the gang and, although we had to turn one of them loose for lack of evidence, we had no trouble in convicting the rest. The famed Newman Brothers gang not only went out of business, most went to the Federal Penitentiary at Fort Leavenworth, Kansas.

CHAPTER FIVE

THE GREAT KETCHUP DECEPTION

A big pistol tournament used to draw the practical jokers like tumble bugs to a fertilizer plant, and I don't recall ever attending one when somebody didn't get the treatment in one form or another. I have always been a blind worshipper at the throne of persiflage and light raillery and, like most practical jokers, I am a dead-cold set-up for anyone who might try to run one on me.

Humor is a strange possession. It is as variegated as a petunia blossom. Any given form of it may make one man laugh until he bloats with the green sickness, while another, seeing and hearing the same piece of foolery, will raise himself angrily to his full height, dust off his posterior, adjust his truss and stride purposefully away, making clucking sounds.

Take me, for example. There are brands of humor which certainly must be funny to millions of people but which go over me like a home run over an outfielder. Jack Benny's program was one of them. Like Gordon Pike, I couldn't possibly see anything humorous about the pronunciation of the words "Azusa" or "Cucamonga" and, in fact, found them both to be fine little California towns. It seemed to put studio audiences into deep, rumbling laughter every Sunday night to hear that Phil Harris liked to belt the bottle occasionally, but this, in itself, wasn't at all funny to me. My list of

HILARIOUS HIGH JINKS

acquaintances boasts any number of brisk lads who could be classified in that category, and although some of their antics after they *have* belted it have almost made me laugh myself into the hospital, the mere fact that they do drink has never struck me as being such a whooping joke.

I have never heard very many Irish jokes that racked me with laughter, nor do I get the call from the odd tricks of speech and spelling of such humorists as Artemus Ward and Josh Billings. I am a man who likes his funny stuff sudden and startling, like the frightful squall of a goosy man when he has been prodded by a determined prankster, or the astounded look of disbelief on a shooter's face when he sits down on a fresh hen's egg, that some light-fingered competitor has slipped into his hip pocket. I like my nonsense for nonsense's sake. With this in mind, AaronQuick and I set up what became known as "The Great Ketchup Deception" at Tampa in 1939.

Wandering through a New York trick store earlier in the year, I had come onto a little mouse trap device that looked like a tea coaster. It was arranged so that when a weighty object placed on it was suddenly lifted off, it would release this small mouse trap device and explode a cap that sounded like a battery of Jubal Early's artillery going off at Spotsylvania.

Our plan was quite elaborate and we set it up between the clubhouse and the lunchstand with the utmost care and precision. First we obtained two benches and put them about 10 yards apart. Then we set the mouse trap device on one of the benches and placed a .22 High Standard pistol on it. Quick put his gun box on the other bench and laid several of his guns out as though he were cleaning them. I took my stand about 20 feet away from the first bench directly in front of the barrel of the High Standard pistol. We then relaxed and waited for our first victim.

He turned out to be a Cuban Naval officer who had come over to the matches from Havana and who knew only three words of English. One of these was "alibi" and the other two "Not ready!" He was walking slowly toward the clubhouse, probably reflecting on an ill-spent night in Ybor City and laying his poor showing at the day's matches on this, when Aaron Quick, timing his play perfectly, asked him in Spanish to please hand him the gun from the bench.

The Cuban, apparently surprised and pleased to hear his native tongue spoken in this foreign land, hastened to comply. When he raised the pistol off the coaster, the cap went off with a black powder roar and I went into my part of the great drama.

I don't believe that Barrymore himself, during his best days as Hamlet, ever executed a death scene with the histrionics that I put on for the quaking Naval officer who was standing there with Quick's pistol in his hand and guilt stamped all over him. I clutched my chest, bugged my eyes out like a tree lizard and, for the *piece de resistance*, as I slowly sunk to the ground, let a mouthful of ketchup (which came from the lunchstand) run slowly out of my mouth over my chin.

This clinched it. If there was ever any doubt in the officer's mind that he had fired a lethal bullet through me, the sight of this red, coagulated liquid drooling over my chin convinced him. He ran to Quick, babbling in Spanish that he was in a strange land...didn't even know the language...had no money for lawyers.

It took me about 10 minutes to get him quieted down after I'd risen from the dead, and finally convinced him I was as good as new. The Cuban Naval officer's reactions were so satisfactory that we decided we'd try it again.

Harlon Carter of the U.S. Border Patrol came whistling down the path and our audience became engaged in other pursuits so he wouldn't get suspicious. As he passed the first bench, Aaron quietly asked him for the pistol and the big explosion took place when Carter lifted it. I went into my act, with death rattles, walling of eyes and slobbering of ketchup and I could see that his mind was actively putting together a defense.

Quick told him, "You've shot him, Harlon!"

HILARIOUS HIGH JINKS

Carter looked quickly behind him and replied, "It wasn't me, Aaron! I heard it come right by me!"

The Great Ketchup Deception finally backfired, as most practical jokes have a way of doing with me. The first two men of our four-man team had fired the center-fire Camp Perry police course with a 295 1/2 average. Pete Chapman was firing with me in the clean-up holes that day and we were to go on the line immediately after lunch. I saw Chapman ambling toward the lunchstand and hastened to get Aaron Quick and our paraphernalia together. I barely got in position when Chapman arrived at the first bench. Quick asked him for the gun, Chapman picked it up, the cap went off and I went into my part of the act. Chapman grinned in disbelief when Quick told him he'd shot me, but when the ketchup began bubbling out of my mouth, he staggered toward me like a delirious man with the breakbone fever.

"Aaron, he *is* shot!", Chapman shouted hoarsely from a dry throat.

We thought it was mighty funny that Chapman was still in a state of high excitement when they called us to the firing line a short time later, but it didn't seem nearly so funny when he jerked a measly 256 over the Camp Perry police course. If he'd even shot a 292, which was much below his average, our team score would have broken the record. I learned something at that tournament. I learned that if you're going to scare somebody half to death, you'd better do it to somebody who isn't on your own team.

I went back to New York from Tampa that same year to work with the raunchy bunch of high-binders who were making it almost impossible for the big-time smugglers to operate. In the early summer, I was ordered to go to the West Coast to meet with the rest of the first team and all of the second team of Treasury shooters for a go at the San Diego and Los Angeles matches.

While in Los Angeles, I had occasion to meet again with Fred Gardner, who by then was Supervising Special Agent of

Customs for all of California and Arizona, with headquarters in San Francisco. He came out to the matches to watch us perform against the highly touted Los Angeles Police Team.

Fred told me that there would soon be a vacancy in Nogales, Arizona. The special agent located there was transferring to New Orleans. He stated that I might be the very one to take his place with my ability to speak Spanish and my previous experience on the border.

When my pistol shooting foray was finally over at Camp Perry, I returned to New York by way of Washington, D.C. where I made an impassioned plea to Tom Gorman, Director of all Customs Service special agents, for the appointment to the vacancy at Nogales.

I told him that my mother and father were getting along in years and I would sure like to be working closer to them. I furthered my appeal by pointing out that I had worked 10 years on the Mexican border, spoke good Spanish and felt that I had a knack for working well with Mexicans with whom I had a great deal of luck turning into informants. He seemed to like my approach, but didn't give me any assurances.

However, a couple of months later, I received my transfer to Nogales, Arizona. I bought the fastest Lincoln Zephyr I could find and didn't hit the ground but twice from the Holland Tunnel to Philadelphia. I was afraid they would wire me, saying, "If you ain't done it, don't do it!"

The New York boys gave me a big going away party at Regan's Bar and poured about five ounces of cheap perfume all over me so my wife would think that I'd been to Nancy's House of Brothelment. It didn't phase her! She was too anxious to get out of New York City and back out West.

CHAPTER SIX

THE FUTURE MRS. ECHOLS

Speaking of my wife, the former Helen Blackman, I first ran into her (literally) when my father moved us from Kiowa County, Oklahoma, in 1921, when I was 13 years old. My Dad had been a big Oklahoma land baron. He had the most barren land in the Kiowa Nation and he finally decided that either he wasn't a cattleman or western Oklahoma wasn't the place to be one. He sold out and drove us to Calexico, California, where he went to work as night captain on the Police Department.

I was in the eighth grade at the time and bought myself a bicycle with money I'd saved from trapping possums, skunks and raccoons on the banks of Sugar Creek where our ranch was located, some 15 miles out of Gotebo.

I was riding my new bicycle on the sidewalk in a very unprofessional manner, the same way I used to ride an ill-fed, but well-trained, cow horse. I turned the corner and ran right into Helen Blackman, one of the prettiest girls I had ever seen, who was also pedaling along the sidewalk on her bicycle. We got ourselves untangled and pedaled off in different directions but I'll tell you there was never a madder girl. Soon after that, we went into high school as freshmen and, despite my efforts at reconciliation, it took me about three more years to effect it, and then it was strictly a friendship situation.

HILARIOUS HIGH JINKS

She was voted the most popular girl in her last three years in Calexico High School and despite the fact I was playing baseball and football, I couldn't get in past the third line with little Helen. However, in our senior year, we played the two leads in the senior class play. It was Booth Tarkington's "Seventeen" and between the first and second acts, we put on a Charleston number that got mighty fine applause.

By that time she was going pretty steady with a boy named Gene McConnell and didn't pay much attention to the amorous attempts of anyone else. I had learned how to play drums by then and was playing in a high school jazz band. We'd play three or four nights a week throughout Imperial Valley for high school dances and other small gatherings. After graduation in 1926, I finally hooked up with a six-piece band which was going to play in Jacumba, California, all summer. Jacumba is about half way between Imperial Valley and San Diego. With the dangerous mountainous roads and rather primitive automobiles, most travelers stopped in Jacumba for the weekend instead of going on to San Diego.

I was playing way over my head with this band and I learned a lot from the piano player, Eddie Hopkins. We had three saxophone players, all of whom could double on clarinets, a banjo player, piano and drums. One of the sax players was Jack Lee who had been one of the early top jazz boys from New Orleans and he had a clarinet solo for the chorus of the Saint Louis Blues that was a real heel-stomper.

The dance hall was rather large and it was one of those dime-a-dance arrangements. We played there on Friday, Saturday and Sunday, afternoons and evenings.

One day Helen Blackman was driving through Jacumba on her way to the coast and she came up to the bandstand to say "hello." She was as pretty as a speckled pup under a red wagon and I excused myself and danced a couple of rounds with her. She left, saying she'd enjoyed seeing me and that made my Oklahoma butt twitch for several days.

The band broke up in the fall and I returned to Calexico

where I picked up with my small band again and also leased a soda fountain on the corner of Second and Heffernan Streets.

On New Year's Eve, 1926, we played for the Governor's Ball in Mexicali, Mexico, across the border from Calexico. There were more than a thousand revelers in the huge hall and at exactly midnight, when everybody began singing and yelling for the New Year, there came the hardest earthquake that had ever hit Imperial Valley. Huge pieces of plaster were falling from the ceiling, knocking people out on the dance floor. The exit door was so small it soon became completely clogged with bodies trying to get out.

I spied a glamorous looking Mexican girl passed out on the dance floor and jumped down off the bandstand, carried her out through a broken window and deposited her on the lawn. Then I went back inside just as another helatious quake hit.

I held on to things until it stopped, and then I noticed that the Chinaman who had been tending bar had taken off for Chilpancingo, leaving all his drinkables rolling around on the floor and under the bar. I hastily grabbed a bottle of Napoleon Brandy and went back out through the window where the Mexican beauty was beginning to come alive. I raised her head and poured a large dollop of the soothing cognac down her throat. She didn't even make a wry face, let alone cough. She sat up, put her arms around me and told me in Spanish that this was the most romantic thing that had ever happened to her and she sealed it with a big, slurpy kiss.

Now, Helen Blackman's father was a very wealthy plumbing contractor and he had built about two blocks of apartments on Rockwood Avenue in Calexico and the little Mexican girl told me that she lived in one of them. She then asked me very plaintively to drive by and see her later that afternoon.

The aftershocks were still being felt when I drove out to see her. As I was driving along Rockwood Avenue by the Blackman Apartments, I saw Helen and a girlfriend of hers standing out on the sidewalks, afraid to enter their homes.

HILARIOUS HIGH JINKS

Helen was home for Christmas vacation from the University of Southern California and I braked quickly to say "hello." She told me that she and her friend and her friend's fiance were going to El Centro that evening to a big show tent to see a play. Tent theaters were quite popular in those days. She asked me if I'd like to accompany them and I immediately forgot all about the beautiful little Mexican girl.

The four of us drove to El Centro, which was 12 miles north of Calexico, and watched the play in the big tent theater. We enjoyed the ride home, reminiscing about our high school days together and I gave her a little kiss when I left her off at her apartment.

About a week later I received a short letter saying how much she enjoyed our evening together. She went on to say that although she supposed she was still in love with Gene McConnell, if she ever got over it, I would sure be her next choice. In addressing the envelope, she misspelled my last name, writing "Echoles" instead of "Echols." I wrote back, telling her that she should learn to spell my last name, as I was going to make every effort to see to it that she would be using it the rest of her life.

It turned out that way, too. I was appointed to the Customs patrol in March, 1928, and in October of that year we drove over to Yuma, Arizona and talked a justice of the peace into marrying us about midnight.

She hasn't used my name for the rest of her life yet, but she's sure got a good start. We'll be shooting for 62 years of marriage in 1990 and during quite a bit of that time she went through the suspense when I took off for work of not knowing if I'd come home alive.

CHAPTER SEVEN
A SLICK HUMBUG ARTIST

To get back to our transfer, we arrived in Nogales after an uneventful trip by automobile from New York, rented a nice home and got our little five year old daughter, Donna, into kindergarten.

I found that there was an abundance of narcotics smuggling in Nogales. Opium poppies were being grown anywhere there was water in the Badiraguato Mountains northeast of Culiacan, Sinaloa, and heroin-producing plants were in operation in many parts of Mexico.

One of the finest men with whom I worked in Nogales was an excellent investigator named Ben White. He asked me if I'd ever heard of a man named Carlos Moreto Cruz in my many years along the Mexican border. I knew quite a bit about Carlos Moreto Cruz, all right. Back in the early 30's he had been one of the slickest confidence operators in Mexico working the border from San Ysidro to Brownsville. He was a real flim-flam man and, as the saying goes, had a paddle that fit nearly everybody's ass.

Along with this, he had a completely guileless face, which of course is a "must" with a fraudulent bamboozler. He spoke excellent English and his deep blue eyes exuded an honesty that would bring the "winchels" to him like straddle bugs to cow dung.

HILARIOUS HIGH JINKS

One of his best licks was the "silver dollar mold" swindle and I knew of several times when he engineered it in Tijuana alone.

It went something like this. He'd meet a prosperous-looking American, usually in the old Blue Fox Bar, and he'd insist on buying the drinks. He'd always pay off with brand-new silver dollars and put the change in his ample pockets. After doing this several times, the patsy would notice that he never used any of the change for these purchases, although his pockets were bulging with half dollars and quarters. He would finally ask Moreto Cruz about this and he'd get a sly wink for an answer. Moreto Cruz would order another round, using new silver dollars and pocketing the change.

Finally, the tourist would ask him again and Carlos would take him outside the bar and away from any possible listeners. "I've got the sweetest little maneuver in the world," he would say. "Here, take five of these dollars and go into the bank with them. Ask the teller to give you a five dollar bill for them."

And he'd hand the man five of the new dollars. The gudgeon would enter the bank, present them to the teller who would immediately hand him a five dollar bill, and out of the bank he would come, anxious to learn more.

"See if you can find a flaw in any of them," Cruz would say, handing him a few coins. The man would examine them thoroughly, dropping them to see if they rang true. Finally, he would notice a small mark on the edge of each where a file had removed a small part of the ridges.

"Here, what's this?" he would ask.

"Yes," Carlos would admit, "that's it. That's the only flaw they have, but any bank in the world will take as many of them as you can stack on the counter."

The next move was to take the tourist to his room in downtown Tijuana. He'd open a steamer trunk with a key and take out a wooden box which was fastened with a heavy lock. He would unlock this box and inside would be a plaster of Paris mold that, when opened, would reveal the perfect imprint, heads and tails, of a silver dollar.

Also from the box, Carlos would take a small vial with a few drops at the bottom. It would have a label on it, written in German.

"This is the secret of the entire operation," he would say. "This is the liquid formula that I get from a German in Karlsruhe, Germany. I melt up a combination of tin, lead and antimony and mold the dollars from it. I can make about 3,000 of them in eight hours. Then with the liquid which comes from Germany in this little bottle, I can mix 10 drops of it with three gallons of distilled water, which I then pour in this trough here," and he would pull a long, shallow trough from his closet.

"Then," he would say, "I put as many of the dollars in the liquid as the trough will hold and in 30 minutes they are so much like silver dollars that no bank will turn them down. Now here," he would continue, pulling out a buckskin bag from his dresser. "Here's 100 of them. They all have the same date as that is impossible to change. You'll also note the small flaw on the edges," and he'd point to the small file marks.

"That is because when I pour the metal into the mold, I must pour it down through this small hole. Then, when the metal cools, there is a small tit on the dollar which must be removed with a file. Let us take this bag full of my wonderful dollars and get bills for them."

He'd put all the gear away and hustle the man to the nearest bank, or to the Foreign Club, a gambling house that operated on the main street of Tijuana in those days.

The cashiers would furnish paper money for the dollars without even giving them a second glance, naturally, as they were authentic, legitimate, silver dollars with small file marks on the ridges. Then Carlos Moreto Cruz would take the victim back to his room again.

"Now, here's my predicament," he would say, and he'd focus those honest, deep blue eyes on the man. "I've got one big fault. I'm a compulsive gambler and although I made over

HILARIOUS HIGH JINKS

$3,000 in the last six months with this wonderful apparatus, I have blown it on roulette and race horses."

The man would usually laugh then and say, "Well, you have the essentials here to recoup your fortune. All you have to do is get to making more of them."

"You're certainly right on that," Cruz would agree, "but there's a catch to it."

He'd pull a notice out of his wallet from the Post Office in San Diego, stating that a package addressed to Carlos Moreto Cruz, from Karlsruhe, Germany, was awaiting him and that it was a C.O.D. package for $3,000.

"If I can get this package out of the Post Office, it has enough of the secret formula in it to manufacture $500,000 that can be changed anywhere in the world for greenbacks."

He would shake his head as though there was no possible way out of his dilemma. Then suddenly, he'd snap his fingers dramatically.

"Tell you what I'll do!" he would say. "If you'll go back to San Diego with me and draw out $3,000 from your bank to get the formula out of the Post Office, I'll make and pass all the money and give you 50% of all we make out of it. You won't be involved in any way except receiving the greenback bills as quickly as I change the dollars at the bank."

After the Simple Simon agreed to do this, then, of course, there was the problem of getting the money from him, and here's how Carlos would do that. In a show of good faith, he would let the man keep the wonderful mold, that had actually taken Carlos about 15 minutes to make, until Carlos returned from the Post Office with the vial of fluid. His reason for not taking the man with him to the Post Office, he would say, was that if there was a police trap set up, they would only get one man, and Carlos had agreed that the man who was putting up the money would entail no risk whatever.

Then, when Carlos got the $3,000, he would take it on the Arthur Duffy, or, as W. C. Fields used to say, he would "grab the money and run for the train."

I asked Ben White what he knew of this man, Carlos Moreto Cruz. He told me that apparently Carlos was out of the flim-flam business and now had 30 ounces of uncut Mexican heroin that he was taking to Tijuana, on the Mexican side of the border, from Nogales, Sonora, where he intended to deliver it to a Los Angeles buyer.

Ben's informer had Carlos' confidence and would accompany him to Tijuana. He had suggested that Ben go to the port of San Ysidro, which is on the U.S. side of Tijuana, and that he take along someone unknown to Carlos who could surveil him in Tijuana and determine whom he met there. The buyer could be intercepted when he crossed the border with the heroin.

Ben asked me if Carlos Moreto Cruz knew me and I replied that, although I knew him by sight, he had never, to my knowledge, seen me nor did he know who I was. Also, I had been away from the border for five or six years. We decided that if he had some prior knowledge of me, the time element would erase it from his memory. We also decided that I would be the ideal man to do a surveillance job on him in Tijuana, so we set up the trip. Ben advised the informant we would await him in a border hotel in San Ysidro, from where I would accompany him to Carlos, who would be awaiting his purchaser in a bar in Tijuana.

Now, unbeknown to Ben and me, we looked almost exactly alike, and when we arrived in San Ysidro and got a motel room to await our informant, we didn't dream of the complications which awaited us.

The informer arrived. It was the first time I'd seen him and his face looked a great deal like an aardvark. He also had an annoying habit of licking his long tongue up into his nose between words. He said Carlos Moreto Cruz was at that moment sitting on the fifth stool from the north end of the Long Bar, waiting for his heroin buyer. The Long Bar occupied an entire block in length and was touted to be the longest bar in the world. It was also full of those wavy mirrors, some of

HILARIOUS HIGH JINKS

which made a person look like President Taft, while others lengthened one's body until he took the appearance of Charles de Gaulle. When I arrived, I got so engrossed in seeing what these strange mirrors did to my contours that I almost forgot about Carlos Moreto Cruz, but I finally located him, sitting where the informer had indicated.

The bar was quite crowded and I sat at a vacant seat about eight stools from Moreto Cruz and ordered a tequila sour. I saw Carlos looking idly at me in the back bar mirror and suddenly his face froze. He got up from his stool, walked down and confronted me.

"Damn you, Ben White!" he stormed at me, his arms waving over his head. "You've followed me all the way over here from Nogales, haven't you?"

"I think you've accosted the wrong man," I told him as calmly as I could. "I'm not Ben White and I've never been in Nogales in my life!"

Carlos Moreto Cruz broke out in a fiendish laugh that made my hair stand up on the back of my neck. "My God, Ben!" he bellowed, "I'd know your hide in a tan yard! I don't know where you got your information on me, nor why you thought you could sit in here without me recognizing you! You need to have your head looked at by a competent physician!" He broke out in that maniacal laughter again.

I began pulling out identification cards and things, trying to prove I wasn't Ben White, but none of it worked. He went out of the Long Bar, whipping his legs with his hat and whooping like a tobacco auctioneer.

I drove back to San Ysidro and told Ben of my misfortune. The informer was still there and he pointed at me dramatically.

"Madre de Dios!" he yelled, running his tongue up into his nose, "I never see this before! I can't tell you apart!"

And I'll be damned if he didn't bawl out with that raucous, fiendish laughter almost exactly like that of Carlos Moreto Cruz.

We gave the Customs inspectors at San Ysidro all the

information we had on Carlos. The informant agreed to work with them on it and Ben White and I drove back to Nogales in a chastened frame of mind and completely subdued in spirit.

On arrival I learned that a Mexican-American friend of mine, Joe Acuna, from Calexico, California, was in town visiting his fiancee who was a clerk in the local Woolworth store. Helen and I invited them to the house that evening for a few drinks and a barbecued steak.

They both seemed to enjoy themselves and next morning, Joe's fiancee met Ben White on Morley Avenue. "Oh, Mr. Echols!" she gushed at him, "I can't thank you enough for that wonderful dinner! You and Mrs. Echols certainly know how to entertain!"

Ben thanked her profusely and she walked on down the street. She was with another local girl who told her she'd been talking to Ben White instead of me. A few minutes later, she ran into me and said what a terrible mistake she'd made, thinking Ben White was me and thanking him for last night's dinner.

I smiled at her in condescension and quietly told her, "I know, honey, I'm Ben White and you just spoke to me about it a few minutes ago."

This really put her in back of a bramble bush. "Oh, yes!" she came back, "of course! Anyone can see that! What's come over me?" and she retreated in complete confusion.

This was getting so good that Ben and I decided we'd go on with it. I called Helen by phone and asked her to drive down Morley Avenue and park near the Woolworth store. When she arrived, Ben and I told her how we had the poor girl about ready for the moonstruck farm.

"Now, here's what we'll do," I told her. "You and Ben walk into Woolworth's arm in arm and see what she does next."

They did and when she saw them together, she knew that at last she'd got hold of Lee Echols, because there was his wife, Helen Echols, right there with him.

She came out from behind her counter and told Ben, "Mr.

HILARIOUS HIGH JINKS

Echols, I've made a definite and complete fool of myself twice this morning. I ran into that man, Ben White, and both times I thought he was you. I just want to tell you both what a nice time Joe and I had at your dinner last night."

When she got off work that afternoon, I was waiting in front of the store. "You'll never fool me again, Mr. White!" she said, smiling broadly. "I've got you all figured out now!"

She never did get it doped out. I lived in Nogales two years and she was as mixed up about it when I left as she was when I first met her.

But I digress. The Customs agents stationed at San Ysidro did a good job of covering Carlos Moreto Cruz after we left and one of them actually saw Moreto Cruz put a package under the hood of the car of the buyer from Los Angeles. They scragged the smuggler when he entered the United States, found the package, jailed the culprit and sent the package to the Customs chemist in Los Angeles for an analysis.

The chemist called back and told them the 30 ounces were milk sugar with a little turmeric added by Carlos to give it the slightly yellowish brown tinge of Mexican-made heroin. Carlos Moreto Cruz was still the flim-flam bamboozler.

CHAPTER EIGHT

THE 62 POUND BAR OF GOLD AND SILVER

I had been back in Nogales only a short while after the Carlos Moreto Cruz fiasco in Tijuana, when a Customs patrol officer in Douglas, Arizona, sent me a copy of a letter he had received from a public stenographer there. He told me a young man named Bert Farnsworth had come into the stenographer's office and dictated the letter and she had saved a copy of it, as it appeared to concern a gold smuggling operation.

The letter was addressed to a Mr. T. Semmes Walmsley in New Orleans and stated that Farnsworth had finally located a huge bar of gold. He would cross the border with it at Douglas and fly it to New Orleans for delivery to Walmsley and his associates.

I telephoned the U.S. Mint in New Orleans and asked them to notify me immediately if a large gold bar was brought to them for sale. Within about three weeks, they called saying they had just received a bar weighing 62 pounds that was mostly silver, but had a gold content. At the prevailing price in those days of $35 an ounce, it was valued at more than $100,000. I asked them to hold it, since it had been smuggled into the country from Mexico.

HILARIOUS HIGH JINKS

I immediately drove to Douglas, which is on the Mexican border, about 100 miles east of Nogales, where I located Bert Farnsworth in the Gadsden Hotel. I told him the game was up, that the big bar of gold had been seized and that, as we were going to indict everyone who had a hand in the conspiracy, it would behoove him to become a Government witness, which might save him a bit of penitentiary time. I told him that he couldn't be with God and the devil both and he agreed to tell me the entire tale.

He said that he purchased the bar from Yaqui Indians in Bacadehuache, Sinaloa, and was to pay them when it was sold to the U.S. Mint in New Orleans. He said he smuggled it across the border under the front seat of his year-old Buick sedan with a flyer who lived in Douglas. He said that he and the flyer, John Woodward, attempted to fly it to New Orleans in Woodward's Stinson airplane, but that they had engine trouble near Hachita, New Mexico, and that Woodward's wife had driven there in Woodward's Ford and that they then proceeded on to New Orleans in the Ford. There they turned the big bar over to T. Semmes Walmsley, the ex-mayor of New Orleans, and a City Councilman named Frank Roder Smith. He said that another member of the conspiracy was the son of a wealthy realtor in New Orleans named Gilbert Vincent, Jr.

I then picked up the pilot, John Woodward, and he, too, "let his milk down," as they say. He said he knew the bar was smuggled. He and Bert Farnsworth tried to fly it to New Orleans, but because of engine trouble in his Stinson monoplane near Hachita, New Mexico, they drove to New Orleans in his automobile, where they turned the bar over to Mr. Walmsley and Frank Roder Smith in the Monteleone Hotel. Woodward said this was his first smuggling venture and he seemed to be very ashamed of himself. He certainly must have been, too, because about two weeks later he took a rented plane up to about 3,000 feet and dove it into the ground, scattering wreckage and himself all over the landscape.

I got in touch with Fred Gardner in San Francisco and told

him of the entire escapade. He told me to take the train to New Orleans, arrest the people there and get them under bond until a grand jury could meet in Tucson. He further warned me that New Orleans at that time was full of crooked politicians and that I should approach Mr. Walmsley with a proposition. If he would go with me to Lake Charles, Louisiana to go before a U.S. commissioner, we would take along a bail bondsman so that when bail was set, the bondsman could put up bail. Further, if he would agree not to fight extradition to Arizona if he was indicted, we would not furnish information about the case to the media in Louisiana.

When I told Bert Farnsworth I was going to New Orleans to arrest the other conspirators in the case, he suggested I first grab the son of the realtor, Gilbert Vincent, Jr., as he was so scared of the entire operation he would sing like a mockingbird and involve the others in the case.

When I got to New Orleans, I put up at the Monteleone Hotel. I called Bill Harmon, the Special Agent-in-Charge for Louisiana, and gave him all the details, including my idea of contacting Gilbert Vincent, Jr. first. Harmon said for me to keep in touch, and that if young Vincent agreed to talk, bring him down to the Customs Office where a secretary would be available.

I called Vincent's home and his mother said he was downtown in Mr. Walmsley's office. Walmsley's office was just across Canal Street from the Monteleone Hotel so I walked there. I told the girl behind the desk that I wished to talk with Mr. Vincent for just a minute and didn't want to disturb Mr. Walmsley.

"Just have him stick his head out the door," I said.

She entered the sacred sanctuary of Mr. Walmsley's office and pretty soon Gilbert Vincent stuck his head out. I motioned for him to come out and when he did, I waved for him to close the door. When he did this, I pointed to a hat and overcoat on a chair.

"Are these yours?" I asked him.

HILARIOUS HIGH JINKS

"Yes," he replied, with a questioning look on his face. I gathered them and motioned for him to follow me out of the office. When we got to the hallway, I showed him my badge and identification and said, "Let's go, Gilbert! We're heading for the office of the supervising special agent of the Customs Service."

We had hardly entered the elevator when Gilbert Vincent was telling me the tale and when I got him down to the Customs house, Agent Jimmy Offutt and I took a 30-page statement from him, in which he gave us the entire story of the smuggling of the big bar of gold and silver. We had Vincent held at the Customs house while I returned to the offices of T. Semmes Walmsley.

I identified myself and said, "Mr. Walmsley, the Customs Service is one of the oldest of the investigating services in the U.S. Government, and, accordingly, we don't need a lot of newspaper and radio publicity to get appropriations. Therefore, I am charging you with conspiracy to smuggle gold and silver out of Mexico, but I realize how the media would blow a charge such as this out of all proportion.

"Accordingly, if you will waive extradition to Arizona if you are indicted, I will meet you at your home at 7:00 a.m. tomorrow. You can have a bail bondsman with you and we will drive to Lake Charles, where I will arraign you before a U.S. commissioner and get a bond set. No one will know of this except you, the bondsman, the commissioner, another Customs agent and myself. The commissioner will be asked to keep it from the press. I'm sure this can be arranged."

Mr. Walmsley looked at me for quite awhile. "Young man," he said, "don't you think you're getting into something a little too big for you to handle?"

I assured him I didn't think so and he agreed to meet me and a bondsman the following morning.

Bill Harmon furnished a car and Special Agent Jimmy Offutt accompanied me on the trip with Mr. Walmsley and his bondsman to Lake Charles.

We had no trouble getting the commissioner to go along with us on not furnishing information to the press, and after we had a bail set on Mr. Walmsley, we had him sign a waiver on going to Arizona if he was indicted. Then Harmon's men picked up Frank Roder Smith and Gilbert Vincent Jr. and executed the same sort of arrangement with them.

I went back to Arizona, wrote a syllabus report covering the entire matter to Frank Flynn, the U.S. Attorney for Arizona, and then went up to Phoenix and discussed it with him. After reading the report, he asked me several questions and said it looked like a perfect case. He had it before a grand jury about a month later and both Bert Farnsworth and I testified.

The grand jury returned a true bill as to all defendants, but just before Frank Flynn could get it to the federal judge for signature, he got a telephone call from the U.S. Attorney General's office. They wanted to know the outcome of the grand jury's investigation. When Flynn told them that the grand jury had returned true bills on all the defendants, he was told to hold it in abeyance until Walmsley and Smith could get out to Tucson and testify in their own behalf.

Later, I talked with the foreman of the grand jury. He told me that the more they testified, the more convinced the grand jury was of their guilt, and the jury came back with another True Bill. However, the Attorney General's office had an open line to Frank Flynn and when he told them the results, he was instructed to fly to Washington immediately and to again hold the action of the grand jury in abeyance. He returned in a few days with a look on his face like a sheep-killing dog. He told me he either had to call the whole thing off or lose his job. He went before the grand jury and told them that, although there was a preponderance of evidence pointing to the guilt of the defendants, the cost of prosecution would be so great and the chance of conviction so small, he would have to ask for no bills for all defendants. This was done, and it put an end to the gold and silver bar smuggling case.

We found out some time later from our agents in Louisiana

HILARIOUS HIGH JINKS

that Walmsley and Smith had aided the Roosevelt Administration a few years back in an investigation of "hot oil" in Louisiana. This prevented Senator Huey Long from running for President against Roosevelt since many of Long's cohorts were sent to the penitentiary. Looking back on it, I decided Mr. T. Semmes Walmsley certainly knew what he was talking about when he asked me if I didn't think I was getting into something a little too big for me to handle.

We had some small comfort in the knowledge that we had seized the car in which Bert Farnsworth had actually smuggled the bar into the United States, the Stinson monoplane which took it from Douglas to Hachita, New Mexico, the new Ford which had hauled it from Hachita to New Orleans, and a beautiful Rolls Royce in which Frank Roder Smith had hauled the bar to the Mint. Not to mention the 62 pound bar of gold and silver.

CHAPTER NINE

THE MAFIA, NARCOTICS AND THE BORDER

Some of the best investigators I have known were special agents with the Customs Service. Harry Creighton was up there among the contenders for the top slot. I first met him in 1928. I believe I'd rather have had old Horny Headed Beelzebub himself after me than Creighton if I'd violated the Customs laws.

In his later years, he became known to all the hired hands along the Mexican border as "Old Man" Creighton, although never to his face. He was canny as a ferret at a field rat's hole, wise as an appellate judge and honest as a bell of brass. He finally wound up as supervising special agent in Houston and Treasury attache in Mexico.

Creighton only had one fault. He liked to run an investigation by telephone from several thousand miles away. Now, in working a narcotics smuggling case, that isn't easy. The plans are fluid and change quickly. The investigator has to change with them and not wait for a man sitting in his suite in the Rice Hotel in Houston to change them for him. But that was about his only fault. That and getting a little mixed up on things as he progressed into his dotage.

HILARIOUS HIGH JINKS

I had occasion to get right into the middle of things with "Old Man" Creighton through my acquaintanceship with Bert Farnsworth, whom I had met in Douglas, Arizona, in the ill-fated investigation of T. Semmes Walmsley, et al.

Bert Farnsworth was born in Colonia Dublan in the state of Chihuahua, Mexico. A group of Mormons moved down there with their various wives when the U.S. Government put a stop to plural marriages in their home state of Utah, and Bert had been exposed to the Church of Jesus Christ of Latter-Day Saints as he grew up. It hadn't taken hold of Bert, however. He said they sent him on a mission to Mexico City, but he got no converts. He returned to Colonia Dublan and told them that if it was true you could be accepted into the Mormon faith after death and thereby enter the Kingdom of the Lord, he'd just wait until then and join up with them later.

Over a warm glass of Bacanora mescal in Agua Prieta, Sonora, I propositioned Bert to look deep in Mexico for possible narcotics traffickers and call me by phone if he learned of any. It wasn't two weeks later when he called me from Guaymas, Sonora, saying he'd met a taxi driver named Tony Rojas, who had told him of two Italians, Salvatore Santoro and Dominic Petrelli, who had purchased four or five kilos of opium from him and had taken it to New York. The taxi driver told Bert that these men had left him an address in New York where he could reach them and had asked him to go to Guadalajara, Jalisco, in an effort to find large quantities of heroin.

I sent a teletype to New York and George Collins advised that Santoro and Petrelli were members of a gang of Mafia hoodlums who were the remnants of the Lucky Luciano and Dutch Schultz mobs and, because they all lived on or near 107th Street, were now known as the "107th Street Gang."

I called Bert Farnsworth, asked him to accompany the taxi driver to Guadalajara and to keep me advised of their activities. I wired him $3,000.

Bert called me a few days later from Guadalajara, saying he

and the taxi driver had located a clandestine heroin manufacturing plant and could immediately purchase eight kilograms of pure heroin at $15,000 a kilo. He said the taxi driver had wired the Italians, using a simple code agreed upon by the Italians before they left. They had heard back from the Italians, saying they would arrive in two days from New York.

Bert called me again after the Italians arrived. The taxi driver introduced them to Bert Farnsworth and told them he was one of the biggest narcotics traffickers in Mexico. They purchased the eight kilos of heroin, sent the taxi driver back to Guaymas and took Bert with them to Mexico City, where they told him they wanted to buy much more heroin than the eight kilos bought in Guadalajara. Bert agreed to help them find it, although actually, he knew less about heroin than he did about milking cow buffalos.

Santoro and Petrelli put up in a suite at the Reforma Hotel and Bert in a room at the smaller Ritz Hotel, about five blocks away. Bert called me again. He was desperate.

"They want 'snow'! What in hell is 'snow'?" he asked.

I told him it was cocaine and he said, "Lee, for Pete's sake, get down here and help me! I'll tell these people you are my brother and that you know even more about narcotics than I do!"

I contacted "Old Man" Creighton in Houston. He was not only Customs Supervising Agent for that District, but was also Treasury Attache to the American Embassy in Mexico City. After I'd explained things, he said for me to come through Houston on my way to Mexico City and that he'd send Customs Agent Ted Simpson to try to cover me down there.

On my arrival in Houston, Creighton called Ted and me to his office and proceeded to give us a lot of advice on our operations in Mexico, all of which was good. Then he told us to call him every night and let him know what had happened and he'd tell us what to do next.

This had an ominous sound, but I'd learned long before that you didn't argue with "Old Man" Creighton. In fact, most of

HILARIOUS HIGH JINKS

the young special agents were as scared of him as they'd be of a charging rhinoceros. Ted and I were the only ones I knew whom he liked well enough that we could occasionally (but not too often) kid the living hell out of him.

"Old Man" Creighton was six feet, seven inches in the air. He had a long face like a dray horse. He had hands on the ends of his spidery arms as big as a first baseman's mitt. His hair and eyebrows were snow white and his eyebrows were two inches long. When he was angry, or even perturbed, he would pull them out with his big, long fingers and stack them up like Kiowa tepees. When angry he could hit the top of his desk with his hamlike hand so hard that dust would fly off his wall picture of Franklin D. Roosevelt.

We arrived in Mexico City and Bert met me at the airport. Ted made himself inconspicuous and we checked into the Ritz Hotel.

That afternoon, Bert took me to the Reforma Hotel and to the suite of Santoro and Petrelli, where I met those dignitaries. Salvador Santoro was a big, fat, young Italian with a nickname of Tom Mix. His head was shaped like a size 14 Dutch oven. Dominic Petrelli was skinny, about 40 years old, with a face like a sea otter. Both of them had their coats off and were wearing Luger pistols in shoulder holsters. A quick appraisal of the weapons showed they were rusted and that they had probably cost about four dollars each, if that.

Bert introduced me as his brother, Jim, and said I'd been operating in narcotics along the entire Mexican border for at least 10 years and the law had never laid a hand on me. They asked me quite a few questions, all of which I could answer satisfactorily. While they were doing it, Petrelli pulled out his Luger and pointed it at the wall. His arm was quivering so badly I thought he was waving at somebody, but Santoro told me, "Dat boid's de best pistol shot in de woild! He can hit a fly at 50 feet!"

"Good grief!" I said, trying to look impressed. "Must take a lot of practice!"

"Nah! Yuh either got it, er yuh ain't got it! Dis boid's got it!"

I had to sit there and listen to this stuff and at that time I had already broken three world records. Petrelli couldn't have hit President Taft at five feet with a Fox shotgun.

Bert and I discovered a doctor in Orizaba who was trying his hand at making heroin and he had six kilos for sale. Santoro and Petrelli wired New York to send a money man and two young Italians arrived four days later in a new Cadillac. Among other pieces of luggage, they had a black bag that contained $90,000 for the purchase. They checked the bag into the strong box at the desk.

Ted and I were calling "Old Man" Creighton every night. He'd wait for us in his suite at the Rice Hotel in Houston and when we'd report to him, he'd tell us what we should do the next day.

The two young Italians disappeared the day after they showed up. Ted gave the maid 10 pesos to let him into their room and he took pictures of all their correspondence and identification papers. Actually, they'd gone to Acapulco fishing, but we didn't learn this until later.

We called Creighton that night and told him they were out of pocket, but that they couldn't be far, as they'd left most of their luggage in the room. He fussed and fumed about us not knowing exactly where they were, but signed off by telling us to let him know immediately when we got them back in our sights.

They came back the next day and, as I was busy with Santoro and Petrelli and Ted was busy covering me, we forgot to call Creighton and give him the news that they were back. He must have worn out the carpet in his suite, awaiting our call. Finally, on the second day, he sent us a wire at the Ritz Hotel.

"Have you found them yet?" and it was signed simply "Creighton."

We wired him back, "No. We've lost our overcoats now."

It wasn't an hour later when he had us on the phone. "Damn

you smart ass young simpletons!" he roared in a voice seething with emotion. "I put both of you on the plane at Brownsville and you didn't *have* any overcoats! Neither of you could find his grandma in a clothes closet, so get back on the job and keep shooting me stuff that's going on down there so I can tell you demented joltheads what to do next!"

He worried all the time about us, but he didn't think it was good for discipline to let us know it. He kept after me to try to find out how the mobsters intended to bring all that heroin out of Mexico. I tried, but they'd grin and tell me they had a foolproof scheme. I told them they were newcomers to Mexico, that what might work in New York City could possibly be one of the easiest traps on the Mexican border, and that my long years of operation should be given some credence when it came to deciding how to cross the border with the heroin. They would get looks on their faces like cats who know how to open milk bottles.

"Don't let it worry yuh, Jim," Petrelli said. "We got a foolproof deal!"

When they bought the six kilos of heroin from the doctor in Orizaba, they sent Bert Farnsworth with one of the young Italians to get it. We'd called Creighton the night before and he told us, above all things, to get samples of it, which we were to take to American Ambassador Josephus Daniels at the Embassy. He, in turn, would ship it to the Customs chemist in Washington through the diplomatic pouch. It would furnish us with the exact anhydrous morphine content of it, which might be good corroborative evidence in a court of law.

This didn't prove easy, as Bert had a hard time getting away from the young Italian on the way back with the six kilos. He finally poured enough Carta Blanca beer in him to force him to go to the restroom before his bladder exploded, and then Bert Farnsworth made his play. We'd told him to get samples from each kilogram and Bert's idea of a sample was a sugar scoopful. When Ted and I met him later in the Papillon Night Club, he had a brown bag of heroin that looked like a steeplejack's lunch. He passed it to us and Ted and I started for the front door. Now, people who look as much like Mafia gangsters as Salvatore Santoro and Dominic Petrelli can't be around Mexico City too long without gaining the curiosity of Mexican narcotics officers. Unbeknown to us, they'd been putting a tail job on them for some time, along with anyone who was associating with them, which meant Bert Farnsworth and me.

When Ted Simpson and I walked out on the street, about five big pug-uglies surrounded us, poking pistols into our slightly overstuffed bellies almost to their elbows.

I had the brown bag about half full of heroin in my coat pocket and one of them who seemed to be the chief said in Spanish, "Where's the man who was wearing the eyeglasses?"

It dawned on me that he was talking about me, as I had just begun wearing glasses and had them on when Bert handed me the brown bag. However, the glasses weren't too comfortable and I'd taken them off and put them in my shirt pocket. I quickly took advantage of this.

"He went out the side door," I said. "We never saw him before, but bought him a drink."

The boss told two of the younger officers to get going and they took off in a high lope. They circled the block and, of course, came back without the bespectacled suspect.

Meantime, the man who seemed to be in charge said, "We're going to search you."

Ted Simpson said, "Don't do it right here on the street! We're tourists down here and don't want our friends to see this. Come to our room. It's just around the corner."

They agreed and when we got to our room, Ted immediately got all five of them in a corner and began a long tirade about how embarrassing it was to have such improprieties performed on us. While he was going through these excellent histrionics, I got so engrossed in his efforts that I almost failed to see his suitcase, sticking out from under the bed, and open. I got hold of myself and slyly dropped the sack of heroin into it, kicking a shirt over the sack.

I didn't get it done a mite too soon, either, as they told Ted that they had all of his conversation they could stand and were going to search us. They grabbed us and went over us from hell to howdy, as the saying goes, and found nothing. I saw an incredulous look on Ted's face when he saw I was clean.

The boss was not only surprised but quite angry at his men's failure to find the brown bag, especially when he'd found my eyeglasses and definitely associated me with the man he'd seen receive the bag from Bert Farnsworth.

He told his associates, still in Spanish, "Let's go take them to the director's house and tell him what happened."

They marched us down to the street and put us in the back seat of one of their cars, the other car tailgating all the way to the director's home.

Ted slid over to me. "Where'd you put it?" he asked, out of the side of his mouth.

"I put it in your suitcase," I told him simply.

"Put in *my* suitcase?" he demanded. "Why the hell didn't you put in *your* suitcase?"

"Well," I explained, "I speak Spanish a little better than you and I figured if one had to go to jail, it would be better if it was you. I could get around and with my Spanish might get you bailed out."

They awakened the director when we got to the house. He appeared at the door in his nightgown and a long nightcap on his head, reminding me of the man in the old poem, "'Twas The Night Before Christmas." In fact, I was thinking of the resemblance and missed the first part of the oration when he found out his men had searched us and found nothing.

"Didn't find anything?" I remember him roaring. "Then why did you bring them all the way up here and wake me?" He was fiery with anger.

"Take them back to their hotel," he said. "I'm sorry,

gentlemen, for this inconvenience," and we were on our way back to the hotel.

Actually, the reason they weren't in our confidence in the first place was that Mexican narcotics agents would trade you black birds for turkeys. If you brought them into your act, they'd figure out how they could make the most money, by working with you or telling the drug traffickers. And if they told the tale to such people as Salvatore Santoro and Dominic Petrelli, things could certainly get lively for Ted, Bert and me. Lively!

We had several false starts the next morning in our efforts to get the enormous sample of heroin to the American Embassy. After considering it in the light of day, I told Ted we'd better try to get some milk sugar and have Bert mix it with the remainder of the purchase, as Bert had cut them down about a half pound, worth about $5,000. We couldn't figure out any way he could get his hands on it again, though, so we dismissed it. After going out of our room with fake packages several times and not being bothered, I finally strapped the heroin to my body under my skivvies and we caught a cab to the Embassy, taking a devious route in case we were being tailed by anyone. We turned it over to the American ambassador and he sent it to Washington in the pouch.

Then we called "Old Man" Creighton. He was morose and sulky.

"What the hell have you two got yourselves into this time?"

"We've been arrested," Ted said.

"Good!" he replied gruffly. "Hope they put you both so damn deep in jail they'll have to shoot frijoles to you with a BB gun!"

"We're too smart for that, Mr. Creighton," Ted said. "They had to turn us loose."

"What did they arrest you guys for, Peeping Toms?"

"No," Ted said, "we had about a half kilo of heroin on us."

"God's lavender drawers!" Mr. Creighton yelled. "How'd you get out of that one?"

HILARIOUS HIGH JINKS

"Lee hid it in my suitcase and they didn't find it. We've turned it over to Ambassador Josephus Daniels and it's on the way to Washington for analysis."

We could hear "Old Man" Creighton chuckling softly. "Well," he said, "you two just keep on going the way you are and it'll be about an even money bet whether the Mexicans send you to the Tres Marias Penitentiary before I have to check into the Texas state looney bin. Call me tomorrow night!"

The next day I got a call from Salvatore Santoro and I could tell by his high, strident voice that he had something important.

"Come on over here," he said. "De boid is here dat's gonna hit dat border wit' de stuff!"

When I got to their suite, there was a swarthy, distinguished-looking man sitting there in a Homburg hat. He had a nose like a huge meerschaum pipe and he turned out to be the Romanian minister to Mexico. Now, Hitler had just taken Romania; King Carol had abdicated and was living in Mexico with his mistress, Madam Lupescrou, and Petrelli told me the minister had been called back home. He said the minister would carry the heroin with his archives and silver through the border at Laredo by train and would deliver it to other members of the mob in New York before departing by ship to Romania. His diplomatic immunity would preclude any possibility of his being searched or intercepted at Laredo.

"How do you like dem apples, Mr. Smart Smuggler?" Petrelli shot at me. He had that damn Luger out again and was waving it around.

I assured them it was the most foolproof scheme I'd ever heard. I couldn't wait to get out of there and over to the American Embassy. I told Ambassador Daniels what their plan was and he said he'd put a stop to it.

He put in a call to the Department of State in Washington, telling them of the plan and asking that the minister's diplomatic immunity be cancelled and that he be searched.

There must have been some mighty high level talks because

they didn't send their decision until two days later, the day before the Romanian minister was to leave for Laredo.

The decision was definitely "no soap." They told Ambassador Daniels that our Government was playing an appeasement role right at that time and trying every way possible to keep out of the war. They said that if the minister was searched and the heroin was found, he would scream that it was planted and this might bring about an international situation.

Ted and I called Creighton and furnished him with this intelligence. He squawked like somebody had pulled a Christmas tree through his crotch, backwards.

"Why, damn it, boys!" he yelled in a high voice, dripping with frustration. "I'll call the Secretary of State on this! This is too much heroin for us to just sit there on that bridge at Laredo and watch it go through!"

It didn't do any good, though. The Romanian minister went through the scheme and the heroin quickly hit the streets of New York.

Creighton then got in touch with the Bureau of Narcotics through the Customs supervising agent in New York. He'd rather have worked with Benito Mussolini. His plan was for the Narcotics people to start buying this heroin, samples of which had been sent to the Customs chemist in Washington. They were to buy from the street peddlers, get the "mules" who were furnishing the peddlers and then, through the "mules," they were to get the lieutenants. Of course, there the chain would have to stop, as the lieutenants were always Mafia members and they would rarely inform on higher-ups.

Meantime, Santoro's and Petrelli's opinion of me and my "brother," Bert Farnsworth, went very high. They'd told me of how they would get the heroin across the river at Laredo and it went through without a hitch. Next they told me their bosses in New York wanted to buy the entire opium crop in the Badiraguato Mountains, North of Culiacan, Sinaloa, next spring. I told them I could arrange it but that I would want to

HILARIOUS HIGH JINKS

go to New York and meet their bosses, so I could have something definite to talk about to the growers when I went to Sinaloa to try to sew it up. They agreed to this and they departed for New York, saying they'd wire me in a few days.

I called Mr. Creighton in Houston and told him about these new developments. "Well," he said. "You've finally got yourself in a fine mess! They've probably already got you measured for your concrete overcoat. I'll do this for you, though, when they call you back and tell you what plane to take, call me quickly and I'll have the Customs boys in New York cover you the best they can.

"Now, see here, Echols," he went on, "if you ever come out of this one alive I want you to stay out of my district! I don't want you and that damned Ted Simpson to ever work together again and, speaking of him, tell him to get the next plane out of Mexico City for Houston! I've got two drawback cases and an undervaluation case I'm going to put him on. He's entirely too loony to work narcotics cases. And," he shouted, "You are, too!" In my mind's eye I could see him pulling out his long, white eyebrows and stacking them up on his desk like tepees.

Two days later I heard from Dominic Petrelli. He wired me to leave Mexico City the following Wednesday and gave me the airline and flight number. He said they'd meet me at La Guardia. I called "Old Man" Creighton.

"I'll call New York," he told me. "Be careful, and lots of luck!" He even sounded sentimental. "They'll cover you the best they can."

Then he got tough again. "Simpson got here. He's on that undervaluation case. It involves 5,000 pairs of guarache shoes from Mexico. He won't be through with that one for six months. Then I'll put him on the drawback cases. You'd better try some of this, Echols. You're too crazy to be working narcotics cases!"

Santoro and Petrelli met me at La Guardia Airport and took me to the Taft Hotel, saying they would pick me up at 9:00 p.m. for a meeting with their top people.

I asked them where the meeting would be held and Petrelli said, "The Cub Room of the Stork Club."

"Good God, Petrelli," I said. "You can't be serious! That's the most conspicuous place in all New York!"

"Yeah, dat's right," he said, "but it's also de most expensive. None of dem damn Customs and Narco guys can afford to drop in dere and do a little eavesdropping on us!"

I assured him it was a stroke of genius and when they left, I hurried to the corner drugstore to call Customs Supervising Agent Roberts. I was afraid to call from my hotel room as it could have been bugged.

When we got to the meeting, I looked about me. We were literally ringed with Customs special agents and secretaries. None of the big boys were there as they were too well known by the Mafia and I heard later that George Collins and Danny Guilfoyle put up a helatious beef because they couldn't come and sit in on the meeting.

I met Charles Albero, alias "Charley Bullets," at that little meeting. He had taken several chunks of lead when Arthur Flegenheimer, alias Dutch Schultz, was killed in New Jersey. I also met Frank Livorsi and Joseph Spitaleri, both old "Lucky" Luciano gangsters, and they immediately began talking things which I could use against them in court.

We made all sorts of big plans and, finally, we did get another kilo of heroin across the border in a hidden compartment of the gas tank of the new Cadillac the two bagmen had driven to Mexico City. Customs inspectors grabbed it at Nogales and we put the driver in jail at Benson, Arizona, completely isolated from bail bondsmen and lawyers, which we could legally do in those days. This gave us *corpus delicti,* as we didn't have much more than the small buys the narcotics boys had made in New York.

We hit a secret grand jury in New York and we were able to indict 52 men on the conspiracy count. Another grand jury in Tucson indicted seven of the top members of the 107th Street Gang on the substantive count. When revealed by the U.S.

HILARIOUS HIGH JINKS

Attorney that they had been dealing with a Customs special agent and several Narcotics inspectors, every one of the 52 men in New York pleaded guilty to conspiracy and received two-year sentences.

The seven ring leaders also pleaded guilty to the substantive count in Arizona. I was staying at the Santa Rita Hotel in Tucson. The evening before they were to be sentenced, U.S. Attorney Frank Flynn and I had a drink together in the hotel bar and then he went upstairs to go to bed. As he reached his room, a door opened across the hall and a man motioned for him to come into his room. When Frank did so, the man said, "I am Benny Siegel, late of New York and now living in Las Vegas."

He pointed to a black bag on the dresser. "That bag contains $50,000, Mr. Flynn. You can pick it up, carry it across to your room and you and I will never see each other again. The only thing you have to do is to ask for probation tomorrow for Dominic Petrelli. This shouldn't be hard to do and the judge should go for it, as all the other six men are willing to take whatever is meted out to them."

Frank Flynn laughed. "Thanks, but no thanks," he said and crossed the hallway and went to bed.

The offer had been made by the infamous "Bugsy" Siegel who, a few years later, was gunned down in Los Angeles and whose murder was never solved. The seven men were sentenced the following day to five to 10 years each.

It didn't seem to teach a lesson to Salvatore Santoro, alias "Tom Mix," since 46 years later in January, 1987, he and six other Mafia nabobs were sentenced in New York to 100 years each in a federal penitentiary. Santoro is now 75 years of age and it is highly doubtful he will ever be a free man again.

About six months after the sentencing in Arizona, I was going through Houston from Florida, where I'd been to the National Midwinter Pistol Matches. "Old Man" Creighton was waiting for me.

"You and that damn Simpson get in my office!" he said.

We sat down and I hope I never sit through such a lambasting again. "I'll have you brash jabbernowls know that I've just returned from Mexico City. And while I was there, I looked up Geronimo Chapas. You idiots reported that Geronimo Chapas knew all about kilos of heroin. Well, I'll tell you this about Geronimo Chapas. He's a cheap, two-bit, ball racker in a stinky little pool hall. Hah!" he screamed, and by this time he was pulling out his snow white eyebrows. "You imbecilic nincompoops gave him 1,000 big, round American dollars! My dollars! Dollars I've got to account for! Geronimo Chapas!" he yelled, his great hands slapping the desk by then and sounding like sledgehammers hitting sheet metal.

"Kilos of heroin!" he hooted. "Geronimo Chapas doesn't know anything about *grains* of heroin! And you two slickers handed him a whole yard of money!"

He went on like this for about 20 minutes and when he finally dismissed us and we walked out in the fresh air, Ted said, "He sure reamed you out good and deep, Lee!"

"Me?" I asked him. "I've never heard of Geronimo Chapas in my whole honest and upright life!"

Ted looked at me in amazement. "I've never heard of him, either," he said, quietly. "Let's get in the record room quick!"

We hurried and looked up the card on Geronimo Chapas. We found it, all right. He was indexed under a different case than the Santoro-Petrelli case and when we pulled his package, we found that another Customs man, Bill Folsom, had been to Mexico City a few months before our arrival and had used Geronimo Chapas as an informant.

We went right in and confronted Creighton with this ripe intelligence. It took another 20 minutes to convince him that neither of us had ever heard of Geronimo Chapas. We finally sold him on it, though, and he grinned at us.

"By gosh, that's good enough for you anyway! I didn't rag you near enough that time when you let the Mexican agents pick you up in Mexico City like a pair of raw recruits! There's probably plenty of other things you got into down there, too,

HILARIOUS HIGH JINKS

that you never even told me about. Maybe this'll make up for it!"

Creighton retired during the early part of World War II and was living in a private club in Phoenix. I was a Navy officer by then and was going through Phoenix with an overnight stopover. I went to see him. He was almost blind but was happy to have me call. We had a drink together and as he settled back in his chair to reminisce and enjoy it, I quietly said, "Geronimo Chapas...I seem to remember him from somewhere."

Creighton rared up like he'd been goosed dead center with an electric cattle prod. "Damn it, Echols," he squawked at me. "You ought to remember him! You and that idiotic Simpson gave him 1,000 of my buck dollars in Mexico City in 1940!"

CHAPTER TEN

A GOOD OPIUM BUST

A short while after the termination of the case against the 107th Street Gang, I received a teletype message from the Bureau of Customs in Washington, ordering me to proceed to Houston, Texas, for an interview with a Commander Rieldaffer of the U.S. Navy.

I went through most of our files in Nogales to try to determine what I would have in common with a Naval officer named Rieldaffer. I found nothing, but when I met him in Houston, he informed me that he was in charge of all Naval intelligence along the Mexican border from Brownsville to San Ysidro. His office had learned that all Japanese intelligence coming out of California was brought by Japanese Americans through the port of Nogales and taken down the coast to a little town in Sinaloa named Los Mochis. He went on to say that a Japanese living in Los Mochis would radio this intelligence to the Japanese fishing fleet, which would then relay it to Japan.

Rieldaffer said the Immigration people were interested in putting a stop to entries into Mexico from the United States by any and all Japanese. If so, the Japanese would undoubtedly resort to renegade Americans or Mexicans taking their intelligence information to the man in Los Mochis. He had discussed this with people in Customs and asked them for the name of an agent who had contacts deep in Mexico who might be able to set an informer into this operation. They had suggested me.

I immediately thought of Bert Farnsworth and told Commander Rieldaffer that I could probably give him a lot of help in his endeavor.

He then told me he wanted to bring me into the Navy as an officer and that he could get me a commission as a lieutenant, junior grade.

I asked him, "What's that?" and when he told me the salary that went with the job, I told him I couldn't afford to take it as I was making more money in Customs. This was in the early Fall of 1940 and I had no idea we would soon be at war with Japan. I couldn't see myself giving up my career in Customs for a position in the Navy that paid me less than I was making in Customs.

The Commander thought this over and finally told me that I was barely old enough to be given a commission as full lieutenant that would pay me a little more than my salary as a Customs special agent. I told him I would go back to Nogales and discuss this with Helen and, if she was agreeable, I would have a go at it. As usual, she told me it was all right with her if it was okay with me.

I filled out voluminous forms and took a Navy physical examination in Tucson. I told the Navy doctor I was a little worried about my hearing, as I had been a pistol shooter for several years and in those days we didn't have the luxury of huge ear muffs that drown out the sound of pistols going off next to your ears. We stuffed .38 caliber bullets in our ears and when our ear holes got too big for them, we'd use .45s.

"I'll give you a hearing examination," the doctor told me. "I don't think you'll have any trouble."

He pointed me away from him, took out two quarters and clicked them together about three feet behind me. "Hear that?" he asked, and I replied that I did.

He backed up a few more feet and I could barely hear a little noise back there. "Hear that?" he asked again and I almost had him repeat his question, it was so feeble.

By the time he got back about three more feet, I couldn't hear the quarters at all and his voice was only a vague murmur.

"I can hear that, all right," I told him.

"Hell, man, there's nothing wrong with your hearing!" he said and he immediately passed me on my hearing test.

I sent in all my papers, together with my physical examination, to the Bureau of Personnel at Navy Headquarters and soon after that I was called to make the grand tour of the summertime pistol matches, winding up in Camp Perry in late August. I checked on my mail on arrival and there was the big brown envelope from the Navy, which I opened quickly. Laying right out before me was my commission, all right, but apparently some junior grade lieutenant had decided that he didn't want some brand new recruit coming into the Navy at a higher rank than he had, and cut it down from a full lieutenant to that of junior grade.

Well, I turned it down when I got home but I did it very diplomatically by saying that since the time I had made application for this honor, things had come up that made it impossible for me to accept. If the international situation changed, I would reconsider.

My mind got off going into the Navy as I got a call from Ray Vader, an old friend of mine, who was Customs Agent-in-Charge in San Diego. He told me he had just heard from Tom Gorman in Customs and that Tom had unrolled a mighty interesting tale. He told Vader that a conspiracy had been hatched in the federal penitentiary in New York between four men who had been doing time on narcotics convictions and who were being released from custody about the same time.

Two of the men were New York gangsters, Leopold Trevino and Louis L. Steelman. A third was owner of a drugstore in Birmingham, Alabama, who had done five years for illegal sale of morphine from his drugstore. The fourth member of the conspiracy was Jesus Varela, a Douglas, Arizona, taxi driver who was also being released.

The plan, according to Gorman, was that the taxi driver would locate opium and heroin in Agua Prieta, Sonora, across the border from Douglas, Arizona, smuggle it into the United States, and the other three men would get together in Douglas to purchase it and get it to New York City.

The drugstore owner, however, decided he wanted nothing more to do with the traffic of narcotics, and he had contacted a narcotics inspector in Birmingham and told him of the scheme. The inspector, a little man who had never worked a narcotics law violation in his life, was an inspector of drugstores and his sole business had been that of keeping drugstore books straight and seeing that all drug sales were legitimate.

Tom Gorman told Vader that the drugstore owner had contacted Trevino and Steelman in New York and told them he was getting out of the conspiracy because of failing health and that his representative, a Mr. E. L. Camp, would call on them in New York for furtherance of the scheme. This was done, and although Camp told us it scared the hell out of him, he bought two ounces of heroin from Trevino and Steelman in New York saying it was for the druggist, who was a helpless addict.

Camp had reported all this to Major Garland Williams, who headed the Bureau of Narcotics in New York City, and Williams had contacted the Customs people in Washington in order to run a joint investigation. Gorman told Vader that Inspector Camp was leaving Birmingham by train on his way to meet the conspirators in Douglas, Arizona and would be coming through El Paso on a Southern Pacific train on the morning of September 20. He directed Vader to proceed by train to El Paso to meet Inspector Camp and get full knowledge of the matter on the train back to Douglas.

Mr. Gorman also teletyped me in Nogales, telling me to meet Ray Vader as he came through Tucson, go with him to El

Paso and back to Douglas, and assist him and Inspector Camp in the case against the ex-federal prisoners.

I met Vader's train in Tucson and accompanied him to El Paso, arriving on the afternoon of September 19. We contacted several of our Customs friends and proceeded to Juarez for an evening of fun.

The following morning Ray and I boarded the Southern Pacific train and had no trouble finding Inspector Camp. He was a little southerner about 40 years of age and it was quite apparent he was completely out of his element working against people such as Steelman and Trevino.

"Why, these fellahs told me they'd shoot innybody who tried to arrest us! They said that with the taxi driver, Varela, they'd set up a company and be furnishin' half the narcotics used in N'Yawk!"

He told us he was also quite intrigued with Garland Williams, the Narcotics Director. "He told me to git right after these people and he kept insisting that I 'bring 'em to justice.' He said to keep him advised every day of what progress we were making."

We told Camp to stay in the Gadsden Hotel in Douglas, as he had heard that Steelman and Trevino were going to put up at a smaller hotel up the street. When we arrived in Douglas, we saw Camp being met by the two New Yorkers. In the little western town of Douglas, they stuck out like Santoro and Petrelli had in Mexico City. Both of them wore wide-shouldered, striped suits and Homburg hats and they whisked little Camp away in a taxi that Ray and I learned later belonged to Jesus Varela, the other member of the conspiracy.

They were having the annual rodeo in Douglas and the street activities were in full swing, making the two New Yorkers even more conspicuous. The Junior Chamber of Commerce formed a sheriff's posse, and anyone caught not wearing western clothes would be grabbed and taken before a "judge," who was actually a local attorney, and fined.

HILARIOUS HIGH JINKS

As Vader and I checked into the Gadsden Hotel, we saw Camp coming down the stairs with Lewis Steelman and they sat down on a large sofa in the lobby. I picked up a local paper, sat down right next to Steelman and began reading it.

"Yuh gotta look out around a little hick town like dis!" Steelman was telling Camp. "Some of dese small-town bulls'll try to put de arm on yuh!"

On the trip to Douglas on the train, we had told Camp to try to make a buy from Steelman and Trevino first, so we'd have them on "sale" as well as actual smuggling. We told him to tell them that his friend, the druggist in Birmingham, would want several pounds of crude opium, if that was what they were going to receive from Varela.

While I was sitting at Steelman's side, he told Camp that they could get him eight pounds of crude opium the following day, for shipment to his friend in Birmingham. He said the cost would be $100 a pound, payable when delivered.

Camp agreed and about that time Trevino came downstairs and he and Steelman started walking down the streets, looking at the strange sights of the Douglas populace dressed in their western outfits. The sidewalks were full of jolly people and Ray Vader and I got in behind them to see how they would fare.

It was hardly any time at all until the posse spotted them. Four of them walked up to Steelman and Trevino.

"Where the hell's your western attire?" one of them asked.

"We ain't got none," Steelman answered with a big grin on his face. "We jist got here."

They were handcuffed and taken to the flatbed truck where the official judge held forth. The first question was, "Where are you two from?"

Steelman, who seemed to be the official spokesman for the duo, replied with another big grin, "We're from N'Yawk."

"All right," the judge, who was quite a clever local attorney, said. "What the hell are you doing in Douglas?"

Ray and I watched both Steelman and Trevino squirm at this

direct approach, but Trevino came back with another big grin, "We're here to see the rodeo!"

"The hell you are!" the judge fired back at them. "This isn't a big enough program to draw people out here from New York. Now tell me the truth! Just what are you out here for?"

Ray and I looked at one another. "That bastard's going to queer the whole operation!" Ray said.

We waited for Steelman or Trevino to answer. They looked at one another, dug their toes in the bed of the truck, and finally Steelman said, "Damn it, sir! We were over at de Grand Canyon and heard about dis rodeo and decided to get over here and see it! Is der anyt'ing wrong wid dat?"

The judge laughed. "Not a thing! I fine you $10 each for not wearing western clothes and I suggest you get right into a store and buy yourselves some before you get picked up again!"

Steelman and Trevino gave a sigh of relief and so did we, and they went off down the street looking for a store. They found one and came out wearing big red bandanas around their necks and a pair of great, big, western hats that were several sizes too large. It reminded me of Danny Guilfoyle in New York with the huge hat we had slipped in his locker.

The next day Varela brought over the eight pounds of crude opium for Camp to purchase, ostensibly to send to his drug addict friend in Birmingham. Vader and I had brought along enough money for this purchase and also for our part of the three-man purchase which the Trevino-Steelman boys wanted to take to New York. This would not necessitate an actual purchase but was enough money for Camp to show the New York boys that he had money to pay for his part of the conspiracy when the opium was delivered. Of course, we expected to move on them fast when we knew the opium was over the border and ready for shipment to New York.

When Trevino and Steelman delivered the eight pounds of crude opium to Camp and he had paid for it, he came down to our room, bug-eyed.

"My God, boys!" he said, "they've delivered it to me and

HILARIOUS HIGH JINKS

I've got it there in my room. I paid them for it and Steelman told me, 'Camp,' he said, 'We never knew you in the pen. We knew a man who you say is your friend. We're selling you this eight pounds of opium for him. If we get blowed out on dis deal, we're goin' to shoot our way out and you jist might be the first target!'"

Camp was as spooky as a man who has dropped his keys on the sidewalks of San Francisco during a gay parade. We gave him a double shot of Jim Beam whiskey and got him quieted down enough to agree to go through with the big delivery the next day. Varela was to cross the border several times in his taxi. If he wasn't being searched, he would go over again, carrying his wife and several of his small children, and when he came back he would have 50 pounds of crude opium concealed in his taxi.

Camp was to await his delivery, along with Steelman and Trevino, in the small hotel up the street from the Gadsden. With a great deal of trepidation, Camp went up to wait for Varela and the cargo of opium. Meantime, we had solicited the assistance of several Customs patrolmen who hid with Ray Vader and me as we waited for Varela and the opium.

Varela showed up right on time and went into the hotel. Soon he returned with Steelman, Trevino and Camp. From our place of concealment, we could see that Camp was holding on to things as he walked and was a little unsteady on his feet.

They began taking bundles out of Varela's taxi and the four of them went upstairs to the room occupied by Steelman and Trevino. We gave them about five minutes and then we banged on the door. We had been thoughtful enough to get a search warrant on the strength of Camp's original purchase, and when the door was opened by Steelman, he had a 9 mm pistol in his hand and seemed ready to use it.

He looked Ray Vader and me in the face. We were both armed with .357 revolvers, cocked and ready. Behind us he could see three Customs patrolmen, with weapons also pointed right at his gall bladder. He dropped the 9 mm and threw up his hands.

We booked Steelman, Trevino and Varela in the Douglas City Jail and stored the opium in the U.S. Customs seizure room. We seized Varela's taxi and put it in the Customs garage. We also found the $800 which Camp had paid for the eight pounds of opium and grabbed that. The following morning we brought the three defendants before the U.S. commissioner, charging them with sale, possession and smuggling of crude opium.

Steelman looked about, "Where's dat little bastard of a stool pigeon, Camp?" he demanded. "Why ain't he in here bein' charged like de rest of us?"

Camp was in an outer room, shaking like a Brahma cow passing cactus apples and Ray Vader went out and brought him in. "Here's your little stool pigeon!" he told them. "Show them your credentials," he told Camp, who forced himself into a great show of braggadocio and whipped out his narcotics inspector's credentials.

The three defendants were held on $25,000 bond and Vader, Camp and I went back to the Gadsden hotel.

On the way back there, Camp said, "Hell's fire! I ain't called Majuh Garland Williams in N'Yawk one time since I've been here! He'll tack my ol' Alabama hide to the outhouse wall! Gotta call him tonight!"

He went up to his room and Ray and I went to ours. We each had a big drink of George Dickel whiskey and Ray picked up the telephone. He told the hotel operator to call Camp's room and tell him that Major Garland Williams was calling him from New York. She did and Camp got on the phone immediately.

"This is Major Williams calling!" Ray said in a stentorian voice. "What the hell are you doing out there, Camp? I haven't heard from you since you got there! Are you lying around in your room drunk?"

"No, no, Majuh Williams!" Camp bellowed in a clamorous

shriek which completely belied his small stature. "We've just made a good-sized buy and a big seizure!"

Ray squawked at him, "Did I hear you right? Did you say that you've just made a *failure*?"

"No, no, Majuh Williams! Not a failure, a seizure! A big seizure!"

I could hear Camp from his room and his voice was that of a Visigoth who had just been stuck through the large intestine with an enemy spear.

"Well," Ray Vader told him, "if you've made a complete failure out there, you might as well pack and split. Get on back to Birmingham in disgrace. I'll report your inactivity to your district chief. And by the way, as you're going downstairs, drop in and have a victory drink of George Dickel whiskey with Ray Vader and Lee Echols."

Camp bellowed and came down to our room immediately, looking shamefaced and sheepish. "Where's that George Dickel whiskey?" he asked. "Pour me a double!"

About a month later, the three defendants pleaded guilty to all charges in federal court in Tucson and, because of their prior convictions, the judge sentenced each of them to 10 years in the penitentiary, to serve one day right after the next.

Inspector Camp was highly commended for his part in the investigation. As he was preparing to go back to Birmingham, Ray Vader told him he was slightly sorry for all the foolishness we put him through by phone in the Gadsden Hotel in Douglas.

"Don't feel a bit bad about that," Camp told us. "A great philosopher named Pascal once said, 'Men are so necessarily foolish that not to be a fool is merely a varied freak of folly.'"

"Now, what the hell did he mean by that?" Ray asked, as Camp boarded the train.

CHAPTER ELEVEN
MORE PISTOL TOURNAMENTS

While all these cases were being investigated in the Arizona District, along with a lot of smaller ones which invariably filled up an agent's desk, I was managing to get in a couple of hours of pistol practice every few days. I was beginning to feel that my shooting was improving quite a bit. I was hearing from the other members of the team and they seemed to be having the same good feelings about themselves. In early March, 1941, when we gathered at Coral Gables for the great Flamingo Winter Matches, our scores proved that we had been right.

At the National Midwinter Matches in Tampa, we began breaking individual and team world records which not only amazed us, but apparently amazed the Secretary of the Treasury. He had his Chief Coordinator, Elmer Irey, write me a letter after we returned to our stations. It was dated March 24, and here's what he had to say.

> Dear Mr. Echols:
>
> Coast Guard Gunner Hubbard, your Treasury Team Coach, has just told the Secretary of the remarkable shooting you and other members of the U.S. Treasury Pistol Team did in the matches at Coral Gables and Tampa.
>
> He wishes to extend his personal congratulations to you for

the part you took in helping to win these matches and establish world records.

There are transmitted herewith world record certificates issued to you and the United States Treasury Team as follows:

National Rifle Association Short Course, Individual .45 Caliber. Won by you with a score of 290 x 300. A new world record.

National Match Course, Doubles, Center-Fire, with Arnvid Anderson. New world record with score of 586 x 300. Your score, 292.

National Match Course, Four-Man Team, .22 Caliber, 1172 x 1200. New world record. Your score, 296.

Camp Perry Course, Four-Man Team, Center-Fire, 1183 x 1200. New world record. Your score, 298.

National Match Course, Four-Man Team, Center-Fire, 1156 x 1200. New world record. Your score, 289.

I wish to congratulate you again on this amazing accomplishment.

> Yours very truly,
>
> Elmer L. Irey
> Chief Coordinator
> Treasury Enforcement Agencies
> Washington, D.C.

I don't know how the other members of the team reacted to copies of this letter, but in looking back on it, I believe I made such an ass out of myself as to have warranted my dismissal from the Service. I even showed it to the Mexican janitor in the Customs house, who told me he had won a prize once in Brownsville, Texas for picking more cotton over a 10-hour period than 50 other pickers. He indicated that his prize far overshadowed my exploits. He was still showing me his techniques on separating the cotton from the bolls using a quick flip of his wrist when I stalked off from him, folding the chief coordinator's letter and depositing it in my hip pocket.

Later that year I went to the Aida Zilker Robinson Matches

at Austin, Texas. This man Robinson married Aida Zilker, a wealthy oil widow, and together they had constructed one of the finest pistol ranges in the United States for the Austin Police Department.

Each year, in appreciation, the Austin Police Department put on a Texas match attended by most of the top shooters in the United States. As usual in those days, along with some mighty high scores, there seemed to be plenty of time for a world of fun and frivolity.

The Kansas City Police Team was there, headed by a fine young shooter named Byron Engle. It will be recalled that this was at the tail end of the Pendergast regime in Kansas City and Byron had come in to help clean up the terrible mess in the Kansas City Police Department. He didn't come in as chief of police, but as administrative assistant, and he helped make a modern and model outfit out of the police department. Many of the innovations that Byron planned and executed were copied throughout the United States. In fact, when World War II ended, General MacArthur personally asked Byron Engle to come to Japan and set up a 20,000-man rural police organization. Byron was there for nine years.

He had a great big, top shooter with him named Francis O'Connor. As the Aida Zilker Robinson Matches progressed, and specifically on Saturday afternoon, Mr. Robinson backed his Cadillac Fleetwood behind the firing line. After the last match was fired, he opened up the trunk, where he had six or seven bottles of different types of whiskey and several cases of cold beer. O'Connor dipped his bill into this assortment to such an extent that when my friend, Aaron Quick, and I wanted to take him to his motel, he had no idea where it was. We had two large beds in the motel where we were staying, so we took him home with us, led him into our room, undressed him and put him to sleep in one of the big beds. Then we bathed, changed clothes and headed for the dance the Robinsons were putting on for the shooters in a downtown hotel.

HILARIOUS HIGH JINKS

We got back to our room about 1:00 a.m. to find O'Connor in the same position we had left him. He awoke the following morning, quite confused about his activities of the previous night. Quick told him that he accompanied us to the dance and that he and a beautiful girl had won first prize in the waltz contest.

"Why," O'Connor expostulated, "I ain't danced a set in 16 years! Was it a toe-waltz or a flat-foot-waltz?"

Aaron quickly figured that the huge O'Connor couldn't have possibly won a waltz contest dancing around on his toes, so he told him it was a flat-foot-waltz.

"Well, that figures," O'Connor said. "That's the kind of dancin' I used to do when I was doin' a lot of it."

When we got to the range, we got several of the female shooters to approach O'Connor, some of them thanking him for dancing with them the night before and one of them, stamping her pretty foot, telling him that he dated her for the prize flat-foot-waltz.

"You just waltzed off from me and took that girl Gloria into your arms and won the damn trophy!"

O'Connor dug his toe in the ground and apologized profusely. "I wasn't myself last night," he said. "I don't know who I was!"

While all this stuff was going on and between matches on the firing line, Byron Engle noticed that I was wearing a 5-X Stetson hat that I had recently bought in Tucson.

"Lee," he said, "throw your hat in the air and let's see if I can hit it with my .38 revolver."

I'd been having so much fun with, and about, O'Connor, that I inadvertently threw it up in the air. Byron took quick aim and put a hole in the crown about the size of a quarter.

I knew Byron Engle a long, long time, and the longer I knew him the more I learned about his basic honesty. I could see that he was really feeling bad when he was able to stick his thumb completely through the hole he had whanged into my new hat.

"Lee," he said, "here's my pistol. I'll throw my hat up there and you have a go at it."

Now, Byron was never known as a fop, or a coxcomb, but he was a sort of Beau Brummel and he was wearing a beautiful Borselino hat from Italy. "Throw 'er up there, Byron! I've never done any of these aerial shots before, so I'll probably miss it," I said.

"Well," ol' honest Byron said, "the gun is a little hard on the pull, so look out for that and when the hat reaches its apex, it will stay still in the air for a split second, and that's when you should touch off the trigger."

He threw it up to about 40 feet in the air and I followed it all the way up and all the way down, and when it flopped into the dust, I eased off the shot and put a dandy hole through both sides of his beautiful Borselino.

"It is a little hard on the trigger!" I told him.

About this time, one of the female shooters came running up and told us that she had just seen Aaron Quick hide his hat in the fork of a pecan tree so we couldn't get a shot at it. Byron and I got a bottle of beer and I shinnied up the pecan tree and poured Aaron's hat full of it. Then Byron got off about 10 feet and shot a hole clear through it. I never saw beer squirt so freely in my life, and two streams of it, too!

Through all this fun, I got on the line when my time arrived. I was doing quite well, but was sure surprised when I learned that I had won the Texas State Trophy by two points over the famous old Texas barber, Jesse Woody.

Jesse Woody was from Stanton, Texas, a little town between Big Spring and Midland, and there used to be a sign just before you got into Stanton, which said, "You are entering Stanton, Texas...3,000 friendly people...and a few old sore heads."

Jesse was one of the friendly people...until he got you on the firing line. He was tougher than the Younger gang anywhere he fired throughout the United States, but in Texas, he'd usually grind everybody out like they had suddenly been afflicted with Meniere's Syndrome. Then he'd go over and sit down on his gun box with a look on his face like a gecko lizard who'd just scared a Cambodian native half to death with his ungodly scream.

It didn't seem long after that before our team was called to the West Coast for the big matches there, then to Chicago, Cincinnati and Detroit, and finally to Camp Perry.

Our luck held out and we made quite a name for ourselves in the shooting fraternity with our world record team scores. I climaxed my career by winning the National Individual Pistol Trophy at Camp Perry.

A few months later the Japanese Navy hit us at Pearl Harbor and the War was on. This put a stop to the pistol matches throughout the country and I was transferred to Laredo, Texas, where the Customs Service was given the enforcement of the Export Control Act and the Trading With The Enemy Act. We were making huge seizures of war material, ostensibly destined for South America or Mexico, but that actually was to be detoured to Mexican ports, loaded on Spanish ships, taken to Spain and then through Spain to Germany to go into the German war machine.

I had just seized a big trainload of lithopone. I had no idea what lithopone was, but I'd checked out the papers in the office of the customs broker who was clearing it through Laredo and learned that it was to be diverted to Tampico and loaded on a ship to Spain.

I hadn't had it under seizure long when my curiosity got the best of me. I went through the Encyclopedia Britannica and learned that lithopone was a very necessary ingredient in the manufacture of paint, so this big shipment was to be used in Germany for making up a concoction to paint their tanks, personnel carriers and airplanes.

I felt pretty good about putting a stop to this little endeavor.

CHAPTER TWELVE
NAVAL INDOCTRINATION SCHOOL

A long about then I opened up the *San Antonio Light* newspaper and there on the front page was a picture of one of my best friends. Henry "Hank" Adams.

Hank had been the all-around pistol and rifle champion of the United States in 1935. When he came back from Camp Perry to San Diego with the big trophy under his arm I decided that was the sort of thing I wanted to do. Hank was the Undersheriff of San Diego County at the time and I prevailed upon him to show me the intricacies of shooting a pistol. Now, here he was, sitting on a coconut stump in a Marine major's uniform, a Thompson submachine gun in his hand and the caption under the photo said, "Executioner to the Japs."

It went on to say that Hank, who was Intelligence Officer in Edson's Raider Battalion, had gone ashore with them on the little island of Tulagi and had left his squad in front of a Japanese house to guard the front door, while he slipped up behind, kicked the door open and killed 15 Japanese soldiers.

My first thought was, "That's for me!" and I immediately sent in an application for an officer's commission in the U.S. Marines, giving them my shooting and investigation background as justification. I heard back from them fast. They offered me a captain's commission and I immediately accepted it. I filled out the same sort of voluminous forms as I had done with the Navy and before I knew it, I had my commission as a captain.

I was waiting anxiously to go to Corpus Christi to be sworn in, when I received a telegram from the Marine commandant's office.

"Where's your birth certificate?" they asked, "we've overlooked that."

I wired back, saying that I was born in the Indian Territory prior to it becoming the State of Oklahoma and that they didn't seem to be passing out birth certificates at that time. I said that the Naval Bureau of Personnel had a letter from my father, stating that I was born in 1906.

Now, this date of birth was a damnable lie, for in order to get into the Customs Border Patrol in 1928 when I was only 20 years of age, I had my father write to them, saying I was a year older.

The Marines didn't pay any attention to this, however. What they did pay attention to when they went through my file at the Naval Bureau of Personnel was the fact I had a dormant commission there for a lieutenant, junior grade, one step below the Marine captaincy which they had sent me.

I got an indignant wire, stating they didn't trade back and forth with the Navy for higher commissions and they strongly suggested I accept the original commission offered by the Navy.

By this time, I was all fired up to go and I sent a telegram to the Navy, saying I would gladly reconsider the commission they had offered me. Before I hardly knew what had happened, Helen, our nine year old daughter Donna, and I were driving from Laredo to Tucson, where they would drop me off to attend a three-month indoctrination school at the University of Arizona. They continued on to Calexico, California, where both Helen's and my parents were residing, after dropping me off at the Santa Rita Hotel.

I swaggered into the lobby where I met the manager, Nick Hall, an old friend from my Nogales days. I told him I had joined the colors and was going to a Navy officers' school the following day and needed a room.

"Lee," he said, "things have changed considerably since you used to come up here to federal court. There are thousands starting school here tomorrow and, to my knowledge, you're the only damn one who didn't have sense to wire ahead for a reservation."

We finally agreed to put me in a room with another of the new officers. After settling in, I went down to the bar where I met up with a cattle buyer from Nogales whom I had known a few short years before and had a drink with him. Then I suggested we buy a bottle and proceed to my room. A mighty grumpy little lieutenant, junior grade met us there. He told me that he had specifically asked for a single room and, without even asking him about it, they'd moved another dummy right in with him.

Before he could unload any more of his anger on me, I poured him an ample libation of Four Roses whiskey and after he'd downed it, he began to get quite friendly. He said his name was John Stansfield and that he was an instructor at Mare Island Navy Yard. He said he was training apprentices in machinery. I asked him where he learned his trade.

"I didn't," he replied. "I just stay a day ahead of them in the instruction book. The commander under whom I work decided that I might have a little more authority over them if I was an officer, so here I am."

He took another drink of the Four Roses. "What do the people at that university have in store for us, Echols?" he asked.

"I'm sure I don't know," I told him, "all I got from them was a mimeographed paper saying for me to be here tomorrow to start training."

"Well," John Stansfield replied, "that's all I got, but I'll tell you one thing, they'd better not try to march me! I'm one of the

HILARIOUS HIGH JINKS

meanest, saltiest little boogers on earth when anybody tries to march me!"

The next morning when we arrived at the University, they set us up in companies and they must have marched us 10 miles before going into the curriculum.

Johnny was in a different company than mine and as he was the shortest one in his company, they had him at the tail end of it. When they straggled in, he was about 200 yards behind the others and dragging his rifle.

He came over to my bunk. "Echols," he asked "can you play a bugle?"

I remembered that I had been a bugler in a Boy Scout troop in Oklahoma many years before, so I told him I could.

"Well," he said, "I noticed this morning that the damnable buglers and drummers play a few tunes out to the stadium as we march along with them, and then, when they get there, they get up in the bleachers and sit around on their lazy butts until it's time to march back to our headquarters and then they play a few lackadaisical tunes and march us back. Now, my idea is, we should get right over there and confer with that drum major and get on that bugle team."

"Can you play one of them?" I asked him.

"No," he admitted, "but I can just pucker up and make out like I'm playing along with the rest of the gold-bricking bastards and they'll never know the difference. They've got about 50 of them in the group."

Stanfield's idea worked out fine. The drum major issued us a bugle apiece and put us right in the front line of the buglers. He didn't even try us out. We started marching out toward the stadium with the two huge classes of new officers behind us, one of which had already been there a month, and I watched Johnny with a great deal of apprehension when the drum major raised his right hand in the air and then quickly lowered it for us to commence playing.

Our first number seemed completely out of place to be played for a Naval unit. It was the old cavalry bugle call that

& DANGEROUS ASSIGNMENTS

summoned the horsemen to the stable early in the morning. I recall the words to it went, "Oh come to the stable, all ye who are able, and water your horses and feed them some corn! And if you don't do it, the colonel will know it, and then you will rue it as sure as you're born!" Of course, no one in the drum and bugle unit was singing it, so it seemed to go unnoticed by the marchers.

My mind, however, was on Johnny Stansfield and how he was able to keep from trying to play his bugle. He was marching right next to me and although he was stepping along right in cadence, he had a look on his face like a man trying to play "Hell Among The Yearlings" on a flute. Not a sound was coming out, but his eyes were bugged out and his cheeks were going in and out like the smoke gun of a beekeeper and I could see that his ruse was working perfectly. The rest of us played several more Jim Dandies on our way to the stadium. Then we were all marched into the bleachers where we sat and told each other funny jokes until 2,000 officers got through parading and sweating. Finally we'd form ranks and lead them back to the barracks to get ready for the classes in Naval lore that confronted all of us for the remainder of the day.

This excellent assignment went on for about a week and Johnny Stansfield was quite pleased. He would lie on his bunk in the evening and sort of practice variations of his facial expressions that would fool the drum major if he ever began checking him out.

And then one day we heard that the governor of Arizona was coming to review the students. The drum major got us together and said he wanted us to learn the bugle call, "Hail to the Chief." Some of his top buglers played it and we were in accord that it was a rousing thing. We learned it quickly...all of us, that is, except Stansfield, and he went through his pantomime so well that no one suspected there wasn't even a small toot coming out of the bell of his bugle.

That evening, however, he came over to my bunk and he

HILARIOUS HIGH JINKS

had a sort of look on his face like a tom cat in heat. "I believe I could play that thing!" he told me. "That's the most rousing bunch of notes I've ever heard, and I just feel that it would come right out of my bugle, if I got a big deep breath and cut loose with it!"

I looked at him in complete amazement. "Johnny," I told him, "you could no more play 'Hail to the Chief' than you could beat Fred Astaire in a soft-shoe dance on a sanded stage. If you dare try one single note of it tomorrow, you'll be out there on that football field, marching in every direction with sweat running down through your crotch like water from the spring at Cut Throat Gap, Oklahoma. Now, Johnny, you just keep on making that awful face like you're actually playing, but don't you dare even blow your breath through that bugle!"

He agreed with me that it was a preposterous idea. "But," he said, "I sure do like the way it reverberates, and I can just fancy myself out there playing it right along with the rest of you as we pass by the governor."

"John," I told him in the most learned manner I could muster, "Samuel Johnson once said, 'All power of fancy over reason is a degree of insanity.' Don't you even breathe through that mouthpiece!"

The next morning, as we moved toward the stadium, we played our regular repertoire of bugle calls. John puckered up his mouth and got that look on his face like a well-trained bugler, working his way through some of his easier numbers.

And then we reached the stadium, where the governor stood on a raised platform, along with Captain Cheedle, the Director of the school. The drum major raised his right arm and lowered it smartly and the bugle players began the rousingly beautiful "Hail to the Chief."

Suddenly a cacophony of dissonance broke loose to the side of me and almost put me to flight. Johnny Stansfield had rared back and blown a blast into his bugle of such caterwauling, discordant sourness as to almost make the governor, to say nothing of Captain Cheedle, fall off the podium.

"Lord Almighty!" the drum major squawked, "what in the name of the ring-tailed Hellion was that supposed to be?"

He brought us to a halt right in front of the platform where Captain Cheedle and the governor were making every effort to regain their composure.

He pointed at the first group of four men. "You play the first part of that!" he ordered, and they played it perfectly. Then he got to the foursome of which Johnny Stansfield and I were a part.

"Now you play it!" he yelled at us.

Stansfield marched briskly up to him, gave him an excellent salute and handed him the bugle.

"Here's your damned, ol' bugle! I'm going back to marching!"

CHAPTER THIRTEEN
GUNS OF THE NAVY AND GRADUATION

That night Stansfield came over to my bunk again. "Can you write?" he asked.

"Can I write what?" I asked him right back, mildly interested.

"Can you write articles?" he went on. "They have a weekly newspaper here and I've learned that the writers on it don't have to do marching. My idea is this. We'll go to the editor, tell him we're experienced writers and we'd like to pick a controversial subject each week. You'll take one side of it and I'll take the other and we'll go from there."

We saw the editor and he agreed to it, which put Johnny completely out of marching for our entire tour of duty at the University of Arizona. I might add that I didn't show up out there, either.

We had a young officer teaching one of our classes and his subject was called "Guns of the Navy." He told us of the big weapons on the battleships and he went into such things as ogive, pentahedrons and quadrilateral arcuation. I would walk out of his class when it was over with my head spinning like a quadrangular cuboid, ambling along on my tiptoes like a penguin on an iceberg.

Finally, he announced that the next day he would explain the functions of the 1911 Colt .45 semi-automatic pistol and I told Johnny Stansfield that he was now getting into a weapon that I would at least know what the hell he was talking about.

"Having broken several world records with that gun," Johnny told me, "maybe you should take over that class."

"Not me, Johnny boy," I said. "A man's never too old to learn new things. I may come out of there with a lot more knowledge than I have now about that intricate little weapon."

The following morning when the young officer got up before the class, he was holding a Colt .45 semi-automatic pistol in his hand. His opening salvo set me back so far I came up with a buggy whip and a pair of high button shoes.

"This gun is strictly for right-handed shooters," he said. Since I was left-handed, this was beginning to sound interesting.

"There are several reasons why a left-handed man can't possibly shoot this weapon," he went on. "The first is, the safety is situated on the left side, making it very hard for a 'lefty' to reach it. But the big problem is the fact that the rifling in the barrel twists toward the right, which means that when the bullet goes through the barrel it is twisting toward the right and at 50 yards, it will hit about eight inches to the right of the bullseye.

"Now, a right-handed man will compensate for this, as he invariably jerks the gun slightly to the left, which moves the barrel over that way enough to where it straightens out the bullet's flight, and instead of going eight inches to the right, it goes right into the center of the bullseye. Now, a left-handed man will always jerk to the right, which puts the bullet another eight inches in that direction, putting it 16 inches to the right of the bullseye at the point of impact of the bullet."

"I've got to go to the head," I told the young officer, as I felt my way out of the room.

I didn't go back, either, and when the lecture was over, Johnny Stansfield asked me, "Why didn't you challenge him on all that? I read the AMERICAN RIFLEMAN magazine and just offhand I can recall the names of several of the best .45 shooters in the country, all of them left-handed."

He began ticking them off on his fingers, "There's Charlie Askins, there's Smitty Brown, and there's you. And," he continued, shaking his finger at me, "you should have really put that bird in his place!"

"Well, not me, Johnny boy," I told him. "I'm married and have a nice little family which I am supporting. Do you think I want to risk getting busted to a sailmaker third, or something equally as non-remunerative?"

There was another way of getting busted, although I didn't learn of it until it was almost too late. Every morning, while the marching was going on, a couple of mighty brisk lads would circulate throughout the gymnasium where we were all quartered, and if your bed wasn't made up better than a Hilton hotel maid could have done it, they'd leave what they called a "bed check" on it.

I'd never made a bed before in my life, and parts were sticking out all over the place when I'd get through with it. Before I knew what was happening, I had received two of these dastardly little notices. I wadded them up and threw them in the wastebasket, but finally learned that if you got three of them, they would demote you to a boilermaker second and that was enough to scare the living daylights out of me.

A few days after I got my second notice, we returned from a class and I went over to my bunk and sat down to rest for a few minutes before my next class. I felt something crackling under me and discovered it was a small piece of paper all folded up. I almost fainted. I felt reasonably sure it was my third bed check and that I would be reporting to the Navy Recruit Depot in San Diego before the week was out.

With no small amount of trepidation, I unfolded the note that said I was to report immediately to Captain Cheedle.

HILARIOUS HIGH JINKS

All of us were not only dressed like yardbirds, we were also treated like them by the officers and even the enlisted men. Whenever we passed an officer with at least two stripes on him we'd usually just feel the hems of his garments and face Mecca. And now, here I was, ordered to proceed immediately for a confrontation with the man with four big stripes on his sleeves!

It was with a great deal of anxiety that I entered into the *sanctum sanctorum* of this ogre. He was sitting at his desk, going over some of his reports, and I gave him the finest hand salute I could muster. I didn't have any idea what sort of title I should use in identifying myself, so I didn't use any.

"Lee Echols reporting, sir!" I said and was actually surprised that my voice didn't go way up in decibel.

He got up, returned my salute and said, "Sit down, Lee. How are you liking the school so far?"

I told him everything was fine and I must have had quite a question mark on my features, as he got down to business quickly.

"How'd you like to go to Mare Island Navy Yard when you get through here, as Officer-in-Charge of the Police Department?" he asked.

"I don't know, sir," I replied, "what is it?"

"Well," he said, "it's the third largest civilian police department in California, next to Los Angeles and San Francisco. You would have quarters on the Island and be in charge of the entire operation."

"Well, sir," I said, "I don't want to sell you a pig in a poke, but I've had very little administrative experience. I'm an investigator with the Treasury Department in civilian life. I spent a couple of years as Chief of about 15 men in the Customs Patrol in Calexico, California, and then I was Assistant Chief of about 60 of them in Puerto Rico for a couple of years. Outside of that, all I've done is investigate Customs violations on the Mexican border and in New York."

Captain Cheedle grinned. "They told me you'd give me a bunch of crap like that," he said.

"Who told you that, sir?" I asked him.

"I had dinner last night with the U.S. Marshal for Arizona and the U.S. Attorney. When I told them I had been asked to find a man going through the school who would fill the bill, both of them immediately said you were the man for the job."

He reached over and put his arm around my shoulder. "Lee," he said, "do you want it or not?"

"Yes, sir!" I told him.

"All right, you can make your plans accordingly. However, you will get out of this school about a month prior to the opening there, so I'll have your orders cut for you to proceed to Frederick, Maryland, for a month. There's an excellent Basic Naval Intelligence school there and it only lasts a month. Then you'll go straight to Mare Island as Officer-in-Charge of the Police Department."

When I got back to quarters, I relayed this intelligence to John Stansfield. "That's good!" he said. "When you get to Vallejo, I'll meet you at the train and put you up with my wife and me until you get your quarters on Mare Island. It may take a little while to effect that."

Many of the boys who graduated with us at Tucson got assignments on merchant marine freighters going up to Murmansk with loads of supplies for the Russians. All of us knew this was a very dangerous assignment and whenever one of them would receive his orders, some smart ass would always come out with, "Sighted sub...glub...glub!" Unfortunately, this proved too true for many of them.

I called Helen and told her of the new assignment and, as usual, she was well pleased. "I'll leave little Donna here in Calexico with your folks," she said, "and drive over to Tucson for your graduation."

The graduation was quite an elaborate affair, but Helen said they hadn't been able to change my Oklahoma cowboy-style of walking. She picked me out immediately among the 2,000 marching graduates.

I must have learned quite a bit of Naval lore at that

HILARIOUS HIGH JINKS

indoctrination school, for I got good grades in every subject. But now, after more than 40 years, the only thing I can remember is the answer to, "What's aft, abaft the afterdeck taffrail?"

The answer is, "Water."

CHAPTER FOURTEEN
MARE ISLAND POLICE DEPARTMENT

The Basic Naval Intelligence School at Frederick, Maryland, proved to be an exceptionally interesting assignment. It consisted mostly of lectures concerning the situation in the Far East and what the Navy and Marines were doing about it.

They told us of the movement through the islands toward Japan proper, the taking of the Solomons and of the heavily fortified Japanese island, Truk, standing in the way of our progress. The plan now was not to try to take it, but bypass it and take the islands behind it until, for lack of supplies, it would die on the vine. Apparently that was the way it worked out. I was well pleased with the information gained at the Naval Intelligence School.

I arrived at Vallejo, California, by Southern Pacific train and was met by John Stansfield. I could see him standing on the platform as our train blew past him and, by the time he walked up to where we were disembarking, he said, "Lee! You went by me so fast I couldn't tell whether you were working steam or diesel! Mighty good to see you! Let's get up to my apartment and drink this situation over!"

HILARIOUS HIGH JINKS

I met his wife and John and I had a nice little reunion. The next morning I went across the bridge to Mare Island and checked in with a Captain Scanlon who was to be my immediate superior.

He gave me the name and address of the officer who was handling housing for the Island and when I saw him, he wasn't very encouraging. "There's only one house available on the entire Island," he told me, "and it's a huge mansion on what we call 'Four Striper Row.' Everyone living on that street has a captaincy in the Navy and I don't see how we can work you into it, with that little stripe and a half you're wearing."

About that time Captain Scanlon called him and told him that by all means, furnish me with those accommodations. "He's got to live on the Island!" he said. "If that's all you've got, then that's what he needs!"

I called Helen that night. "Drive on up here, honey," I told her. "We've got the finest quarters on the Island and we're getting it for my housing allowance of $125 a month!"

The Navy handled the moving of our household effects from Laredo to Mare Island and they got there about the same time I did. We moved in immediately when Helen and little Donna arrived and one of my first official acts was to get Helen and myself all prettied up to call on Admiral Friedel, who was the Commandant of Mare Island Navy Yard. I was all decked out with my blue uniform and grey gloves and Helen was beautiful, as always, in a modest little evening dress. We presented ourselves at the door of the Admiral's spacious quarters and I handed my card to the Filipino houseboy.

The Admiral and his wife were very gracious to us. He told me my job would be somewhat aided by the fact I was relieving a lieutenant commander, formerly an officer in a Kansas police department, who had set up good, working arrangements of span of control and chain of command. I had been somewhat worried about that, for I knew little about administration, and those were two of the main factors in handling any sort of operation as large as this.

"Would you and Mrs. Echols care for a highball?" the Admiral asked.

We said we would, and within a few minutes, a lackey of some sort came out with a tray containing four bourbon highballs, at least that's what the Admiral called them. They turned out to be from a wartime bottle labeled "Black Shield." It was fairly well known throughout the U.S. as "Black Death" and was made from distilled prune wine, or something equally as terrible. It tasted worse than a medicine my mother forced down me when I was a little tyke in Oklahoma, called "Black Draught."

Helen and I had gotten into something almost as horrible as this during Prohibition. A mighty good Customs friend of mine, Carl Eifler, and I had seized 1,400 cases of alleged Vat-69 scotch on the beach at San Onofre, California. We put all the smugglers in jail and on our way to the Customs seizure room with the truckload of booze, I accidentally kicked off a case of it at our house.

Neither Helen nor I had ever tasted Scotch whiskey before, but we opened a bottle of it, and got busy. We were sick in bed for three days and Helen hasn't been able to even smell it from that day forward. We learned that the whiskey was concocted on a rum boat off the coast of Ensenada and made from sugarcane alcohol, distilled water and creosote dip. This Black Shield whiskey wasn't quite as horrible as the concoction bottled on the rum boat off Ensenada by the pseudo chemists of the Prohibition era, but it was well up there among the contenders.

Helen and I dutifully drank our highballs and Mrs. Friedel, on seeing us perform our part of the tableau, lifted hers to her lips and took two huge swallows.

Her eyes bugged out like a woman in the last throes of Riggs Disease. She let out a loud reverberating belch and fled into the bathroom where we could hear her retching and vomiting.

The Admiral took a couple of dainty sips of his drink. "Lieutenant," he said, and his voice quivered with honest emotion, "it is impossible to obtain any kind of whiskey in the San Francisco Bay area which is drinkable. I apologize for this, but you will encounter the same situation as you get settled down."

I told John Stansfield about this the following day. "Don't you have some police in San Francisco which you must oversee?" he asked.

"Yes," I told him, "I have 80 men up there who are guarding a lot of new radar equipment which arrived recently."

"Well, let's go up there and check on 'em," Johnny said. "I've got an idea where we can get some good bourbon and get it quick."

He told me he knew of a man who was the distributor of Old Granddad whiskey for all of northern California. "We'll go in and put a pitiful tale to him."

His plan was to confront this man, tell him we were emissaries of Admiral Friedel and that the Admiral asked us to inquire if it would be possible to get two cases of Old Granddad whiskey each month for little private parties for returning Navy officers whose ships had been shot up in the Pacific and were getting repaired at Mare Island.

We worked our way through two or three secretaries and finally into the presence of the whiskey man. Johnny explained our situation.

"This is a different deal entirely than the regular Officers' Club," he said. "The Admiral just wants to have a few little private parties for these officers to sort of raise their morale before they go back into the Pacific."

"How many cases would the Admiral want?" the man asked. "This is a hard assignment, boys! Any whiskey I turn over to you people means I will have to cut one of my best customers down that much."

"I'm sure the Admiral understands that," Johnny agreed. "Accordingly, we are only asking that you sell us two cases a month."

"I'll go, boys," the man said. "I'll let you have two cases

right now and I'll sell it to you monthly at my cost. I think this is a wonderful effort, and I'm glad to help out on it."

When we got back to Mare Island, Johnny took one case and I took the other. When the Admiral returned my call, which he was obligated to do, I asked him if he and Mrs. Friedel would care for a bourbon highball. He hemmed and hawed about it, but before he realized what was happening, I had four made up and presented one to each. He sipped it gingerly and roared, "Where in the world did you get whiskey that tastes like this? I haven't tasted anything like it since I got to Mare Island!"

I told him I had a little secret deal with the distributor and that if he wanted about four bottles a month, I would let him have them.

This pleased the Admiral no end and actually, it put him in the conspiracy, whereby if Johnny and I ever got questioned about it, we'd refer the questioners to the Admiral!

The situation at the police department was going along fine, except that there was a great deal of thievery among the vast amount of workers on the yard. Recruiters had gone through the South and brought back thousands of laborers who were helping build submarines, sub tenders and escort vessels and others who were helping repair crippled ships with all sorts of holes in them.

Many of these workers were hiding small tools and other gadgets in their clothing when they walked off the Yard and were selling them locally for almost as much as they would make in salary in six months.

The workers walked across a short bridge to the mainland at Vallejo when they left the yard at quitting time. They had to pass through a police check and show their identification badges. I acquired an x-ray machine, which we set up about 30 feet behind the policeman who was checking the badges, and every man who passed through it was x-rayed. If the x-ray showed an unusual amount of solid things about this body, other than the general assortment of bones, the officer taking

HILARIOUS HIGH JINKS

the pictures would press a button. When the man arrived at the checkout station, he was ushered into a private room and given a body search.

Within a month after we set up this arrangement, we had seized tools and other small concealable articles valued at more than $100,000 and we had the Vallejo jail bursting at the seams with candidates for the federal penitentiary, none of whom had any idea how we were catching them.

In the meantime, Helen and I settled down to a fine social life on the Yard and met many friends with whom we have kept in contact ever since. It wasn't easy for most of the four stripe captains to adjust to having an upstart lieutenant in a beautiful house on their lane, but they usually relented when they learned my job required living on the Yard.

Every once in awhile, my police officers would encounter a senior officer, driving home from the Officers' Club at a rather high rate of speed and would have to pull him over. This happened one night when Johnny Stansfield's boss, Captain Moore from Alabama, was wheeling along in a mighty fast, illegal fashion. One of my best police officers sirened him down, told him he was going very fast through a residential district and asked for some identification.

Captain Moore, a deep-South man if there ever was one, didn't particularly care for a young civilian police officer demanding things from him while he was driving home from the Officers' Club.

"Why, young man!" he said in a loud voice, "I'll just get out of my car and cane you! I just can't stand to be talked to like that!"

The policeman laughed. "Captain," he said, "there's no reason for us to have any problem at all. We are both doing what we can to further the U.S. war effort and I can tell by your rank that you must be doing a wonderful job. Just pull over there to the side of the road and let me in and I'll drive your car and take you home."

Captain Moore fussed a little, but he finally agreed and was driven home. In the meantime, the officer had radioed ahead to have another officer pick him up at the home of the Captain and take him back to his radio patrol car.

On arrival at his house, Captain Moore was still very indignant and he browbeat the officer, still talking of "caning" him.

The following morning, I read the officer's report and called Captain Moore. I told him that for the morale of my department, I would have to insist that he come over to the police station and personally apologize to the officer. I would have the man in my office at noon and would await his appearance.

He showed up, right on the button, cold sober and apologetic. He apologized to the man, thanked him for his courtesy and introduced himself to several of the high ranking members of my chain of command.

"You people are doing a wonderful job," he said. "And I know it isn't easy."

I found it amazing how this little episode got out among the policemen. I became a *persona grata* immediately.

One of my main difficulties was keeping the force built up to its full strength. Every few days some of my young, robust men would get drafted and we'd have to find replacements for them. This was so hard to do there was a saying that whenever a man applied for a job, we'd disrobe him completely, bend him over and put a doctor at each end. If they couldn't see one another, he was a Mare Island policeman!

I began to learn that there were wild birds in great abundance within a few miles of Mare Island. There were pheasants behind every bush between Vallejo and Sacramento. There were ducks all around the bay area and quail and doves in the Marysville section.

The big problem for a game bird shooter, however, was the fact that shotgun ammunition was impossible to obtain legally. They were black marketing shotgun shells in San Francisco from one to five dollars each, but the dealers had nothing but empty shelves.

HILARIOUS HIGH JINKS

I got to thinking about all my friends in the ammunition business and I wrote a plaintive little epistle to my good *compadre*, Dave Flannigan, Manager of the Peace Officers Section of Remington Arms in Bridgeport, Connecticut.

I told him about the abundance of feathered game and the scarcity of material with which to shoot it. I suggested that he look around the Remington Ammunition Works and, if he could find anything from a box to a case of 12 gauge shells that had so far escaped the war effort, ship them to me with a bill.

I got a telegram saying, "Things look good. Letter follows." Then I got one of the most formal letters I'd ever received, from one of the Vice Presidents of Remington Arms. It said,

Lieutenant Lee Echols
Officer in Charge
Mare Island Police
Mare Island, California

Dear Lieutenant Echols:

We have just finished manufacture of a large quantity of shotgun shells, using steel heads instead of the usual brass.

We have given them extensive factory tests and find they hold up quite well. However, we are sending you, under separate cover, a case of these shells with the request that you give them exhaustive field tests, looking for squib loads, malfunction of primers and any other faults which might show up in them. Please advise us of the outcome of your experiments.

Sincerely,

Dave Flannigan
Remington Arms

Then he attached a note to the letter which said, "Lee, please excuse the formality of this letter. We had to do it that way to get around red tape and Government regulations."

The pheasants and ducks didn't have things so easy for awhile after that.

CHAPTER FIFTEEN
ALMOST OFF TO WAR

I had been at Mare Island about a year when I got a phone call from my old friend, Carl Eifler, that led to quite a change in my life.

I first met this fabulous man when I worked in the Customs Patrol. I was with a couple of other patrolmen and we were checking the bays and waterways south of Los Angeles for possible liquor smuggling on boats. We were in Newport Beach about midnight when a police car accosted us. A young giant of a policeman got out to see what we were up to. We identified ourselves and he got to talking to me about the Customs Patrol and how on earth he could get into it. He said his name was Carl Eifler and that he had worked on the Los Angeles police force for three years before taking his present position with the Newport Beach Police.

"You don't look that old," I told him.

He laughed, "I'm not," he said. "I lied about my age and got on the Los Angeles police force when I was 17 years old. They didn't learn it until three years later, but I still was only 20, so they had to let me go. I've been on this job now for over a year so I'm finally 21 years old."

"Well," I said, "they're hiring men, all right. They want big ones, so I guess you could qualify there, but they also want them to be about 35 years old."

He put his flashlight on me and looked me over. "How did you fill the bill on either of those?" he wanted to know. "You look like you're about 18 and you wouldn't weigh 150 pounds carrying half the books in the Encyclopedia Britannica."

"I fudged a little about my age," I told him. "And the way I got by on my size, I made such a nuisance of myself, breaking in on private meetings and things of that sort, they finally hired me to get me out of their hair."

I gave him the name and address of Collector of Customs Schwaebe in Los Angeles, who was doing the hiring, and we drove away.

It wasn't a month until he joined me in Calexico on the Mexican border and we worked together for practically the next six or seven years. We made a lot of big alcohol seizures during Prohibition. After Repeal, we went right after the narcotics smugglers. We were fortunate to acquire several excellent informers and finally were assigned together as investigators for the Customs Service in three districts, Los Angeles, San Diego and Arizona.

I was made Officer-in-Charge of the Customs Patrol in Calexico in 1935. We continued to work together until early in 1936, when Carl was transferred to Honolulu as Chief Inspector and I went to Puerto Rico to help organize a 60-man Customs Patrol.

Carl had become interested in the Army Reserve back in 1929. He got a commission and attended a lot of their meetings in San Diego which were handled by then Colonel Joe Stillwell, later known as the great General "Vinegar Joe" Stillwell in Burma.

The one thing I could hardly stand about Carl Eifler was that he was absolutely fearless. This wouldn't have been so bad in itself, but I'll be damned if he couldn't talk me into going with him on some of the scariest predicaments imaginable.

For instance, during Prohibition, the alcohol smugglers had

prepared a small landing field a couple of miles north of Rosarito Beach below Tijuana. They would take big trucks loaded with alcohol out there and the big trimotor Ford planes would fly in from up the coast, set down on the field, load up with 700 gallons of alcohol and fly back to their home fields.

Now, it was Eifler's idea, and he made it sound mighty simple, that we would drive down, hide our car in a canyon about a mile from the field, rub burnt cork all over our faces, crawl in almost onto the field, get behind some bushes and then, with a pair of field glasses, figure out the numbers on the planes.

This in itself didn't sound so scary, but the smugglers had three shotgun guards who would patrol the landing strip and kick behind every bush of sufficient size to hide a U.S. Customs man.

We got to know these shotgun guards after repeal of Prohibition and every one told us they would have filled us with number four buckshot if they'd have found us and that, since they were paying the police a huge figure to operate there, they would have been proven justified.

One night we crawled in to where we could almost, but not quite, read the numbers of the plane being loaded, and Carl whispered, "Let's change our position to that bush over to the right."

We crawled over to it just in time to see a big, burly Mexican come up to the bush we had just evacuated. He kicked all through it with his cocked *escopeta* at the ready. I almost had a bowel movement, but I could hear Eifler chuckling as he got airplane numbers.

After we'd get the numbers from the plane, we'd crawl to our car and drive back to San Diego where we had a book with the location of every airplane in California. It would tell us where each particular plane was located, using the numbers we'd obtained in Mexico. We'd drive up and stake out the field for several nights and when it came in, bouncing along with five gallon cans of alcohol throughout the plane and even

HILARIOUS HIGH JINKS

stacked up around the pilot, we'd move in on him and say, "Surprise!"

One night Eifler and I were lying on a trail in the Tijuana River bottom that led out of Mexico, when we heard the unmistakable sound of alcohol cans coming down the trail. We rose just in time to apprehend 10 Mexican smugglers. They were wearing canvas newspaper bags, each of which carried two five-gallon cans of alcohol in the front and two in back. We had them lined up and were feeling them for weapons when a flanker appeared out of the brush and put a pistol on Carl and me.

"Get up your hands!" he ordered, "or I'll shoot the damn sheet out of you!"

Eifler, without saying a word, walked quietly over to the gunman, pushed the gun to one side with his left hand and hung a right on his jaw, knocking him back into the bushes, his pistol flying into the air. When we got to him, his jaw had been broken on both sides. We had him in the hospital 10 days before we could even get him to the U.S. commissioner for arraignment.

A lot of this stuff was running through my mind when Helen called me to the phone in Mare Island, telling me Eifler was on the line.

I remembered he had been called into the Army just before Pearl Harbor and was a Captain in charge of a company when the Japs hit. Shortly after that he had heard about the newly-formed intelligence unit called the Office of Strategic Services, or OSS. He maneuvered a dead-head ride in an Army plane to Washington, D.C. where he confronted General "Wild Bill" Donovan, the Director of OSS, with the proposition that he should be sent immediately to Burma, where his old friend, Joe Stillwell, now a General, was in charge of all U.S. troops in that area.

Donovan said he would talk with the General and get him to bring Eifler under his command to set up espionage units behind Japanese lines in Burma, using trained natives to assist him, along with a group of some 150 Americans. They would gain enough intelligence about the Japanese in Burma to give enormous support to the Americans and the British who would eventually move through Burma and put the Japanese out of business.

Donovan and his top people saw the possibility of this operation. They sent Eifler to Burma where, after prolonged discussions with General Stillwell, the operation was put in effect. It was called "OSS Operation 101" and was probably the most effective OSS maneuver of the War.

Eifler had written me several times from Burma and, although he didn't give me many details, I could see that he was having a lot of luck with his operation and that he had been promoted from a Captain to a bird Colonel in less than three years by "Vinegar Joe" Stillwell, probably the toughest Army general on promotions.

It turned out that Carl was calling me from San Francisco and he said he wanted to come up to Mare Island and see me. We invited him to have dinner with us and spend the night.

When he arrived, he looked over our quarters, located in the most prestigious section of the Yard. "How'd you like to go to war?" he asked me.

"I'd like it fine," I told him, "but I tried awhile back to go out as damage control officer on a destroyer and the Admiral wouldn't hear of it."

"I can have you out of here in three weeks," he said.

Eifler had put on a lot of weight since I had last seen him. He must have weighed well over 250 pounds and not much of it was fat. He sat down in one of Helen's beautiful dining room chairs, leaned back in it and looked me right in the eye. He leaned back a little too far and broke the back legs of the beautiful Queen Anne chair, right up even with the seat.

By the time we could get him off the floor and we'd all quit laughing, I asked him, "What sort of death-defying act are you going to get me into now?"

HILARIOUS HIGH JINKS

He started telling me about it and I'll be damned if it didn't sound like it would be the easiest operation imaginable. He said he wanted me to get together about 10 men, many of whom I'd known most of my life, people whom we could trust implicitly, both for their integrity and ingenuity.

"You will all go through the OSS indoctrination schools, which will take about three months."

"What dastardly movement have you got in mind for us after that?" I asked him.

"We have learned that the Germans are bringing 'Heavy Water' out of Norway," he said. "They are taking it to their nuclear scientists in a little town in Bavaria. Through our operators in Switzerland, we know that they are moving fast on cracking the atom and our assignment will be going into Bavaria, kidnapping their top scientist there, bringing him out through Switzerland and flying him to a submarine which will bring him to the United States. There the Manhattan Project scientists hope that, by combining their knowledge with his, they can solve the great riddle of the atom."

I started to ask him all sorts of questions, but he silenced me with a wave of his hand. "Our operators in Switzerland can give us extremely valuable information about the whereabouts of this scientist and even furnish us with a guide who will take us right to him."

He sounded convincing, and before I knew what I was doing, I agreed to get the 10 men together while he, through General Donovan, would get me transferred from Mare Island to the Office of Strategic Services in Washington, where I would be Chief Investigator for this strange operation.

For starters, I picked out two men Helen and I had gone through high school with in Calexico. One was Pete Aguirre, one of the best football players Calexico had ever had and one of our best friends. He was, at the time I was to contact him, a First Lieutenant in the Army, stationed at North Camp Hood, Texas. The other was Ross Wantland, also an ex-football player and good friend and now with a construction gang in the Aleutian Islands.

Each of them replied, "Get busy. I'll go!"

Eifler and I had a fine friend in Hawaii. He was in the Customs Service and Eifler had worked with him prior to being called into the Army. His name was George Roberts and I had known him quite well in the pistol shooting business. He had come to Washington for the tryouts for the Treasury Team, made our second best team and had gone with us throughout the United States on our pistol shooting forays.

Then, of course, I grabbed up Johnny Stansfield and a young man who was working with him in his training program named Hal Johnson. Turning to my friends in Customs, I propositioned Eddie Cleveland, with whom I had worked in New York and later in Laredo, Texas, and Harold Slack in Brownsville. Both of them agreed to come with us at top sergeant rank.

Eifler said he would bring some of his best men from Burma into our group and that they would consist of Floyd Frazee from Parkersburg, West Virginia, an Army Major who had been Carl's Executive Officer in the Burma enterprise; Major Vincent Curl, who had run one of the Cachin natives units behind Japanese lines in Burma for a couple of years; and a Major Phillip Houston, who was a Signal Corps instructor.

I also enlisted one of my Mare Island police sergeants, Bill Amick, and before I knew it, I was in Washington with all the recruits, getting ready to start through the OSS training schools.

Helen and little Donna had a try at living in El Paso for a couple of weeks after we left Mare Island, but it didn't appeal to them, so they changed their address to Calexico, where Helen got a job as a bookkeeper in an accounting office.

We all went through the OSS schools and while so engaged, Colonel Eifler went to Switzerland, where he made all the arrangements to bring the German scientist out when we put the grab-job on him in Bavaria.

HILARIOUS HIGH JINKS

About the time we completed the OSS schools and were ready to begin our hazardous assignment, I'll be damned if the Manhattan Project didn't crack the atom, obviating the necessity of our kidnapping the German scientist. Our venture was scrubbed—thank God!—and that idiotic Eifler almost cried when he told us about it!

CHAPTER SIXTEEN

THE KOREAN ESPIONAGE OPERATION

It wasn't long until Carl Eifler called us together again. He seemed to have gotten over the terrible thought of not leading us into Bavaria.

"All right, boys," he said, "we've got a new assignment, and it's got to be one of the best in the war! As you all know, there are thousands of Koreans living in the United States. Most of them are here on student permits and there isn't a damn one of them who wants Japan to be running their country.

"Our assignment is this. We will go through the Immigration files on the West Coast and learn the names and addresses of every Korean who has come into the United States in the past 15 years. Then we'll check out the best looking prospects and here's how we'll do it. Lee here will form investigative groups of four people each: two investigators, one wire-and tape-recording man who can also set up phone taps, and a girl stenographer who can put all the things we get over the phone taps and the room tapes on paper.

"When they find a good prospect, they will contact him, wherever he is living, and interview him. He will usually never meet but one of the investigators, but the other three people will, of course, be busy. He will be told of the possibility of being chosen to go back into Korea on a mission for his country and also for the United States. He will be asked, if chosen for his mission, where he would prefer to go and whom he would like to take with him. Then he will be asked what information he feels he can get within the chosen target and before he knows what's happening, it will appear that it's his idea instead of ours.

"Occasionally," Eifler continued, "some of the ones whom we feel should be leaders will suggest others whom they feel should be the boss of the operation. Then he will be asked to contact this person and even go to meet him. When he does, the room will be set up in advance, along with a tape recorder and a phone tap, and the crew will be there ahead of him to prepare all this.

"With my connections with the Los Angeles police," Eifler said, "we can set up a deal with the Biltmore Hotel whereby we can get our prospective agents put up there for a few days before we put them out for their training program."

"Where are we going to train them?" Pete Aguirre asked.

Eifler got a big smile on his face. "You'll never believe this, but I've made a deal with the Army whereby we'll train them on Catalina Island!

"Now, we know," he went on, "that we may lose some of the units to enemy action when we put them into Korea, so the answer to that will be for us to keep the various groups of espionage agents completely separated from one another while they are going through the training process. This can be effected by training up to four or five groups of them at the same time on Catalina Island, but in different coves and hideaway places.

"My plan on putting them in the Biltmore Hotel for a few days when they arrive from the East Coast and the Midwest, prior to getting them out to Catalina, is that a great many of the Koreans in the United States live in the Los Angeles area and a lot of them throughout the United States know one another.

"After we decide on a recruit, we will bring him to the Biltmore and tell him he can call up any of his Los Angeles friends in the next few days until I arrive to confer with him, but under no circumstances is he to talk with friends about the possible assignment. Then, of course, we will bug his room and if he gets too chummy about this possible assignment with any of his friends, he will be told that the program has folded because of lack of funds and he will be sent home with the admonition that when we get the program refunded, he will be contacted again."

It worked immediately. I set up the four-person investigative groups and it didn't take us long to recruit the four secretaries to go all over the country with the investigative units.

Things got funny quickly. For instance, Eddie Cleveland and his little group tied into a Korean in Detroit. He seemed like a mighty fine prospect and Eddie brought him back to Los Angeles to meet with me. We put him up in the Biltmore Hotel and although he met with many of his old friends in the Los Angeles area, he never told any of them of his future plans.

However, he had the same affliction which appeared to trouble all of them, although he seemed to have been hit with it in the extreme. It was simply this: no Korean can pronounce the letter "L." They invariably pronounce it as an "R." When he would meet with Eddie Cleveland, he would shake hands, saying, "Oh, Mister Creerand! How are you getting arong with your pran? How is Rieutenant Eckers? How is the Kerner?"

This kind of stuff got so funny, Eddie would run him in every chance he got and have him go through his repertoire. However, aside from this fault of mispronouncing a vital English letter such as "L," he turned out to be one of the best recruits we got on the teams.

The problem of landing all these agents on the Korean beaches began to assume rather large proportions. We learned that the Japanese had put radar devices everywhere and they could reach out at least 30 miles and detect our landing operations.

Carl Eifler, always the ingenious dreamer, came to me one day. "Lee," he said, "we've got to get some baby submarines that we can put on each side of a submarine. We've got to put them in steel containers so that if the sub has to submerge quickly, they won't go to pieces. They've got to hold a pilot and have space on each side of him for an agent, lying down. We can have the submarine that carries these two devices surface 30 miles from the coast, outside of radar range, put the baby subs on the water with a crane, get the four agents and the pilots in them and go abreast to the landing site on the Korean coast.

"Now, Lee," Carl continued. "I've already got the plans drawn for these little subs and their steel containers. They are being constructed at the Wheeler Boat Works in Coney Island, New York.

"We have one little problem, Lee. How can we defeat the radar with the exhaust and intake pipes that we must have, sticking up above the little underwater boats to keep them functioning?

"Now, there's a man in New York, staying at the Taft Hotel. His name is Waterbury and he is in charge of all the radar installations on the East Coast. I want you to get back there and show him our problem. I'll bet nine pesos to a bottle of that phony Vat-69 whiskey that he can figure out how we can defeat radar in getting those two little boats to the Korean beach!"

I told Carl I would leave immediately to meet with the radar man and see what he could figure on these two tricky little pipes that would have to be above the water line as they advanced on the Korean shore.

"All right," Carl said, and then, as an afterthought, he went on with a grin, "I almost forgot to tell you. You have been promoted to a full Lieutenant as of the first of next month."

I went up to New York and Eddie Cleveland went with me

as he had a recruit there he wanted to talk to before he came out West. We found the radar man and I told him of our planned underwater boats and our problem in trying to defeat the Japanese radar.

"Let's go out to the Wheeler Boat Works at Coney Island and have a look at them," he said, and we took the subway to within about 10 blocks of where the construction was taking place.

It turned out to be one of the coldest days in New York and, even with our collars turned up and our hands in our pockets, we almost froze to death.

When we got to the site, the radar man looked the boats over. "You people are a bunch of dummies!" he said, laughing. "Any kid could figure this little problem out. All you have to do is wrap these pipes with steel wool. Then when the radar beams hit them, instead of bringing its message back, it breaks up like a hammer-hit egg!"

We started back toward the subway entrance and Eddie and I both felt a little miffed at the way the radar man had ridiculed us. The cold hit us again and we were going into the wind and shaking. There was a man on the first corner selling baked sweet potatoes at a nickel each. Eddie Cleveland and I stopped and bought 20 hot potatoes from him.

The radar man couldn't understand what we intended to do with that many sweet potatoes, but we showed him quickly as we marched into the wind. We stuffed one in each of our ten pockets and had a built-in heater system which completely defeated the ice cold northerner sweeping down through Long Island.

"How'd you guys think of that?" the radar man asked.

"You sure are a dummy," Eddie Cleveland told him, "any kid could have figured this out!"

And as an old Oakie friend of mine once said, "He jist sorta grinned. He seen we had him!"

CHAPTER SEVENTEEN

THE KOREAN PROJECT ROLLS ON ... AND ABRUPTLY ENDS

By this time our espionage program was really rolling. We had four units in training on Catalina Island, the little underwater boats were delivered and we were running training escapades all over California.

We were giving them extensive training in espionage, subversive activities, radio communications and the usage of codes which were extremely hard to break. We taught them weapons, unarmed combat, map reading, demolitions, cover, security, informant information, compass, arrival in Korea, recruiting establishment of headquarters, sketching, jungle-craft, cryptography, ambushes, intelligence reports, landing men and materials by surface and undersea craft, defense measures, railways, selection of targets, night firing, photography, countermeasures by the Japanese and how to defeat them, planning attacks, raids, aircraft iden- tification, secret inks, propaganda and who knows what all else.

One group which had progressed well with their training picked as their target the U.S. Naval Air Station near Seeley, California, in Imperial Valley. Their assignment was to

HILARIOUS HIGH JINKS

infiltrate the target, learn how many fighter planes and bombers were stationed there, where the radio installation was located and the building where the bombs were concealed. There were four members of the unit and they planned on entering via San Pedro harbor using the underwater boats and then, by thumbing rides and using Greyhound buses, they would go to Imperial Valley and set up a camp along the East High Line Canal, from where they would operate.

I drove to Imperial Valley where I met with Sheriff Bob Ware. I told him of the planned operation, although I didn't tell him the target, and that if any of his men picked them up, they were to make every effort to have them tell their true identity.

"They won't be in Imperial County an hour before they'll be picked up, and we'll try to get their story after that," he said.

The four men were to carry false papers, showing them to be Chinese, born in San Francisco. Just before their departure from Catalina Island I told them what the Sheriff of Imperial County had said. Their leader, a brash little buy from Seoul who had spent several years in Chicago, laughed.

"We'll see about that!" he said.

They got through the submarine nets and traps in San Pedro Harbor, out on the Coast Highway with their baggage, including a small radio, and before long were stopped by a lone Immigration Border Patrolman who was driving from Los Angeles to San Diego. He inspected their documents, decided they were authentic and gave them a ride to San Diego. From there they took the Greyhound bus to Imperial Valley and when they reached the East High Line Canal, about five miles from their target, they left the bus, walked upstream about a mile and made camp. They radioed in code to Catalina, giving their position and stated that they were proceeding with their assignment.

Their leader walked back out to the highway, caught a ride into El Centro and proceeded directly to the sheriff's office. There he met Rodney Clark, the Undersheriff, and identified himself as a Chinese from the San Francisco Bay area. He told Clark he was working in a shipyard there and had a week off that he was utilizing to get out to the U.S. Naval Base at Seeley to visit his brother, an enlisted Navy man, who was working there as a cook. He asked Rodney Clark how he could get out there and Rodney, out of the goodness of his heart, told him, "I have a deputy who lives in Seeley, very close to the Navy installation. He's getting off duty and will be driving home. I'll have him take you out there."

This was done, and as they were in a marked sheriff's car, they had no trouble getting through the guards at the outer gate. When they arrived at the main office the Korean asked the deputy to wait for him while he found out if his brother was still assigned to the station. When he returned, he had a "lost soul" look on his face and said, "We're too late. He's been assigned to the Great Lakes Training School."

And then, as he got in the car, he said, "My brother has told me so much about this great air base, would you mind driving me around and explaining it to me?"

The deputy agreed and the Korean made mental notes of all the planes, while the deputy pointed out the radio quarters, the building where the bombs were kept, and then graciously hauled the agent back out to where the highway crossed the East High Line Canal. They shook hands, wished one another all sorts of luck and the Korean walked back upstream to the camp, where they radioed all this information back to Catalina. They broke camp, waved down the next bus for San Diego and had no trouble in returning to their base on Catalina Island.

The other groups were having the same sort of luck and it began to look like we had an operation that would work in Korea.

Carl Eifler and I sat down and prepared a report for General Donovan and the OSS Planning Board, advising where each of these groups would operate within Korea. We went into detail about recruits whom they would enlist in Korea and send for training in the two advance bases we would set up, one in

HILARIOUS HIGH JINKS

Northern Luzon and the other in Okinawa. By this time we were recruiting older Koreans and training them to serve as instructors on these bases.

The OSS Planning Board told Eifler that they had finally received a plan that seemed completely workable. They went on to tell him that most of these proposals were merely schemes, but this one was a definite plan, and they approved of it 100%.

The plan went to the Joint Chiefs of Staff and after a couple of weeks they, too, approved it, subject to the approval of the area commanders in the Pacific. Admiral Nimitz was the first to give his approval and he made some recommendations that we include in our plan exactly how many people would be in our rear echelon, that is, the Koreans who would be running the bases in Northern Luzon and Okinawa and the Americans who would be in the South Pacific, running the entire operation.

General MacArthur took the plan under con- sideration for several weeks and finally replied, saying that he never had accepted an OSS plan before, but he was intrigued with this one, particularly with the man who would be parachuted into a valley in North Korea. The man's family had the entire valley and he planned to set up a landing field where American flyers who were shot down in Japan and Korea could be secretly brought in by our agents and flown out.

Our only hold-up was General Wedemeyer. He had to give his approval in order for the one-man unit to be parachuted into northern Korea to set up the secret landing operation.

In the meantime, many young men who had volunteered for OSS and who had gone through the various training schools were beginning to hear rumors of our operation and would look up Colonel Eifler in an effort to get on our team. Since we had almost as many people as we needed by then, Eifler would pull a little Jim Dandy on them. He would look them over and say they weren't anywhere near tough enough to be in his organization. This would stand up the hair on the back of their necks. They'd tell him they were just about as rough as people come and would demand to know what they could do to prove it. Eifler would then tell them to hit him in the stomach as hard as they could.

Now, although Eifler's stomach protruded a little because of his enormous size, it was still mightily buttressed by muscle. When the prospective recruits laid into him with all their might, he would laugh and say they couldn't possibly qualify for his operation.

This sort of backfired on him one day when a man whose nickname was "Hercules," showed up and requested a job with our unit. This "Hercules" had just got back from about two months' training at the parachute school at Fort Benning, Georgia. He was also as big as Eifler and his arms were muscled up like the hind legs of a quarterhorse.

"I don't think you are tough enough for my outfit," Carl told him, sticking out his size 52 chest. "If you think you are, I want you to hit me just as hard as you can, right in my belly. That is the best way to decide on you."

Hercules looked him over. "My God, Colonel!" he said. "I can run my fist through your belly and tear out your backbone with it!"

Carl glared at him, stuck out his ample jaw and said, "Let's see!"

I don't believe I've ever seen a harder blow struck than the one Hercules laid on Eifler. He started from way back, used his mighty shoulder muscles to propel it and when it landed right in the middle of Eifler's stomach, it sounded like a great sledge hammer banging on a giant bass drum.

I watched Eifler's eyes, and they crossed about a foot in front of his face. He got hold of himself quickly, though.

"You can't cut it in my outfit, Hercules!" he said. "There isn't a man in my outfit who can't hit harder than that!"

As Hercules left in disgust, Carl said, "Run things around here, Lee. I've got to lie down for awhile."

It didn't seem to teach him anything, however. A week or so

later, in the Biltmore Hotel in Los Angeles, we were having a sort of impromptu Christmas party. A lot of our investigators were there, some with their wives who lived in the California area. We also had a couple of beautiful little sisters there. One, who was with Hank Adams, was a sort of Class B movie star, playing in western movies. The other was a ballet dancer who weighed about 100 pounds.

After about four big Christmas Tom and Jerries, Eifler pulled the shoes off the little ballet dancer and lifted her on top of a highboy dresser. He laid himself down on the carpet below her and ordered her to jump down on his belly.

"My goodness, Colonel!" the poor girl said, "I'm liable to go through it clear to your backbone!"

"That's what a great big man told me in Washington a while back," Carl said. "He said he could run his fist through my belly to my backbone. He couldn't anywhere near do it and I don't think a cute, little ballet dancer like you can, either. Go ahead and jump!"

The little dancer did and I'm here to tell you, when she hit on Carl's belly, he broke wind, which actually rattled the big bay windows in the suite. He jumped up with a look on his face like a man would get when he learned he was terminal with the yellowjack flu.

"Did you hear *that*?" he demanded.

"*Hear* it?" I asked him. "I've heard thunderous bombilations before, but if you'll allow me to quote Shakespeare, 'the thunderlike percussion of thy sounds' were almost too explosive for human ears to hold up under."

He didn't hear the last of my description of his unbelievable crepitation. He was running straight for the bathroom.

Our training operation continued and we anxiously awaited the signal to move with it. It was about the middle of July, 1945, when we finally got word from Donovan's office that General Wedemeyer had given his approval. We were ordered to prepare for the movement of the four units we had ready, take them individually to San Francisco, stake them out in various hotels and wait for advice on how to proceed to the South Pacific. All necessary gear was brought to the Bay area, including the underwater boats, radio equipment and clothing of Japanese and Korean manufacture.

And there we were on August 6, when the atomic bomb was dropped on Hiroshima, Japan. This didn't quite bring the Japanese Empire to its knees, but the one dropped on Nagasaki three days later did the trick.

OSS folded its tents like the Arabs and silently did away with its operations. Within three weeks we had dispersed our secret agents, paid them off and sent them home. One of them had been given some mighty fine plastic face surgery by a Jewish doctor who had escaped the wrath of the Nazis and wanted to do something for our cause. The secret agent had a round face with no bridge at all to his nose and the surgeon had raised the bridge with a couple of plastic insertions. Then he lengthened his face by putting a couple of them under his chin. The agent's own wife didn't recognize him when he came out of surgery. He looked more like a Mohawk Indian than a Korean and he had planned to ride into his little home town where nobody would recognize him unless they were contacts.

Well, during the hullabaloo of getting the operation closed down, he came and told me he wanted his old face back. Actually, the "Mohawk Indian Look" was a great improvement on the face the Lord had blessed him with. I pointed this out to him, but he wasn't satisfied. I finally told him the plastic surgeon had got away from us somehow and he'd just have to go along with his new face. His wife joined me in convincing him he looked a hell of a lot better than he had before and, using her to buttress my allegations, he finally agreed, ending a rather messy scene.

CHAPTER EIGHTEEN
HUMBUGABLE "HOWLIN' MAD" SMITH

When I got back to Washington to end my career with OSS, I learned that I still had about six or seven months in the Navy before I could get out on points. However, this was assuaged somewhat when I learned I had picked up another half stripe in rank, making me a Lieutenant Commander.

I called a good friend of mine in San Diego, Captain Perkins, who was Chief of Naval Intelligence in the area. He had been boss of the Immigration officers and was stationed at San Ysidro when I was working around there in the Customs Patrol in the early 30's. I told him I had run out of race track with OSS and still had some time to go before I could return to civilian life. He asked for my serial number so he could wire a request and sent me to the Bureau of Personnel to request a transfer to his office in San Diego.

"By hitting them from both ends like this," the Captain said, "you'll be on the train tomorrow." And I was.

Once in Kansas City I wired my old friend, Henry "Hank" Adams, to tell him I was arriving. "Hank" had been in seven major landings in the Pacific before the War ended and had

HILARIOUS HIGH JINKS

recently changed his beat from that of a Marine Lieutenant Colonel to his old job of Undersheriff of San Diego County.

Hank met me at the depot. I was to stay with him and his new bride until I found quarters. He said San Diego was so full of people you couldn't get a reservation at the Helping Hand Mission without a request from President Truman.

On the way to his house he told me that his old friend, General Holland "Howlin' Mad" Smith, had returned from the Pacific and was now Commanding Officer at the Marine Recruit Depot in San Diego. He said the General was having a party that evening at his residence. Hank had been invited and he would call General Smith and get me invited, too.

Smith agreed to Hank's request and that evening as we drove over there, Hank said, "Now, Lee, there's something about General Smith that few people know. He's an absolute and complete gudgeon for a slight-of-hand trick."

Hank knew I was quite dexterous at making a quarter disappear by holding it between my first two fingers, running it down the edge of my thumb and turning it slightly to where I could hold it well down in my palm between my index finger and my thumb. By using this technique, all sorts of things are possible, such as throwing it through a hat and picking it off a person's clothing.

"Now, when we get there and I introduce you to General Smith," Hank continued, "I'll hand you my big western hat and you ask him if he's ever seen a man throw a quarter through a hat. From then on, you'll absolutely have him in your power."

I was completely dubious about this. I'd never gone up against a four-star before with a whizzer such as this, and frankly said so.

"Don't worry, Lee," Hank said. 'You'll have him, all right. He'll forget about his party."

When we entered the residence, a Filipino houseboy took our cards and the famous General came to greet us. He was of medium height but showed great strength in his shoulders. He

130

wore steel-rimmed glasses over his small, shoe-button eyes and his face crinkled with genuine pleasure when he saw Hank Adams.

"This is Lieutenant Commander Echols, General," Hank said and before the General was finished greeting me, Hank had handed me his hat.

I gulped a couple of times and my throat felt like I'd just swallowed a dollop of wine vinegar. It took me three false starts to say it, but I finally came out with, "Ever see a man throw a quarter through a hat, General?" and my tone was in a much higher decibel than I had expected.

His eyes squinted up in a sort of incredulous scowl and I feared Hank had tricked me.

"Why, no, Commander," the General finally said, curious now. "I don't believe I ever have."

I took Hank's big hat and made a motion as though I was throwing the quarter at the crown. Actually, I ran it down my thumb and rested it in my palm. At the same time I snapped my middle finger off my index finger of the hand with which I was holding the hat. This made a loud sound as though the quarter had actually hit the crown of the hat. Then I turned the hat over, slyly releasing the quarter into the crown and picking it up to show him.

A complete metamorphosis took place with General Smith. He got an artful, Machiavellian look and his little beady eyes screwed up more than ever.

"Hey, now! Do that again, young man!" he demanded. I did it again and he shook his head in complete disbelief.

"Get in this room here!" he ordered, propelling me by the arm. "I'll get to the bottom of this!"

He hustled me into a small room off the entrance hall and demanded that I do the trick some more. This time, instead of finding it in the hat, I plucked it off his shoulder.

"Hey, now, that's not fair!" he shouted. "I was looking for it in the hat! Now get on with it! Show me some more! I'll catch you this time!"

HILARIOUS HIGH JINKS

He kept me in the room for half an hour, forgot about his guests and had me go through my repertoire dozens of times. He never had an inkling of how it was done and finally his wife, Ada, came to the room and practically dragged him out.

I got well acquainted with the fiery old General. We made several forays into Baja California below Mexicali with Hank Adams, Hank's brother, John, Brick Lowe and John Rutman to hunt geese in the lower Colorado River basin.

On one of these trips, we stayed all night in Calexico before going into Mexico. My father had asked us over to his home for cocktails that evening.

After the first drink, which we were enjoying in the den, General Smith disappeared. He didn't come back for about half an hour and we began looking for him. We found him in the living room, surrounded by my nine year old daughter and the neighborhood kids, playing marbles on the rug. He was in a violent quarrel with my daughter. It was his turn to shoot and she had yelled, "Knuckles down, bony tight!"

"I'm already losers," he screamed back at her. "You've outsmarted me on every turn and you want me to shoot 'knuckles down, bony tight' so you can get more marbles from me!"

He fussed and carried on, oblivious to our arrival, but our daughter prevailed and he grudgingly agreed to do it her way, and of course, missed his "taw."

When the kids won the remainder of his marbles, he came into the kitchen for another drink, mumbling about how they'd ganged up on him, cheated him unmercifully and busted him out of the game. The children were completely enthralled with him.

I am firmly convinced that there never lived a finer fighting General nor a tougher one. I'm also convinced he was the world's greatest "winchell" for a magic trick. I suppose if he'd ever seen a complicated one, like sawing a woman in half or making an elephant appear on the stage behind a small sheet, he'd have pulled out his sword and fallen on it like he forced hundreds of Japanese officers to do when his Marines overran their islands.

In 1952, the National Rifle Association of America held its Annual Meetings in San Francisco and General Holland Smith was invited as the key speaker. Hank Adams and I were there and we learned that the General had arrived from his home in La Jolla and was staying at the St. Francis Hotel.

At that time, the public relations representative for the NRA was Paul Cardinal who had been an Army Major during World War II. Paul knew that Hank Adams and I were friends of the General and asked if we'd accompany him and make the introduction so he could officially greet the General and assist him prior to the dinner meeting. He told us the General was waiting in the lobby of the St. Francis.

Hank and I readily agreed. In the taxi on the way to meet General Smith, we could see that Paul was quite nervous about meeting such an illustrious personage.

"Be very much on your dignity," Hank told him sagely. "When we get in the lobby, assume a stiff military bearing and as you march up to the chair where he is sitting, immediately go into a smart military salute with a sharp clicking of your heels and hold it until he puts you at ease."

"Oh, he's a stickler for decorum, all right, Paul!" I cut in. "March up there like a well trained soldier. When he sees the type of salute you can perform this long after your military life, he'll take you to his heart!"

Now, without Paul's knowledge, Hank and I had a pair of those big rubber masks you can pull quickly over your head in our overcoat pockets. Mine was a replica of Mortiner Snerd and Hank's was that of a giant, orange-faced baboon.

When we arrived at the St. Francis, we saw General Smith sitting in a corner by himself, reading *The Wall Street Journal*. We pointed him out to Paul, pushed him out in front and watched him go into his military cadence. His shoulders were squared, chin in, chest out and his rhythmic meter was in perfect timing as he marched briskly toward the General.

HILARIOUS HIGH JINKS

"Great day, Lee!" Hank whispered as we dropped back to put on our masks. "Paul could qualify as Honor Guard for the Tomb of the Unknown Soldier!"

We barely had time to get our ghoulish masks on before Paul hauled up in front of the General's chair. He put his right elbow out and brought his arm up in the finest salute I'd seen since I got out of the Naval Officer's Training School. His heels went together with such a crash of leather as to bring the eyes of the house detective on him. Paul's eyes were bugged out and his mouth was drawn down in an expression that said, "I'm here, Sir, and ready!"

Hank and I slouched behind him, wearing our masks. We must have looked like a couple of escaped padded cell patients from the idiot rookery. The General looked up from his paper at this panorama, squinted hard at the rigid Paul Cardinal and then his gaze fell on Hank and me. By this time, we were doing a sort of stomping dance we hoped would be reminiscent of the victory scalp dance executed by the Mescalero Apaches.

The General watched this scene for almost a minute, his little beady eyes scrunching up in complete disbelief. Finally he said, "I don't have any idea who this flawless fool in front is, but that pair of addleheaded jobberknowls behind him have got to be Hank Adams and Lee Echols. There isn't a living human in the civilized world who could drum up a situation like this but them!"

Paul whirled on us, so brittle he seemed to be breaking up, and when he saw how he'd been had, he walked slowly over to the wall. He put one arm on the wall, leaned his head against it and started beating the wall with his other fist, as strangled cries came from his throat.

I kept in touch with the grand old General until shortly before his death. I sent him birthday greetings when I was Sheriff of Yuma County, along with a deputy sheriff card and an invitation to go quail hunting on the Indian reservation near Parker, Arizona.

He wrote the following letter that I have kept for years,

Dear Lee:

Please do not judge my appreciation of your birthday card by my tardiness in thanking you. I often thought about our hunting trips and you and Hank Adams and the amazing magic tricks you could perform. It seems years ago. As age creeps up on me, I have given up golf, hunting and all forms of strenuous exercise. Actually, I feel as well as I have for many years, but I do tire easily.

I appreciate my sheriff's card and especially the friendly spirit that prompted it. Should you ever come this way, I would be highly pleased if you would drop by. I appreciate hearing from you. There is nothing comparable to a friendship between strong men. Immodestly, I place myself in your capacity.

> With all good wishes,
> Your old friend,
>
> H. M. Smith

He died before I saw him again. His last years were spent in La Jolla, California, with his wife, his grandchildren and his flowers. An unbelievable man. He and his beloved Marines brought the Japanese Empire to capitulation, but he couldn't figure out how that quarter got in Hank's hat, and had to shoot "bony tight" and lose all his marbles when a nine year old girl ordered it.

CHAPTER NINETEEN

FROM NAVAL INTELLIGENCE TO THE NRA

My six months' tour with the Naval Intelligence Office in San Diego went by so quickly and pleasantly that I was amazed when it was over. I worked on several assignments with a Lieutenant Commander Turrentine. In assessing him and his methods, I decided he was probably the fairest minded man I had ever worked with. He has been a U.S. Federal Judge in San Diego for about 25 years.

One of the first cases concerned a chief petty officer, stationed at Miramar Air Base near San Diego, whose job was that of reassigning enlisted personnel returning from the Pacific and who had some time to serve before they were eligible to get out of the Navy.

Now, as these men had been in the war zone for a long time, they had invariably saved up quite a sum of money and this chief petty officer figured out a nice way to get some of it. When one would appear before him for reassignment, he would find out the sailor's home of record. Then he would show him the nearest Navy installation to his home and advise that for $250 he would assign him there until his Navy time was up. He was picking up several thousand dollars a day with this little operation. We were able to scrag him when five of us, dressed as enlisted men with papers showing we had just come off a returning carrier, appeared before him for our next assignment. I was dressed as a chief petty officer and although I'm completely adverse to bragging about myself, I sure looked like a salty, old seafaring dog.

I told him my home was in Waukegan, Illinois and he quickly said he could shoot me directly to the Great Lakes Naval Training Station for $250. I agreed to this, paid him off with marked money and Lieutenant Commander Turrentine came along right behind me. Turrentine bambozled him, also, and so did the next three men and then we, as the saying goes, put the big britches on him. I don't know whether his home town was up in the State of Washington, but that's where we sent him to the federal penitentiary.

We worked on a commander who was a dentist. He was being released from the Service and his idea was to furnish his civilian office with Navy dental equipment. He hired a drayman, who was cleared to take cargo off and on the Navy Recruit Depot, to haul his two dental chairs and everything that went with them past the Navy guards at the entrance and on the Santa Fe Depot, from where they would be shipped to his home in Texas.

The Navy guard at the gate wasn't too satisfied with the papers shown him by the drayman to clear the equipment off the yard. He came to our office and I was assigned the case. It was a simple matter to break the commander and he not only went out of the Navy with a dishonorable discharge, but he had to serve hard time for his discrepancy.

These seemed like penny-ante deals after my two years' assignment in Mexico on the 107th Street Gang and our OSS assignment. I was mighty glad when my time was up and I was able to get out of the Navy and return to my old job as Special Agent with the Customs Service, even though it was in Laredo, Texas. I might state that most Oakies look on Texas as "Baja, Oklahoma."

Heroin, opium and marijuana were all crossing the border from Mexico in great quantities and my work took me all over Texas running down the perpetrators.

I quickly found out that although my salary hadn't improved much since the time I went into the Navy, neither had my travelling per diem. I seemed to be on the move most of the time on six dollars per day. I'd spend that much before I got my bags into a hotel in Houston, Dallas or Austin and I began to wonder if there wasn't something else I could be doing.

In those days, the federal retirement was unbelievably small. Regardless of your grade, you worked until you were 70 years of age and then got out of the service at the stupendous retirement of $100 per month!

I was mulling this over in late August of 1946, when I got a phone call from C. B. Lister, the Director of the National Rifle Association in Washington, D.C.

He asked me if I could get a couple of weeks off and come back to Camp Perry, Ohio, to write the article about the pistol matches for the AMERICAN RIFLEMAN magazine. I told him I would have sufficient annual leave to make the trip and he insisted that I leave Texas a little early and come by the NRA in Washington, as they wanted to see me on a matter of great importance.

I couldn't figure what that could be, but arrived about three days before the Matches began at Camp Perry and was ushered into a meeting room where I found most of the top NRA officials waiting for me.

They asked me to sit down and Mr. Lister said, "Lee, I don't know whether you've heard this or not, but the NRA has grown from about 80,000 members at the beginning of World War II to over 300,000. We have decided that our membership is large enough to warrant field managers throughout the United States. Their jobs will be to help gun clubs get organized, furnish them with architectural plans for club houses and range construction, and talk to university classes, gun clubs, service clubs and city council members, among other things.

"These field managers will also help our friends in local, state and federal elective offices in combating ridiculous gun control laws that will be presented all over the country, now that the War is over.

"Now, Lee," Lister said, with his big, wide grin. "We've picked you out as a hot prospect for one of these jobs. We know your present grade with Customs and we are able to offer you a 15% raise over that."

"Now, wait a minute, Mr. Lister," I said. "In my present job I travel most of the time. I only get six dollars a day for this travel and it costs me much more. I can see that the field manager's job will entail a great deal of travel. If I consider it, I would have to know what my daily amount would be in the way of per diem."

Lister gave me that great grin of his. "Why, Lee," he said, "you wouldn't get any per diem for your travel."

"Then how in the world can you hire people to run all over the United States on their own money?" I said.

I think everyone in the room laughed at this except me. "Here's how that will be managed, Lee," Lister said. "You will set up an office, hire a secretary and we will start a bank account for you wherever you decide to locate your office. We will start your bank account with $5,000 and you will voucher us for whatever you have spent during that month's period. That means office rent, secretary's salary, your salary, office expenses, mileage on your car and your travel expenses.

"Now, this means that whatever you spend, you can voucher for it back to NRA. However, if you wind up having to pay $100 for a dinner with a group of enthusiastic members, you will have to tighten up your belt for a few days to amortize it.

"If you would consider taking this position, Lee, walk over to the big map there on the wall and point out an area where you would like to serve as field manager."

& DANGEROUS ASSIGNMENTS

Guy Echols, Lee's father, was an Oklahoma cattleman and later Chief of Police of Calexico, California, for 20 years.

The Border City Rhythm Kings Jazz Band in Calexico, California, 1925. Lee is at the drums.

HILARIOUS HIGH JINKS

The U.S. Customs Border Patrol for San Diego and Imperial Counties, 1929. Lee Echols is third from left, front row, and Carl Eifler is third from right, same row.

Special Agent Johnnie Hooe (right) and Lee Echols (left) with 156 pounds of crude opium seized after a gun fight with Mafia members, New York, 1939.

Mel Rogers, fellow Treasury Department Team member and sometimes the butt of Lee's jokes, once complained that it seemed like every time he shot the lowest score on the team, they broke a world record. Replied Echols, "I don't remember you ever shooting low man on the team!"

HILARIOUS HIGH JINKS

The renowned Smitty Brown with his trained ape checking one of *their* targets at the Midwinter International Tournament in Tampa, Florida, 1939.

The famous U.S. Treasury Department Pistol Team, holder of every team world record, pictured at Camp Perry in 1940. Left to right, Lee Echols, Arnvid Anderson, Mel Rogers, Charlie Hubbard (coach), Al Meloche and Pete Chapman.

& DANGEROUS ASSIGNMENTS

Echols turned his M1911 pistol and his remarkable skills to winning the 1941 National Pistol Championship at Camp Perry.

HILARIOUS HIGH JINKS

Lee Echols, shortly after he entered the U.S. Navy, proudly displays many of his shooting trophies and medals.

& DANGEROUS ASSIGNMENTS

Colonel Carl Eifler (left), and General "Wild Bill" Donovan, 200 miles behind the Japanese lines in Burma.

HILARIOUS HIGH JINKS

Lee, winner of the Texas State Pistol Championship in 1946, shown with his trophies and medals.

& DANGEROUS ASSIGNMENTS

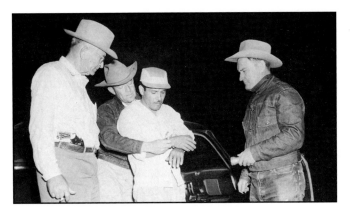

Pete Newman, Yuma Sheriff in 1953, apprehends a heroin smuggler as Customs Agents Charley Cameron (left) and Lee Echols look on.

A drug smuggler is questioned by Lee Echols (left) during an opium bust in Yuma, Arizona, 1954.

HILARIOUS HIGH JINKS

Lee's wife, Helen, and granddaughter Juanita, holding a jewelry box bought in Bolivia and authenticated as a present from Napoleon to Josephine.

& DANGEROUS ASSIGNMENTS

Lee Echols and friends offer a panoramic view of the 34-foot Anaconda snake (skin) that he "almost captured," then killed, while on assignment in Bolivia.

Yuma County Sheriff Echols (center) with his Deputies, 1961.

HILARIOUS HIGH JINKS

Public Safety Advisor Mike Salcedo (right) and Lee Echols stop off in Havana for a visit with Hernando Hernandez Hernandez (center), Chief of the Cuban National Police. Hernandez, a long-time pistol shooting friend of Echols, was later executed by Castro's forces.

Captain Viriato Brito Pilier of the Dominican Secret Police was one of the bravest officers with whom Lee Echols worked while on assignment in Santo Domingo in 1965.

& DANGEROUS ASSIGNMENTS

Helen and Lee Echols learning to dance the *merengue* in Santo Domingo, 1963.

HILARIOUS HIGH JINKS

Byron Engle, Director of Public Safety, Agency for International Development, congratulates Lee upon reaching 30 years of Government service. Lee continued with the Government for another eight years.

Lee Echols put on his famous pistol shooting exhibition at a fundraising barbecue for his friend, U.S. Congressman Duncan Hunter, in El Cajon, California.

& DANGEROUS ASSIGNMENTS

Lee came from a family of law enforcement officers. His father was Chief of Police of Calexico, California, for 20 years and carried the Colt single action .45 (top of frame). One of the badges belonged to Lee's grandfather, a Deputy U.S. Marshal in the Indian Territory.

HILARIOUS HIGH JINKS

Lee Echols with friend. The inscription reads, "To Lee Boy, come back to the Ranch! Bring your pistols! Best Wishes, Ronald Reagan." (Another Lee high jink. All for $5 and a cardboard figure.)

U.S. Vice President Dan Quayle with Lee Echols in San Diego, California, February, 1990.

& DANGEROUS ASSIGNMENTS

I got to thinking I'd never been talked to like this in the Customs Service! They handed me a pointer and I made my way to the big map. I pointed out California, Arizona, New Mexico, Nevada, Oregon and Washington. And, as an afterthought, I pointed out part of Texas that covered El Paso.

"Well," Lister said, "that all makes sense. You probably know more members and shooters in those areas than in any other part of the United States." And then he put a real dream request to me.

"Now, go over to the map and point out a place where you'd like to set up your office," he said.

I turned over two spittoons getting to San Diego with my pointer!

"We'll put you to work as soon as you get through with your Camp Perry assignment," Lister said. "We'll pay for the shipment of your household effects to San Diego and you can get busy setting up your office immediately."

"Now, wait a minute," I interjected. "Mr. Lister, there are a lot things contingent on my taking this position, although it certainly sounds interesting. One of them is my wife, Helen. I never take any sort of new position or even a transfer to another locale, without talking it over with her. I think she will go for it, but I'll have to find out.

"Another thing, I have several important federal court cases coming up between now and the end of the year in Brownsville and Laredo. If I accept your fine offer, it will have to be after they are concluded.

"As soon as I get back to Laredo, I will talk this over with Helen and if she is agreeable, I will be able to turn myself over to the National Rifle Association early in January."

"That all makes sense," Lister said. "We'll hold everything in abeyance until we hear from you in Laredo after you and Helen have talked it over."

"You'll need a good secretary," he said.

"I already have one in mind. Her name is Virginia Smith and she's the best secretary in the office of the collector of

HILARIOUS HIGH JINKS

Customs in Laredo. She lost her husband when the First Marine Division went ashore on Guadalcanal and I think she'd like a change of scenery.

"I'll get on up to Camp Perry and write the article for the AMERICAN RIFLEMAN."

As the meeting broke up, Mr. Lister said, "By the way, Lee, just because you'll be writing the article about the pistol matches doesn't mean you're barred from shooting in them."

I told him I hadn't done very much shooting since the War began but I might try my hand at it for a few of the matches.

I tried it but didn't do anything outstanding except for the .45 slow-fire match. This was a 20-shot match, slow-fire, at 50 yards on what they call the standard American target. I had won that match in 1941, the year I won the Custer Trophy. I had a good day and won it again with what at that time was a Camp Perry record.

I wrote the article for the RIFLEMAN, went back to Laredo and talked the new deal over with Helen. We were both in accord that it would be a good change, especially when we spoke of the small travel allotment the Government was furnishing and the niggardly pension system they had in effect.

I called Mr. Lister and told him we were going to accept the position and that I would let him know when I was finished with my court cases in Brownsville and Laredo.

While I was in Laredo, still waiting to be subpoenaed for federal court in Brownsville, I read in the *Laredo Times* that there was a Thanksgiving pistol turkey shoot being held at Zapata, about 40 miles from Laredo. I talked with my two old shooting buddies on the Treasury Team, Aaron Quick and "Spot" Osmer, both of whom were working as Customs special agents in Laredo. We were just back from the National Matches at Camp Perry and hot as depot stoves and decided we'd go over and see what they had going in this turkey shoot.

I told Aaron and Spot to keep our beautiful guns in the car until we learned what the deal was, and we walked over and asked the man who was running the shoot to describe it to us.

"Well," he said, "you get three shots for a dollar. You shoot at a clay pigeon at 50 yards. If you hit it, you get to shoot again and you are allowed to win two turkeys for your dollar if you can hit two clay pigeons with three shots."

Aaron Quick got a cagy expression on his face. "Suppose we get lucky?" he said. "Suppose we begin winning several turkeys, will we be barred from shooting for any more?"

The man laughed. "Listen, friend," he said. "There have been men shooting out here all day and nobody has won a turkey yet. Let's put it this way, I have 13 turkeys. You boys shoot for them until I run out of turkeys or you run out of money."

There were several old cowboys out on the line, shooting in a whangety-bang manner with single-action .45 pistols. Their bullets would either hit the sand some 20 feet before they got to the clay pigeon or go clear over the backstop and cut branches off the trees behind them.

We went back to the car and got our equipment. We won all the turkeys he had in less than three minutes and made fun of Quick all the way back to Laredo for missing one of them with his first shot.

We furnished turkeys to our Customs friends for a nice Thanksgiving Dinner. About four months later, I was getting a haircut in a Laredo barber shop. When it came time for the barber to shave around my neck, he laid his razor right on my jugular vein.

"Do you remember me?" he asked and I don't believe I've ever seen a more malevolent expression on a man's face.

"No," I told him, trying to edge away from the razor, but having no luck as he followed my jugular with it.

"I'm the son-of-a-bitch you won all those turkeys from in Zapata a few months ago!" he said and raised the razor as if he would not only sever my jugular with it, but might also go clear through my brain stem and scar it up somewhat.

"Now, there was nothing personal about that!" I cried as I

HILARIOUS HIGH JINKS

jumped out of the chair. "We just went over there and got lucky! How much do I owe you? I don't need my neck shaved!"

He laughed and wiped off his razor. "They're still talking about it over there in Zapata," he said. "You boys sure showed those cattlemen how to break clay pigeons!"

CHAPTER TWENTY
SALVOS IN GUATEMALA

My wife, Helen, and Virginia Smith were real good friends and when we discussed NRA's job offer with her, she said, "Let's go!" I called the NRA and said we were ready.

Helen, little Donna and I drove to San Diego, rented a nice two-room office, found ourselves a new apartment, called Virginia and asked her to come to California. She did, liked it fine and, since she had two small children and a Mexican maid, we began looking for a house for her. In those days right after the War, a veteran could buy a house using a Government loan, but they had overlooked the possibility of the widow of a veteran having that same privilege. "Virgie," therefore, wasn't eligible for a Veterans Administration loan. However, I was, so I used my benefit and bought a nice home for her in National City, south of San Diego. Our household effects were shipped from Texas by NRA and we were in business.

I believe that of all the interesting jobs I have had, the one with the NRA had them all beat.

The best part of it was that I didn't have anything to sell. I just traveled around my district, giving things away. New clubs were clamoring for help to build club houses and ranges and I offered detailed plans in great abundance. I helped clubs

HILARIOUS HIGH JINKS

set up tournaments and refereed big matches throughout my district. I talked before Rotary, Kiwanis, Lions and other service clubs. I set up junior rifle clubs throughout the several states I had under my jurisdiction and helped them get places to shoot through their city governments.

With the help of local shooters, we convinced the City of El Paso to construct a pistol range in an abandoned rock quarry. It had 50 air-operated targets and a beautiful club house. In my hometown of Calexico, California, the Chamber of Commerce helped us build another fine range. We held big annual international pistol tournaments there and attracted shooters from all over the United States and several top teams from Mexico.

And then one day in early 1950, I got a phone call from C. B. Lister. "Would you like to go down to Guatemala for about a month," he asked, "to help run the pistol and rifle matches for the Sixth Pan American and Caribbean Olympic Games?"

"Just say when," I said. "I'm rarin' to go."

"All right," he said, "you'll be going down there in about a week. You will be joined there by General Sid Hines, Colonel Paul Roberts and your old friend, Phil Roettinger."

All this sounded mighty fine to me. Sid Hines was an old Army shooter and a tank commander in World War II. Paul Roberts had worked in civilian life with the Western Ammunition Company as their West Coast representative and stayed in the Army after the end of the War. Phil Roettinger was one of the top shooters in the U.S. and I had known him since he was about 23 years old. He later became a range officer at Quantico and eventually a Marine Colonel with a lot of service in the Pacific during the War.

All of these men were well qualified for the assignment and I was happy to tag along to Guatemala with such a group. It is quite possible that I was chosen for the assignment because of my ability to speak Spanish.

A girl asked me recently if I could speak Spanish and I told her, "I speak it just like I do English," and a good friend of mine, Don Perry, told her, "And if you listen to him speak English for about 15 minutes, you can tell that he doesn't hardly speak Spanish at all."

The DC-6 settled by the head like a hog in a bean field and circled between the great volcanos of Agua and Pacaya. It roared past Lake Amatitlan and onto the long runway of Guatemala City Airport. I thought of the three men I was to work with while I was disembarking. They had the knack of being able to recognize a funny situation when they saw one and they happened in Guatemala, with hilarious regularity.

Three businesslike young men rushed up to me at the airport lobby and asked if I was Mr. Echols. When I replied in the affirmative, one of them stepped forward and greeted me in a dignified manner.

"Meester Echols, my name is Luis Escobar. I am on the welcoming committee for the Oleempics! Your room is ready and you will find it to be the finest in all Guatemala! Your meals will be served on the preemises!"

By this time I had noticed a second emissary who was chomping at the bit and had pushed his way in front of Escobar. "My name is Jesus Cordoba, Meester Echols," he said, bowing very low. "Your baggage will go through without inspection."

The third greeter, who was almost apoplectic by this time, pushed the other two into the background. With a look on his face like the late King George of England presenting the medal of Stonehenge Antiquity to an underling, he said, "If jew want quetzales to spend while jew are here, jew shall have them!"

And he spread out his hands in a gesture such as a magician might use when he is showing an audience that he has nothing to hide.

At that time I had no more idea what quetzales were than I did how to knit a crewneck sweater, but I wasn't long in learning that a quetzal was legal tender and at that time was worth a round, silver dollar. It is also a small Guatemalan bird, green as a ripe lime and sporting a tail like a Saks Fifth Avenue hat. There were more of the paper ones flying around Guatemala than the feathered ones.

The judges for the different events were to be quartered at the nurses' school. I learned on arrival that none of the others were there yet, but that Phil Roettinger and his wife were expected within the hour. They had entered Guatemala at Puerto Barrios by steamer from New Orleans, and were coming across to Guatemala City on the narrow gauge railroad that day.

Phil Roettinger was a shooter whose physical appearance never gave him away as a great bullseye man. With a few notable exceptions, your top handgunner is a stocky, short-armed fellow with an easygoing disposition. Phil had the latter attribute, but there the comparison had to stop. Phil was high like a pecan tree and gaunt like a hungry timber wolf. He looked like a lot of bones with the meat scraped off and his arms were long enough to fasten his garters while standing at attention.

The desk clerk notified me when Phil and his wife checked in, and after about 20 minutes, I knocked on their door. I had one of those large trick noses with eyeglasses that made anyone wearing them look like Groucho Marx. When Phil opened the door, face covered with lather, I opened up on him. I had decided he missed out on the welcoming committee by entering the country at Puerto Barrios, so I tried to give him the nice treatment I had received at the airport.

"Meester Roettinger!" I roared in the enthusiastic manner of my friends awaiting me on arrival. "My name is Julio Torreon. I am on the welcoming committee for the Oleempics!"

I was watching Phil closely while handing him this stuff and I could see that he hadn't seen through my disguise. I decided to really pour it on.

"Meester Roettinger," I said, shaking his hand like a Swiss milker pumping the mammary gland of a dairy Durham, "we haf read about your wahnderful shooting! You haf shot on the Oleempics at Lahndon!"

Phil smiled, returning my handshake with one equally as friendly. I could see he was genuinely pleased to learn that he was so well known in Guatemala.

"Did you hear that?" he yelled to his wife. "They've heard about me way down here!"

His wife stuck her head out the door, with cold cream all over her face and her hair up in curlers. She gave me a quick glance and said to Phil, "You'd better recount your beads, Lengthy. That's Lee Echols you're talking to." Phil was a little jumpy over it for two or three days.

By the time Sid Hines and Paul Roberts arrived, we had begun meeting the various shooters and delegates. It was becoming apparent that this was to be quite a tournament, with 10 countries and insular possessions entered. We heard more variations of Spanish and English than I thought existed. Many of the shooters were old friends of ours. We knew most of the Mexican team, the Cubans—this was nine years before the Castro takeover—and some of the boys from El Salvador. I knew the Puerto Rican delegation and we spent several enjoyable sessions together drinking deeply from the pitcher of memory.

The fun really started when we held our first delegates' meeting. A Guatemalan named Jose Guirola was chairman of the meeting and he started off very conscientiously, running the meeting in Spanish. Then, after quite a bit of argument, mostly because some Spanish words had different meanings in the various countries, he would meticulously translate the discussion into English for the benefit of Dr. Benito Machado who, despite his Spanish-sounding name, was the Jamaican delegate and knew no Spanish at all.

However, after the arguments reached the arm-waving stage, Guirola forgot to do any translating and the various delegates would go into great detail in Spanish, using colloquialisms found only in their particular countries and that were entirely misinterpreted by the others. These misunderstandings led to louder and more turbulent speeches.

HILARIOUS HIGH JINKS

Finally, after about 20 minutes of this, with all the delegates talking at once except for Dr. Machado who was sitting there, half amazed at it all, Guirola would turn to Machado. He would explain the discussion, tell him that some motion had been proposed, discussed and voted upon and then he would advise Machado of the outcome of the vote.

This went on for some time. Finally Benito Machado asked for the floor. When the hullabaloo died down enough for him to be heard, he said in a voice filled with tender solicitude, "Gentlemen, I know the hour is getting late and I am beastly tired. I have flown from Kingston today through rawther nawsty weather. This may have something to do with influencing me in my feelings but it just doesn't seem quite cricket for you chaps to discuss these various problems in a language with which I am entirely unfamiliar, make motions concerning them and only *then* translate your decisions to me."

This justifiable complaint was well received and in almost no time Machado was again getting the current gist of the discussions instead of a translation after the vote.

The practice sessions at the beautiful Guatemala range showed that although Benito Machado had never fired in a match, he was a very "close holder" and was racking up some slow-fire, free pistol scores that would have been creditable tallies at Buenos Aires or London.

However, when the free pistol match was held on opening day, Machado came face to face with a formidable enemy of match shooters that had been laying waste to top scores since the invention of the rifled barrel, and known to the trade as "Buck Fever." Machado went down under this initial assault, allowing "Old Buck" to cover his entire body with a set of hoarfrost shakes that were unbelievable to behold. Machado walked off the line, confused, perplexed and completely beaten.

"How'd you make out, Benito?" Phil asked.

Machado forced a small, sick grin and replied, "I think if I

& DANGEROUS ASSIGNMENTS

hadn't gotten so blahsted frightened I'd have soundly beaten all of the bloody boogers!"

Nevertheless, he was quick to reassemble his wits and went on to win the .22 national pistol match and the .22 50 meter rifle event.

Humberto Medrano was not so fortunate. Humberto was one of the top shooters from Havana, and Roettinger and I had shot with him many years at the great Florida matches. The Coral Gables matches had been stormed by an attorney named Clem Theed and Roettinger asked Humberto, "When did you see Clem Theed and the boys from Coral Gables?"

"Clem Theed and the boys from Coral Gables, bah!" Medrano snorted. "I saw this fellow at Jacksonveel," and his face lit up with instant displeasure. "They were in the hotel room and they had a bottle of this stuff, what do you call it?" Then he remembered and answered his own question, "Old Kentucky Dad!" he beamed.

"I had a Havana shooter with me named Montez and he drink the Old Kentucky Dad...and he drink the Old Kentucky Dad...and finally he raise up and spread the arms and he beller, 'America! Cuba! Friendship!' and he fall over on his back, boom. We have to carry Montez up three floors to his room." Medrano shook his head at the ghastly thought. "Clem Theed and the boys from Coral Gables! Bah!" he said.

Medrano got off to a flying start in the .22 national match course. He shot a 97 slow-fire, a slick 100 timed-fire and only dropped two points his first string of rapid-fire. He was shooting for a 295 and the awful look he assumed for the firing of his last string of rapid-fire drew a goodly crowd of curious spectators.

If they were looking for an exhibition, Medrano didn't disappoint them. He fired his five shots in such a wild manner that Benito Machado beat him with a score of 279. I watched Medrano and he looked like he had just learned that the island of Cuba was breaking up and sinking in the Gulf of Mexico. I stopped him as he walked off the line.

HILARIOUS HIGH JINKS

"What happened to you, Medrano?" I asked.

He stopped in his tracks, set down his gun box and said in an earnest, quivering voice, "We Latins shoot from deep in the heart...and you...you fellows...you shoot from the guts!"

As I walked away from him, he had already started to cry.

Sid Hines and Phil Roettinger served as range officers for the service rifle team match and, since they didn't speak Spanish, it was decided that we would get an interpreter for each of them. Since then Roettinger has lived many years in Mexico and speaks Spanish like a Madrid lawyer, but in 1950 he couldn't say "adios" in Spanish.

The interpreters were to stay with them throughout the match and help straighten out any difficulties. We were fortunate to get a young Guatemalan for Sid who had attended school in the States and who spoke very good English. Our efforts were not so fruitful, however, in our quest for Phil's man, and we finally settled for a rangy boy from British Honduras named Reginald Bushnell. He had come to Guatemala as a broad jumper with the team from Belize and, either by accident or design, had wandered out to the rifle range.

We found that he spoke very little Spanish, or English for that matter, and although we tried him out in most of the languages used in the Western Hemisphere, none of them seemed to be particularly native to him. In addition, he had a sly, skeptical expression about the entire procedure as if to indicate that he didn't believe one bit of it. If we were putting on this treacherous hoax to try to straw-bail him, we were wasting a lot of time, as he was completely wise to our little trickeries.

He watched with incredulous suspicion as the practice targets came up from the pits 300 meters away and the shooters prepared their equipment on the line. He even assumed a tolerant little smile as the firing began, indicative of his willingness to indulge our puny attempts at raillery.

The shooting had barely started, however, when all hell, in

its strictest sense, broke loose at the targets assigned to the Cuban Army Team. It broke loose in loud, staccato blasts of words over the field phone assigned to Captain Sebastian Garcia Herrera, the Delegate and Coach of the Cuban Team, and the mighty blasts were coming from the throat of the good Captain himself. He would scream into the phone, the veins standing out on his forehead like war roads on a map of Anzio Beach.

Then he would quit talking into the phone, slam down the receiver and start talking *at* it. His voice would rise like the ululations of a water buffalo and diminish to the bubbling cry of a swimmer with a green apple cramp. Then he would go through it again and finally would rush up to Phil Roettinger and roar.

Phil's interpreter maintained his tolerant, tongue-in-cheek smile through all this, as if he knew that this, too, was part of the hoax being played on him.

After Captain Garcia Herrera had rent the air like bagpipes and doodle sacks for fully 15 minutes, Phil finally asked his British Honduran assistant what in the name of a bountiful God ailed the Captain. Bushnell looked up at Roettinger with a "you're- not-kidding-me-big-boy" look on his flat face.

"He say," Bushnell said slowly, "that when his men throw at the 'blanc' they don't pull the 'blanc' down fast enough."

Bushnell stayed the rest of the day, following Phil around with a look of sheer disbelief on his face. I'll bet he went back to British Honduras feeling pretty smug in the thought that, whatever our little scheme was, we didn't put it over on him. Not a damn bit.

CHAPTER TWENTY-ONE

BACK WITH CUSTOMS

When the Guatemalan matches were finally over, I bade everyone goodbye and got back to San Diego just in time to go to Calexico for the big pistol tournament. I liked my job with the NRA more all the time. There was one small problem, however. Although the U.S. Government could offer me only $100 a month when I retired at age 70, the NRA couldn't offer me a thing except Social Security, and at that time I didn't even know what that was.

About that time the FBI got what was called "The Hazardous Duty Retirement Act" through Congress. It allowed any Government employee working in a gun-carrying job to retire at age 50 with 20 years' service. I was giving this quite a bit of thought when we attended the NRA convention in San Francisco in the Fall of 1951.

Helen, Virginia and I were there and it was one of the best NRA conventions since I went to work for them five years before. A group of us were in our suite at the St. Francis Hotel when I got a call from Larry Fleishman, the Customs Supervising Agent in El Paso.

"Lee," he said, "you've probably heard of our new Retirement Act."

"Yes," I said, "I sure have! It's a mighty good one and I sort of wish I'd stayed in!"

HILARIOUS HIGH JINKS

"Well," he said, "here's your chance. I've just received word from the Bureau of Customs that we're going into an austerity program and that we may not be able to hire new people for two or three years. However, I've gone through your personnel file and find that you have 19 years with Customs and that your retirement money has never been drawn off.

"I have two openings right now," Fleishman continued. "One of them is in Brownsville and the other in Laredo. You'd better grab one of them and get back in harness again. You can't afford to blow those 19 years, when all you need is one more and then go looking forward to being 50 years of age, or even more, which of course would improve your retirement mightily. What do you think of it?"

I told him that I was extremely glad that he had thought about me and didn't see how I could possibly turn it down. However, I also said I didn't much like Laredo or Brownsville, but that I might have an answer to that problem.

Larry had a Special Agent in Yuma, Arizona named Harold Slack who had worked for me in OSS during the War. "Now, Harold Slack," I said, "is from Brownsville and so is his wife. How about me going down to Yuma and putting the charm on him and getting him to take the vacancy in Brownsville and I'll slip into his hole in Yuma?"

Larrie laughed. "That sounds fine with me if you can manage it," he said, "but if you can't, you still have too much to lose if you don't take one of the two vacancies. I'll give you a week to let me know and then I'll have to start filling them or lose them."

"I'll sure let you know and thanks for thinking of me," I said.

After I hung up I went directly to see Mr. Lister. I explained the opportunity.

"Lee," he said, "I don't see how you can turn it down. We have no retirement except Social Security and this will set you up for life, if you stay with it long enough."

I drove down to Yuma with Helen and talked with Harold

Slack. He immediately agreed to accept the position at Brownsville, but he had a slight problem with it. He said it would cost at least $200 to make the change, even though the Government would pay for the move, and he thought I should pay him that much to balance expenses of the transfer. I could see my old friend, Slack, was giving me the "boots and saddles" for my $200 and I remember he was quite a dice shooter. He knew nothing about handling them, but he invariably got into dice games, usually losing his walk-about money.

Unbeknown to Harold, I had learned to handle fair dice when I was a kid and on the bum. My brother and I had run away from home when he was 14 and I was 13 and went through 14 states, returning home just in time to start school during the Fall session.

I paid him the $200 that he demanded to accept the transfer, and while we were talking, I threw a pair of big red dice on the table.

"I'll shoot $10!" he yelled, and it took me about 10 minutes to get my $200 back, using what is known as "The Kansas City Whip Shot."

I checked into my new station at Yuma, Arizona, in early 1952 and had been there only a few days when I met an Immigration Border Patrolman named Charlie Cameron. He was born in Ajo, Arizona, on a cattle ranch. His mother was a descendant of the California Spaniards and he learned to speak Spanish at an early age. He was also one of the best men I had ever known to seek out and enlist good informants.

I tied in with him and we had a lot of luck in the Yuma area with narcotics cases. After we had worked together for about six months, I tried to get him in the Customs Service. Despite Larry Fleishman's dire predictions about not being able to get any new agents aboard for the next few years, Charlie Cameron was made a Special Agent rather quickly.

By this time, I was involved in the quarter horse racing business in a rather small way. I'd met a man in Yuma named

HILARIOUS HIGH JINKS

Wayne Brand who was a rancher. He had owned some of the finest running quarter horses in the country. One of them had been Hard Twist, who had won the Quarter Horse Championship of the United States in 1947.

Wayne owned a colt by Hard Twist named Yuma Twist and I had a filly by the famous stallion, Joe Reed II, named Lila Reed. We were breaking them at his ranch on the Indian Reservation along the Colorado River.

I was going strong with my friend, Charlie Cameron. He had developed three excellent informants. We were making fairly large narcotics seizures every couple of weeks when I got a phone call from a special agent in Nogales. His name was "Bud" Bump and I had played football and baseball in Calexico High School with him. I had also used what little influence I had in getting him into the Customs Service many years before.

Bud told me he had been having a lot of trouble in his efforts to arrest one of the biggest opium traffickers on the entire Mexican border, who also happened to be chief of detectives in Nogales, Sonora, at that time. His name was Guillermo Ocio Lopez and they had run agents at him twice but he figured them out both times. Bud thought the reason was that they spoke everyday, common Spanish in their negotiations and Ocio seemed quite aware of the fact that almost every Customs investigator was well versed in Spanish.

"Now, Lee, I have a suggestion that may alleviate any suspicions on Ocio's part. We have an informant here who can introduce a prospective buyer to him and you and I have a very good friend over in Calexico who can speak excellent Spanish. He's black and this should ease any feeling Ocio might have that he's again dealing with somebody who wants to put him in the penitentiary.

The man I have in mind is Freddy Brown and I'm sure he thinks enough of you to come over here with you as your interpreter."

I had known Freddy Brown since he was a small boy in

Calexico and Bud Bump was certainly right when he said we were very good friends. Freddy ran a barbecue shop in Calexico and had spoken Spanish all his life. I told Bud I'd drive over and see if Freddy would accompany me to Nogales and help set the trap.

"That sounds fine," Bud said, "Ocio has just received 25 pounds of smoking opium and he's looking for a buyer."

I drove over to Calexico where my friend, Freddy Brown, was very agreeable to the proposal. We called Bud, saying we would leave for Nogales the next day and would use Freddy's car, as my Customs car might be recognized by the wily Ocio.

We met the informant when we arrived in Nogales and he advised us to get a room at a motel some two miles from the border, on the highway to Tucson, and that he would bring Ocio to meet us. Our plan was to tell Ocio we owned a house of prostitution in San Francisco and that many of our customers were opium-smoking Chinese. Freddy was to do all the talking and interpreting.

In those days it was almost impossible to get a sizeable roll of money as a "flash roll" from Customs. To show a peddler that we meant business and had the money for the buy, we usually used what was called a "Michigan roll," a dollar bill wrapped around a corncob. Actually, we would get a few hundred dollar bills, a lot of twenties and then a great deal of smaller bills. We'd put the big ones on the outside and only give the seller a quick flash of the hundreds on top of the roll, then tell him that when he delivered the narcotics, we'd let him count the money.

Bud feared this wouldn't hold water with the foxy Ocio and he borrowed $25,000 from a wealthy Nogales cattle buyer, so our bank roll would not only look real, but was.

The informant brought Ocio to the motel. He was a cagey one, all right. He tried two or three times to get me to speak Spanish but I was able to hold off. He went outside and looked over Freddy's car. It was a fairly new Lincoln and Ocio examined the license plates carefully to see if they had been put on recently. They hadn't, so that seemed to satisfy him on that score.

We showed him the vast amount of cash that we kept in a drawer of one of the nightstands. We were to pay him $1,000 a pound for the 25 pounds of smoking opium. He finally seemed satisfied that we were legitimate. He said two elderly women would bring the opium across the border in their underwear the following morning.

He left for Nogales, Sonora, and Bud Bump and Agent Ted Simpson checked into the motel about four rooms down from ours.

"Now, when the women show up with the opium," I told them over the phone, "I will taste it first to make sure it's opium. Then I'll send Freddy out to his car, ostensibly to get a can opener so I can dig down into the opium to see that the middle of it isn't penoche brown sugar. Actually, we won't give a hoot if it is and if the outer coating is opium. I'll send him out to the car to let you boys know that they've delivered it and at least part of it is opium.

"When you see Freddy coming out to the car," I continued, "get right down here and we'll put the big britches on Ocio before he shoots me right through the gallbladder. I think he was carrying a pistol under his shirt, but I couldn't be sure. I fell right in front of him and pulled myself up on his legs, but he backed away from me before I could feel around his belt."

"If you have to make your play before we can get there," Bud said, "watch those two old hags. The informant says they're as dangerous as Ocio and one of them might pull a pistol from her brassiere and shoot you while you're covering Ocio."

That night an Arizona Highway Patrol car parked on the highway about 30 feet from our room and I feared it might spook Ocio off. But I had Freddy tell Ocio about it the next morning and ask if he thought they were covering our transaction.

"No," he said, and then he turned to me and in his very

faulty English said, "Las' night I stay in the booshes...I look with *my eye*," and he pulled down his lower eyelid to where it looked as though his right eye would fall out. "Nahting to worry about!"

Then he reverted to Spanish and told Freddy, "Las mujeres estaran llegando en menos de dos o tres horas." ("The women will be arriving in less than two or three hours.")

We sat around and waited...and waited...and waited, and finally when two o'clock in the afternoon came, without thinking what I was doing, I called out in Spanish to Guillermo Ocio.

"Parece que ellas no van a venir. Que bastardo eres!" ("Looks like they are not going to come. What a bastard you are!")

I'm not sure which of the three of us jumped the highest when we realized I was talking in Spanish. Ocio pointed at me and yelled at the top of his lungs at Freddy Brown.

"El habla Espanol mejor que nosotros!" ("He speaks Spanish better than we do!")

I got hold of myself quickly. I told Freddy to explain to him that as a child I lived in San Antonio Texas, and learned a few words from the Mexican kids, but I couldn't put them into a complete sentence.

Freddy covered me in a wonderful manner. He told Ocio he was absolutely sure I had just come out with a childhood expression I had learned in San Antonio, and that I couldn't speak Spanish at all. Ocio finally began to believe him and I'll be damned if he didn't start trying to teach me Spanish.

About that time the old Mexican women appeared at the door. Ocio let them in with great aplomb. Each of them carried a two-pound coffee can. Ocio took both cans and ceremoniously handed them to me.

"Aqui esta el opio!" ("Here's the opium!") he said, and as I took the cans he held out his hands as if he was awaiting the handcuffs.

I told Freddy, "Tell this man we are here to buy 25 pounds

161

of smoking opium. This piddling amount is not for us! We have a connection in Juarez who can furnish us 40 kilos if we need it. We will leave right now for El Paso and deal with a man whom we know. A couple of two-pound coffee cans of smoking opium! That's too small a deal for us!"

Freddy translated and Ocio laughed. "We were just checking on you!" he told Freddy. "If you had been Customs officers, you would have arrested me and the two women and then you would have found that the coffee cans truly contain coffee. Now we believe you are levelling with us. The women have the opium concealed about four blocks back toward the border, and they'll put it in their underwear and bring it here immediately."

Freddy patiently translated and I tried to be mighty frustrated about the lack of trust Ocio had in a pair of genuine opium purchasers. Before we had the whole thing straightened out, the old hags were at the door again.

"Aqui esta el opio, Senores! Finalmente!" ("Here's the opium, gentlemen! Finally!")

He sent the two women into the bathroom and I allowed them only a few minutes until I went in, too. I realized they would probably testify in court that they had no idea what they were bringing into the United States, so as they were pulling plastic bags and tobacco cans of smoking opium out of their garments, I asked, "Es puro opio?" ("Is it pure opium?")

"Si! si!" they said. "No le tenga miedo a este! Es opio puro y listo para fumar!" ("Yes! Yes! Don't be afraid of it. It is pure opium and ready to be smoked!")

I pinched off a little from one of the cellophane sacks and tasted it. It was opium, all right. I turned to Freddy Brown.

"Go out to the car and get a can opener. I want to dig into these sacks and make sure that they don't just have opium on the outside and something like penoche on the inside."

Freddy translated and then left the room. I waited several minutes. Ocio and the two women were getting a little restless.

Finally, I said, "Well, I'm sure it's opium."

"Si, Senor!" Ocio said, "Es opio puro!" ("Yes, sir! It's pure opium!")

"All right," I told him and I pointed to the nightstand. "I have the money right there."

I walked over to the nightstand and instead of the big roll of money he had seen me put in the drawer, I came out with a .45 semi-auto loaded with hollow-point bullets and aimed right at the brisket of Guillermo Ocio Lopez. He looked at me for a second then raised his hand to his forehead.

"Madre de Dios! Este es!" ("Mother of God! This is it!")

I remembered what Bud Bump had told me about the women. I watched them out of the corner of my eye. Suddenly, I saw one of them start reaching into her brassiere. I moved my pistol slightly, so it would still cover Ocio, as I still didn't know if he was armed, but would also put me in good line to blow the woman off the wall if she came out with a gun.

Sure enough, I saw her start to pull some sort of metal thing out of her brassiere and I started my squeeze. It turned out to be a Prince Albert tobacco can full of opium that she was trying to steal and take back with her to Nogales to resell.

About that time, Bud Bump, Ted Simpson and Freddy Brown came through the door. The action was over.

Guillermo Ocio and the two old women pleaded guilty in federal court in Tucson. I was there as a witness in the event they decided to change their plea.

There was a Narcotics Drug Enforcement Act at that time that called for a minimum sentence of five years for a deal such as this. The two women were given five-year sentences. Ocio, being the head man in the operation, was given 10 years. As he marched out of the courtroom between two determined-looking U.S. deputy marshals he spotted me sitting in the spectators' section.

"Ah hah!" he yelled, pointing to me. "You no speaky Spanish, hah!"

CHAPTER TWENTY-TWO

BOLIVIA, THE FIRST LATIN AMERICAN ASSIGNMENT

In late 1956, Byron Engle, Director of Public Safety, Agency for International Development, phoned me. "How'd you like to go to a country in South America as chief police advisor?" he asked.

"That sounds mighty interesting," I told him, "but I'm working under that Hazardous Duty Retirement Act and if I went down there with you, I might lose that '20 year retirement at age 50' deal. Have you gone into that with the Civil Service people?"

"No," Byron said, "but why don't you fly back here and we'll go talk with the commissioner of Customs about it and see if he'll be amenable to letting you go on loan for a two- or three-year tour of duty? If he's agreeable, then we'll go see the Civil Service folks and find out if a loan from one Government agency to another is feasible. If you'll buy your own airfare, I'll reimburse you for it when you get here."

I told him that I could possibly get a "dead-head" ride from the Air Force as they had planes flying from Yuma to Washington quite often.

It turned out they had a big plane going to Friendship, Maryland in a few days and I could go on it, provided I had

HILARIOUS HIGH JINKS

written orders to Washington. Since I was practically my own boss, I wrote my own orders to Washington for the conference. I boarded the plane two days later for Maryland.

Byron met me at the airport in Friendship, Maryland and the following day we went to see the commissioner. He was agreeable to let me go on loan, but insisted that he put it in writing.

"There might be a man sitting in this chair who has never heard of you in his life when you get back," he told me. "We'll write a letter about it, guaranteeing your job when you arrive. By the way," he asked, "where the hell are you going?"

I'd forgotten to ask!

"He'll be going to La Paz, Bolivia," Byron said. "We have operations in quite a few countries in the Near and Far East, but this will be only the second one in Latin America. We have one doing well right now in Guatemala and I'm sure this one will prosper, too, with this left-handed pistol shooter in charge."

We took our story to the Civil Service. After going through tomes of regulations, they decided it could be done and that I would be able to come back to my Hazardous Duty Retirement Act job when I was through in Bolivia.

Helen and I sold our house when I got back to Yuma. Our daughter, Donna, had married in 1952. The marriage lasted long enough for her to have a beautiful little daughter named Juanita. She remarried a professional cowboy named Sam Kennedy and they turned up about a year and half later with identical twin daughters whom they named Kathy and Karen. They were living in St. David, Arizona, near Benson.

I flew back to Washington to go through some more schools. There I met Mike Salcedo, the young Los Angeles Deputy Sheriff who was to accompany me on the tour to Bolivia. We had about a three-hour meeting with Byron Engle who told us that the minister in charge of the 15,000-man Carabinero Police Force and the 1,000-man traffic police was a leftist and bordered on being a Communist.

"You'll have to be very careful," Byron told us, "if he even suspects you're down there fighting Communism, he may send you home before you even learn how to drink *chicha*."

"What the hell is *chicha*?" I asked, mildly interested.

"It's a native drink made out of kernels of corn. The squaws chew them up until they get them into a sort of coarse corn meal, saturated with spit. Then they spit it all out in a large bowl and when they get it full, they let it ferment. Then they pour it off and that's *chicha*."

"I can't wait to get down there!" I said.

Changing the subject, Byron asked, "How well do you know Hernando Hernandez Hernandez?"

"I know him very well, of course," I replied.

Hernandez was the Chief of the National Police in Cuba and had been a member of their pistol team for many years. I had fired with him in Florida, Camp Perry and Havana many times.

"Well," Byron said, "he has a young captain who graduated from the University of Pennsylvania Traffic School. He is running traffic courses in Havana and it might behoove you and Salcedo to drop off in Havana for a couple of days on your way to La Paz, and see if you could get a traffic school started there and send about 40 or 50 students to it from Bolivia. This would smooth out any suspicions that the minister might have about your intentions, and then you can gradually work into the secret police operations and the main body of Carabineros and go to training them in modern police methods and tactics."

I agreed this would certainly be a beginning that should keep the minister from declaring us *persona non grata* before we even learned how to drink *chicha*. I put in a telephone call to Hernando Hernandez Hernandez in Havana, advising him that we were coming through on our way to Bolivia and would stop off for a couple of days. This seemed to please Hernando. We were good friends and I asked him how the Castro Revolution was progressing.

"He's a young upstart and he'll never get his Communist

followers out of the mountains and down here where we can get our hands on him," Hernandez said.

This was in March, 1957 and it took Castro a year and nine months to do just that. When he finally did, nobody "got their hands on him."

We were met by Hernandez' public relations chief, a member of the pistol team, who took us to the International Hotel.

"The boss is busy as can be with the Revolution," the PR man said. "We'll meet you this evening about seven and take you around the City. We'll have a drink at 'Sloppy Joe's' and dinner at one of the fine night clubs. We have a deal with Hernandez to meet him at 10:00 a.m. in the morning at his office."

This suited us fine and we had a nice rest before the onslaught on Havana that evening. The Public Relations Chief sure put us through the ropes. Havana had many excellent night clubs in those days and the City was booming with American tourists from the East Coast.

We were picked up the following morning by Cuban police and escorted to the office of Chief Hernando Hernandez Hernandez. The police station was well sandbagged with machine guns behind every bag. He gave us a big *abrazo* and told me how happy he was to see his old, left-handed shooting *compadre*, "Meester Ecklies."

We told him of our mission in Bolivia and suggested that if his traffic school could help us, we would probably send 40 or 50 traffic police to go through their three-month training program. He was very agreeable to this, but suggested that if it was possible, he would like to send his top instructor down to Bolivia to study the problems that would confront him in the training program. I could see the sense of this, as I knew La Paz was a city of steep, high hills and worn-out automobiles. Traffic police had a monstrous job with traffic flow. I told him I would contact him as soon as the program was set up.

Chief Hernandez took us to the airport the following day and saw us off. We flew across Colombia and landed in Peru, where we changed planes and then crossed the Andes to the highest commercial airport in the world above the old Spanish city of La Paz, Bolivia.

The airport is almost 14,000 feet above the sea and a group of the friends I had made when I went through the AID indoctrination course in Washington were there to meet us. One of them had an ominous tank of oxygen in the event any of us keeled over.

We could see the city down in the huge valley and the taxis swarmed around us in a manner that seemed to border on suicide, but none of them went over the precipice. Our friends took us to a hotel downtown and, after a nice dinner in an adjoining restaurant, the beds were mighty comfortable.

The next morning, Mike Salcedo and I went to the American Embassy to meet the AID Director who turned out to be a fine little Irishman named "Dinty" Moore. He gave us some excellent offices in the Embassy and said the new Ambassador was arriving that day and would present his credentials to President Silas Zuazo that afternoon.

On the way back to the hotel, we met a police colonel on the street and told him we were the new public safety advisors who were going to work with the police for a couple of years. He was happy to meet us and invited us to walk over to the Palace to see the magnificent old buildings. Mike had his camera with him and after a few photos of the surrounding terrain, the colonel took us inside the Palace. Before we knew what was happening, he introduced us to President Silas and told him of our mission. The President was busy preparing for the new Ambassador to call and present his credentials.

About that time Ambassador Bonsal and his entourage arrived in their morning coats and striped pants. President Silas gathered his people and lined them up in a row before Mike and I knew what he was doing.

"You haven't met the Ambassador, either," he told us, "this will be a good chance!"

And there we were, in our baggy suits in need of pressing

after our long trip. When the President introduced us to Ambassador Bonsal, he grinned from ear to ear and shook his head in disbelief.

After the greetings were over, Mike and I slipped out a side door. "Well," Mike said, "let's get back over to the Embassy and turn in our resignations before they fire us!"

At the Embassy, the charge d'affaires grabbed us and took us into the Ambassador's office. The Ambassador got up and shook hands with us.

"I want you to answer this truthfully, how in the world did you work it?" he asked.

I told him it hadn't been prearranged at all, it just sort of fell into place and we couldn't get out of it.

"Well," he said, "you fellows are certainly off to a good start down here. If you handle your assignment as aggressively as you did the introduction this morning, you'll do mighty well!"

It didn't take Helen long to find a beautiful penthouse apartment about two miles from the Embassy. Mike's wife and two small children soon arrived and they, too, found a nice residence further down the valley.

We learned a lot of things very quickly about living conditions in La Paz. One of the first was amoebic dysentery. It was so prevalent in the area that it was necessary to filter and boil the drinking water. And going to a nightclub for a little relaxing fun was completely out of the question. The Bolivians thought that when water was frozen into ice cubes, the germs were automatically frozen to death and there was nothing more to fear. It didn't turn out that way, though. Instead of freezing them to death, I think it just made them sexy. Anybody who drank a highball containing nightclub ice cubes was almost a cincher to be going out of La Paz in the next couple of weeks on a stretcher.

Accordingly, all the entertaining was done in homes. This made for a bond of friendship among the American Foreign Service crowd that was much stronger than in most foreign countries.

& DANGEROUS ASSIGNMENTS

As Byron Engle had suggested, we went to the Carabineros' headquarters, met the chief and most of his top-ranking officers and told them our first assignment would be to help the traffic police. They couldn't understand and I didn't blame them, but I said we'd be through with the traffic people in about three months and then could get busy with the Carabineros.

Next we met the chief of the traffic police and several of his top-ranking assistants. They were very enthusiastic about the proposed traffic school in Havana. We told them to pick out about 40 young men for the class. Then we contacted Hernando Hernandez Hernandez in Havana and asked him to send the young Cuban officer to La Paz to survey the problems. We sent him a round-trip air ticket and he arrived within a week. The survey didn't take him long. There were many problems to solve, but he told me he had the answers and would be able to set up the class in Havana and start within two weeks.

The time came for the students to leave for Cuba and you never saw such pandemonium. None of them had ever been out of Bolivia before and the hullabaloo that took place getting them packed and out to the airport was unbelievable. It took about 10 police cars to haul them up the long drive to the airport and at least 10 of their suitcases, heavily packed and tied with strings and ropes, fell off the cars and broke open on the road.

The police finally had to make the pilot hold up departure for about half an hour until they could get the bags loaded, tied back together again and on board. And off they went to Havana.

CHAPTER TWENTY-THREE

WE LOSE OUR DONNA AND GAIN A NEW DAUGHTER

While the young traffic officers were training in Havana, Mike and I concentrated on the traffic chief and his top people. When the trainees returned we moved on to the huge body of Carabineros, who welcomed us with open arms.

The Carabineros had the same flaw in administration as the traffic police, only worse. The chief asked me, "How many men have you ever had under your jurisdiction?"

I told him, "Five."

"Heavens!" he said, "I have 15,000!"

I explained to him that wouldn't fly; that no man could run an organization that large by himself. I told him of the intricacies of span of control and chain of command and it didn't take long until he was lining up duties for his top assistants that would take a lot off his back. We taught his colonels the same thing and they gave more responsibility to their captains, lieutenants, sergeants and even corporals.

We set up training schools all over the country. We got them about 50 used Jeeps from the U.S. Army and Mike set up driving schools. We built pistol ranges throughout the country and trained the men to shoot, making instructors out of the ones showing the most aptitude.

Then we started with their so-called secret police. We taught

HILARIOUS HIGH JINKS

them advanced methods of surveillance, interrogation (without the use of violence), infiltration of the Communist Party and sent three of them to Puerto Rico to learn fingerprint classification and filing.

We hadn't been in Bolivia but a few months when we heard from Sam Kennedy, our daughter's husband. He told us Donna had cancer and was to have a mastectomy within a week. Helen packed her bags and flew to Arizona to be with Donna and the three little babies. After the operation she flew back to La Paz.

She had only been back a month or so, however, when we received another call, saying Donna's cancer had moved down to her liver and that it was terminal. Helen flew back immediately and I showed the telegram to "Dinty" Moore. He arranged for me to fly to Washington for a conference, with a 10-day stopover in Tucson, where Donna was in the hospital.

I'd only been there a few days when Donna passed away. We were able to adopt her four year old daughter, Juanita, as she was by a different father than the one and a half year old twins.

Because of the adoption laws in Arizona, it was necessary for Helen to lease an apartment in Yuma so the State's adoption people could call on her occasionally to see that she was raising little Juanita in accordance with their regulations. I went to Washington and conferred several times with Byron Engle, who gave me a lot of good advice on the continuance of our program in Bolivia. I bought a new car in Washington and drove it back to Yuma for Helen and then flew back to La Paz.

CHAPTER TWENTY-FOUR

THE WORLD'S BIGGEST SNAKE

A few weeks later, I was in Santa Cruz, Bolivia, building a pistol range. Santa Cruz is the third largest city in the country and sits on the edge of the Green Hell Jungle on the banks of a slow, brown, sluggish river. It has the most beautiful women and the best looking men in all of South America.

I was sitting in a bar having a drink when a man sat down beside me. In the course of the conversation he told me he was a cattleman on the Beni River, one of the big tributaries of the Amazon. About five miles up the Beni River from his ranch house there was a hole in the river bank in which an Anaconda snake lived, possibly the biggest snake in the world. They had known of his existence for at least 50 years, and 50 years ago he was the same size.

"How big is he now?" I asked.

He looked me squarely in the eye. "He's over 10 meters long," he said.

I had been studying about these Anacondas and, according to my sources, the largest one in existence was in the Hamburg Zoo in West Germany and it was 33 feet in length.

I told the cattleman this and he replied, "This one is bigger than that. He comes out of his hole about every three months, throws a loop around a big steer, drags him into the river, drowns him, drags him back onto the bank and devours him.

HILARIOUS HIGH JINKS

Then he crawls back into his hole, digests him for about three months and then comes out again, looking for another meal. To our knowledge he has killed and eaten nine natives. About 10 or 11 of them have disappeared on jungle trails and we believe he dropped on them from trees.

"Now, I have a deal," he continued, "with the Bronx Zoo in New York, to capture this big snake and get him up there where they will put him in their Zoo as the world's biggest snake. The railroad comes right through my property and I have a small depot station where I ship cattle to market. If we can just get him over to the station, we can get him on a train to Brazil, put him on a ship in Rio and move him right up to New York. What I would like for you to do when you get back to La Paz is to talk with your Foreign Service people and try to figure out a way to capture this big snake and get him to the railroad."

The thought struck me immediately on how to get him out of the hole. Mike and I were training riot control police and we had an abundance of tear and sickening gas. We could shoot about three blasts into the snake's hole and he would probably come out. But, of course, the big question would then be, "What do we do next?"

I went back to La Paz. For the next six weeks, at every Embassy cocktail party, the sole topic of conversation was, "How do you capture a snake that is over 10 meters long?"

To make things even scarier, the cattleman said he was, at the very least, as big around as a 55-gallon oil barrel!

We came up with half a dozen ideas and all were abandoned. Finally a young man from Albuquerque, New Mexico, who was with the AID Mission as an agricultural advisor, called me one evening. His name was Dave Thornburg and he had a wonderful idea.

"I'm going to Lima tomorrow on business," he said, "and there's a place there where they make zippers. They tell me they will make them in any size required. Now, I'll get them to make two, about four feet long and about four or five inches wide. Then we'll buy a roll of canvas and take the zippers and the canvas out to the pants manufacturing plant here in La Paz. We'll have them make us a cotton-picking sack about 40 feet long and big enough around that we know the snake will fit in.

"We'll regiment our attack well. We'll have a zipper at each end of the sack and have a head zipperman and a tail zipperman. When you fire the tear and sickening gas into the hole and the snake can no longer stand it, he'll come slithering out for some fresh air. He'll see the cotton-picking sack at the entrance to his hole, but he'll also see daylight at the end of it. He'll go right into it and when he does, the head zipperman can close his zipper quickly, the tail zipperman can close his and then we'll have him!

"Now," Dave went on, "the problem of getting him to the railroad can be solved like this. Along with the cotton-picking sack, we'll have a long pine tree trunk lying right alongside the sack. We'll have heavy cotton rope around the sack at intervals of about 10 feet. It will also be wrapped around a pine tree and we'll have three rope-tying men in position. As soon as the zippermen do their job, the rope-tying men will immediately tie the cotton-picking sack to the pine tree, and we'll have enough Indian helpers to get him up between a couple of Jeeps and drive him the five miles to the railroad. It's going to be a mighty simple operation if our people are well trained."

Well, since no one had come up with anywhere near as plausible a solution to our problem, we began recruiting and training our force. Dave Thornburg had the zippers made, we got the roll of canvas, and the pants manufacturer made the huge cotton-picking sack. We appointed Ed Broughton, the AID Mission Personnel Manager, as the head zipperman and a six feet, five inch man, Darwin Bell, who was the Business Manager for the AID Mission, as tail zipperman. Mike Salcedo was to fire the tear and sickening gas into the hole and three stalwart lads were the cotton rope-tying team.

I phoned the rancher on the Beni River and told him we were ready for the onslaught. He asked us to fly to Oruro the

HILARIOUS HIGH JINKS

following Saturday and he would have two Jeeps and a carryall waiting for us. He said we could drive to his ranch in about four hours and he would have a fine barbecue and an evening of fun for us, including Indian musicians and dancers. I told him we would need about 10 Indians to accompany us to the site of the snake's residence.

We made it to his ranch without incidents. The next morning he gave us 10 Indians, armed with machetes. We drove up the river to the site and, as we got near the hole, I noticed a huge track on the ground, right through the brush and over big bushes that stood in the way. I pointed this out to one of the Indians and he said the snake had been out foraging the day before, but hadn't found anything.

"He didn't find anything?" I demanded. Here was a track about four feet wide and he hadn't found anything!

"No," the Indian said. "If he'd found something to eat there'd be a track much wider than that."

We got our paraphernalia out of the Jeeps. The Indians had cut the pine log the day before and had it in place away from the hole. We laid the big cotton-picking sack alongside the hole and put the big cotton rope around the sack and the tree trunk in loops about 10 feet apart.

We were ready. I stood about 20 feet away with a Colt Python revolver in hand, loaded with .357 Magnum hollow-point bullets. The rest of the men were at their posts. I waved to Mike to fire the three tear and sickening gas shells into the hole and, when he did, we could hear ol' Big Boy wiggling around among the bones of some of his choice dinners. He couldn't stand it for very long, however, and soon came wriggling out.

As his head reached the entrance to the hole, he looked down inside the 40-foot sack and saw daylight at the other end. He began his slow entrance into the sack and we could see the contours of his body as it worked its way down to the end. When he reached the end, the head zipperman gave a quick jerk of his zipper and one end of the sack was closed. The tail zipperman did the same and we had the big snake well caught up in our canvas trap...or so we thought.

In order to be sure the snake would enter the sack, we had made it quite a bit bigger around than we imagined the snake could possibly be, and it gave him about a foot and half of slapping room. He hit the sack with half a ton of meat, hide, bone and muscle and split it about half way along the length. The next thing any of us knew, he was out of the sack and free.

Out of the entire crowd he picked me to come after. A drunk will do that. He'll pick me out of 50 people and always wants to either waltz or fistfight me and usually winds up doing both.

The snake slithered along silently, right toward me, and every once in a while he'd raise himself to where his head was about eight feet in the air. He'd run his big, blue tongue out at me, and it must have been well over a foot long. When he'd get his head back down and start at me again, I'd put my pistol right on his headbone and start my squeeze. I knew the pistol had exactly a three and a half pound trigger pull and I'd hold on to what pressure I'd put on the trigger. Then when he'd get back down to earth and start slithering at me again, I'd continue with my squeeze.

I remember thinking, "If you ever made a dead center 10, Lee Boy, you'd better make one now or you'll wind up an hors d'oeuvre for this monstrosity!"

When he finally got about 12 yards from me, I eased off the shot. It took about a third of his brainpan out. He went up into a big loop and fell against a mahogany tree about the size of a small telephone pole. He shattered it like a match stick. I rushed in and got two more shots in his head and he wiggled and slithered off into the jungle and got all mixed up in the vines. He writhed around in there for almost an hour before he quieted down enough for the Indians to go in with their machetes and cut him loose from the vines.

It took all 10 of them to drag him out onto the banks of the river where we measured him. He was exactly 34 feet, six

HILARIOUS HIGH JINKS

inches long. We rolled him over on his back and started to skin him. His belly was so armor-plated we could cut through his skin with an axe, but couldn't sever the skin from the rib structure. We finally had to settle for skinning him out from the sides of his belly, thereby losing about a third of the width of the skin. However, he was still about three and a half feet wide.

It's a very odd thing that none of my old shooting friends believe this story, even when I roll out the hide and show it to them. Most of them are big game hunters and they have their homes full of old, musty, stuffed bears, lions or tigers lying around on the floor snarling at you. Some of them have elephant tusks up to eight feet long and I've never questioned them as to the authenticity of their trophies, despite the fact that you can buy these large, ferocious animals already tanned and stuffed. But when I tell them of the big Anaconda episode in my life and how the damnable thing almost ate me before I could shoot him, they invariably look at me like a bull at a bastard calf. Even when I roll out the huge hide, almost the length of a swimming pool, they still don't believe it.

The story has been written up, however, in at least three books and numerous magazine articles. The writer of one of the books was my good friend, David Atlee Phillips, who some years later was Chief of Station with the Central Intelligence Agency in the Dominican Republic. When he retired in 1976, he started the Association of Former Intelligence Officers. David wrote an excellent book about his experiences in the CIA, using fictitious names for many of the people he wrote about.

In relating the snake story, he called me "Al" and said that he never believed any of it...even went so far as to call me a liar. He said that he hurt my feelings somewhat and that I went into my garage and unrolled the awful thing in front of him. He still couldn't make himself believe the story. A few years later, however, at a party in Washington, he met the Assistant

Secretary of Labor who told him he was in Bolivia at the same time and that he knew me.

"What about that big snake story he told me about?" David asked him.

The Secretary looked him dead in the eye. "I was the tail zipperman!" my old friend, Darwin Bell, replied.

CHAPTER TWENTY-FIVE
NIXON COMES CALLING IN BOLIVIA

Things were rolling very smoothly for us in Bolivia. We had schools all over the country. The Carabineros went all-out for the training programs. Byron had sent us a secretary from San Antonio and the goose, as the saying goes, was hanging high.

However, a study of Bolivia's history would have shown us that it couldn't last. Bolivia had been free from Spain since 1825. During those years they'd had more revolutions than freedom. Many of the revolutions had been successful, but they had lost three actual wars. They lost their only seaport to Chile and even Paraguay defeated them in the Chaco War.

The war clouds gathered in 1958 when the leftists began asserting themselves. I was in Sucre, the old colonial capital, helping the police with their riot control training program, when I saw people gathering in the park. I wandered over and a loud-mouthed agitator was up on a box, shouting at the top of his voice.

"Do you see this tall tree right here?" he yelled and pointed to a huge mahogany growing in the park. "We're going to hang every American in Sucre on those inviting limbs."

HILARIOUS HIGH JINKS

I looked all around and decided I was the only American in Sucre. I exited quickly.

The ruckus had begun on my return to the capital. They had outfitted thousands of Indian tin miners with guns and they began their march on the American Embassy. The Carabineros, fairly well trained in riot control by then, moved to meet them. At first they tried to quell them with tear and sickening gas, but it didn't work. The revolutionaries were too well armed and when they began to shoot, the Carabineros returned fire. The Indians reached the front door of the American Embassy before the police, aided by the army, turned them back. Several hundred of the revolutionaries were killed and they destroyed many cars in the Embassy parking lot. The police and army finally stopped the revolution, but of course feelings ran high on both sides.

About this time, Vice President Richard Nixon and an entourage of about 30 people came through on a goodwill tour of South America. A Secret Service officer arrived about a week before the Nixon party and in a meeting with the chief of the Carabineros and me, told us that Mr. Nixon wanted no show of force. It was his desire to make the visit as cordial as possible and to assure the people that he was strictly on a mission of goodwill.

I told the Secret Service officer this sounded very good, but that it wouldn't work in Bolivia. The Carabineros chief backed me, adding that if Mr. Nixon came to La Paz, he would have the highest security he had ever seen. If he wouldn't accept it, then he shouldn't come. The advance officer didn't like that too much, but as he had no choice, he agreed to it.

We figured that if there was an assassination attempt on Nixon and his party, it would probably occur on the winding road leading into La Paz from the airport. We put 10 or 12 officers in civilian clothes at every crossroad to mingle with the huge crowd as the entourage wound its way through the city. We parked carryalls nearby to haul away the dissidents and, as soon as an agitator got busy, the plainclothes police were to move in, grab him and take him downtown to the jailhouse.

We surrounded the entourage with police cars. Machine guns bristled from each car and they rolled down to the American Embassy without incident. Every place Nixon went while he was in La Paz, he had complete and heavy police coverage, although he didn't seem to like it. I met Nixon at the Embassy along with a big, young colonel who was with him. The Colonel was Vernon Walters and they said he could speak seven languages fluently. I never heard him speak any of them except Spanish, but if he could speak the others as well, he must have been an excellent linguist.

I followed Walters' career. Some of the many positions he held were that of Assistant Director of the Central Intelligence Agency, Ambassador to the Near East, and American Ambassador to the United Nations, replacing Jeane Kirkpatrick.

I have kept in touch with him and in a letter after his last appointment I said, "We are now in mighty good hands. They can't slip around talking in foreign tongues, thinking you won't understand them!"

The Nixon entourage went from La Paz to Lima, where the dissidents threw rocks and skinned up several of the Secret Service guards. Then the entourage went to Bogota, Colombia, where, with no police protection, they nearly lost their lives. The Carabineros felt justifiably proud of the manner in which they protected the Nixon party in La Paz.

Early in 1959 I was again in Sucre when I got a telephone call from our Embassy in La Paz. They had a cable from my mother in Calexico, California, saying that my father had died in his sleep the night before. It was impossible for me to get back for the funeral, or to help console my mother, but Helen and little Juanita went immediately from Yuma and Helen did her usual excellent job.

My tour of duty ended in April, 1959, and the Embassy personnel gave me many going away parties. The party I'll always remember, however, was given by the Carabineros.

HILARIOUS HIGH JINKS

After the flowing speeches, they presented me with a Bolivian license plate and I'll be darned if it wasn't Number Two!

The Chief told me, "The President has to be Number One, but you'll always be Number Two in our hearts!"

Then the Minister of Foreign Relations, Victor Andrade, presented me with the following letter,

REPUBLIC OF BOLIVIA
MINISTRY OF FOREIGN RELATIONS

La Paz, Bolivia
4 April 1959

Honorable Lee E. Echols

Dear Mr. Echols:

    It is my desire at this time to confirm in this correspondence what I have already expressed to you in person.

    It is the wish of this Government to bestow upon you our highest decoration, to-wit: "The Condor of the Andes," in sincere recognition for your services that you have rendered so faithfully to this Government. Upon completion of your trip to the United States, I will appreciate it if you were to inform us of your destination, so that we may have the pleasure of sending our representative to personally present this decoration.

    Wishing you every success in your new position. May I repeat, my kindest personal regards and good wishes.

                                  Victor Andrade
                                  Minister of Foreign Relations

This was really something, as the Condor of the Andes was a huge, solid gold medal weighing at the very least a half pound. However, I couldn't accept it as long as I was working for the U.S. Government. By the time I got around to asking them for it, the Bolivians had changed governments five or six times and, even with the help of U.S. Congressman Duncan Hunter, Ambassador Edwin Corr, and Rey Hill, former AID Director to Bolivia, that big chunk of gold still rests in the archives of the Bolivian Government.

CHAPTER TWENTY-SIX

THE PAN AMERICAN GAMES

After getting reacquainted with my wonderful wife and our daughter, I got right back in the middle of things in Yuma. Charlie Cameron and a couple of special agents from Nogales and I made a huge seizure of crude opium in Phoenix and arrested four smugglers.

We put the defendants in jail and stored the opium at the Federal Building until we could get it to the Customs house in Nogales the next day. Since it was about 2:00 a.m. by then, we had a few victory drinks in my room in the El Rancho Motel and went to bed about four in the morning.

At 6:00 a.m. my telephone rang. I jumped out of bed, hung my shin on one of the bedposts and skinned it from my knee almost down to my ankle bone. I knocked over the lamp by my bed and broke the globe and finally made it to the phone. When I finally got the receiver off the hook, the wackiest, weirdest and undoubtedly the most abnormal conversation ever held over Mr. Bell's invention took place.

When I yelled, "Hello!" this high, hysterical voice, dripping with idiocy responded, "This is Mayor Daley of Chicago speaking!"

"Fine," I replied. "I'm King Gustav of Sweden. I'm lying up here in bed with Queen Marie of Rumania. And," I said as an

HILARIOUS HIGH JINKS

afterthought, "if I'm going to get up at this time of the morning, I'll get a paper route!"

There was a lot more of this idiotic prattle passed back and forth and I finally awakened enough to realize that I was actually talking to Mayor Daley. He apologized profusely for calling so early, saying he'd forgotten about the time change.

"I'm actually calling to ask if you will come to Chicago in a couple of weeks as Chief Range Officer for the pistol and rifle matches of the Pan American Games. The people at the National Rifle Association recommended you highly and I ran you down through your wife in Yuma."

"Mayor Daley! A thousand pardons for my smart-ass remarks," I told him. "If I have not offended you, give the commissioner of Customs a call in Washington to get his approval and I'll sure be there."

The commissioner approved and Helen, little Juanita and I drove to Chicago where we spent about three weeks running the matches for the Pan American Games.

Dozens of my old friends from Latin America were there, including the Cuban Pistol Team. I had heard that when Fidel Castro took over Cuba, my old friend Hernando Hernandez Hernandez, the National Chief of Police, had escaped on the second plane to leave Cuba after Castro made his triumphant entry into Havana. He made it safely to Miami.

"It didn't last long," one of them told me, sadly. "Castro contacted Hernandez by telephone and told him he had found that Hernandez wasn't cruel to prisoners. Castro told him if he'd come back, everything would work out well."

Hernandez fell for it. Of course, this was prior to Castro's statement that he would be a Marxist Leninist until the day he died.

"He flew back," the shooter said. "Castro's boys had a welcoming committee at the airport. They escorted him off the plane, put him against a wall and filled him with .30-06 bullets."

Back to the Games. The big U.S. Army Team from Fort

Benning, Georgia, was there and, as usual since World War II, they dominated the matches.

Soon after World War II the Army formed the Marksmanship Training Unit at Fort Benning. Every time an Army recruit showed promise as a shooter, he would be shipped directly to Fort Benning. The routine went like this. They'd get him up at daylight, feed him and then take him out to the range where he'd shoot, under good supervision, until he almost had to be pulled out of his hulls with a derrick. The same procedure was followed when they'd recruit a machinist who showed promise. They'd send him to Ft. Benning and make a gunsmith out of him.

As a result, the Marksmanship Unit made such profound advances in accurizing the old Colt .45 semi-automatic that it would shoot like a .22 rifle. In fact, no one was shooting revolvers in the center-fire matches. The .45 pistols were every bit as accurate, without the inconvenience of cocking after every shot in the timed and rapid fire matches.

While I was at the Games, I met a man who would not only become one of my best friends, but also give me unbelievable help in my chosen field for the next couple of years.

He was a huge, six feet, five inch giant named George "Tex" Ferguson and he was there with the shooters from Fort Benning. He was a Sergeant Major E-9, the first one I'd ever met, and was wearing more ribbons and medals than I'd ever seen on a human being. On his left breast, arranged in sequence, were the following medals: Distinguished Service Medal, Silver Star, Bronze Star with one cluster (showing he'd won it twice), Purple Heart with no less than four clusters and Army Commendation, along with general campaign ribbons to include both the Asiatic Pacific and European theaters. In addition, he wore the Infantry, Paratrooper and Rifle and Pistol Distinguished Marksman badges. To top it off, he had a whole gaggle of foreign decorations as well.

He was not only a man of matchless modesty, but also had a lively sense of humor. Although he was born in Texas, he had

HILARIOUS HIGH JINKS

spent a great deal of his early life in Yuma County, Arizona.

Since I was planning to retire from the Customs Service soon and run for Sheriff of Yuma County, I began to take quite an interest in this huge soldier. Especially when I learned that, in addition to his helatious war record, he had a degree from USC in criminal investigation. I began to think that he'd make a fine under sheriff if I were elected. I told him of this possibility and asked when he could retire.

"I can get out most any time now," Ferguson replied, "and the possibility sure sounds interesting."

I made arrangements to keep him current on my plans and when I got back to Yuma, I learned from my sources in the Department of Defense that Ferguson was born in Hamilton, Texas, graduated from high school in Duncan, Arizona and attended Arizona State Teachers College and later, St. Mary's College in San Antonio, Texas.

He enlisted in the 158th Infantry Regiment of the Arizona National Guard and when it was federalized in 1940, he was called to active duty and transferred to the 45th Infantry Division. Ferguson was platoon sergeant, bayonet expert and instructor in hand-to-hand combat at Fort Sill, Oklahoma. He had mastered the intricate art of knife fighting from his Comanche grandfather and taught many of our war heroes the art of jungle fighting.

Shortly after Pearl Harbor, Ferguson went to Australia, where the Bushmasters 158th Combat Team was getting ready for its move through the South Pacific. He went through the Solomons and the New Guinea Campaigns with this bunch of rough-stuff dispensers and was finally sent back to the States with two wounds in June, 1943. He didn't stay hospitalized for very long, however, and in May, 1944, left for England with the advance party of the 95th Infantry Division.

Ferguson hit Normandy in June with a special reconnaissance unit and continued through France, Luxembourg, Belgium and Germany, where he saw action with the Fifth and 95th Divisions.

At the height of battle in Germany, he received multiple bullet wounds throughout his body. The severity of his wounds was such that he was evacuated to England and he spent the next three years in hospitals in England and the United States. They put 1,341 stitches in him to sew him back together. He was declared dead at one time. As the corpsman was tying an identification tag to his big toe, Ferguson rared up and asked for a bourbon and water highball, with just a touch of lemon. He received, among other things, a wonderful letter of commendation from General George Patton.

This was the man I had on tap as my under sheriff, should I become Sheriff of Yuma County.

CHAPTER TWENTY-SEVEN
ECHOLS FOR SHERIFF

B ack in Yuma, I began preparing to go to Phoenix to appear before the Federal Grand Jury on a number of cases that Charlie Cameron and I had handled in the Yuma area.

A good looking young man walked into our office and introduced himself. He was a lawyer who had arrived in Yuma while I was in Bolivia. He had been an Air Force lawyer and opened his law practice after he left the Service.

His name was Jeff Richards and he was from Kentucky. He had his law degree from the University of Kentucky, joined the Air Force and served as an intelligence officer during the Korean campaign. After the Korean War, he had been stationed in Phoenix, met and married a young nurse and they had one daughter.

Richards' main reason for coming to see me was because he represented an 18 year old man who had been arrested coming back from San Luis, Sonora, with about five or six marijuana cigarettes in his possession. He said that if the boy pleaded guilty or was convicted, he would serve a minimum sentence of five years in the federal penitentiary because of the Federal Narcotics Control Art.

Jeff thought this was too tough a sentence for a first conviction and for such a small quantity of marijuana. I agreed

HILARIOUS HIGH JINKS

and told him I was going to Phoenix the following morning and, if he wanted to, he could accompany me. We'd see the U.S. Attorney and find out if he would agree to transfer the charges to State court where, Jeff said, the boy would plead guilty and take whatever sentence was handed down by the court.

The U.S. Attorney agreed and the State court sentenced him to three months in jail.

A few months after that, I made one of my worst mistakes, and I've made some colossal ones. I announced that I was running for Sheriff of Yuma County and retired from Customs with 22 years of service, plus four years as a Naval Officer during World War II.

Now, Yuma County had been practically wide open to prostitution and gambling since statehood in 1912. These two professions invariably get into the hands of outside gangsters, something usually unknown by run-of-the-mill residents in a community, and they bring in narcotics like flies to a bucket of buttermilk.

There were four ex-sheriffs and an incumbent in Yuma, all of whom were very wealthy. One or two of them had been to the penitentiary on income tax fraud, but no one seemed to mind.

I ran on a "Clean Up The County" campaign and assured the voters that if elected, I would clean up Yuma County to the point where you couldn't get a bet on your weight.

Jeff Richards came over to see me. He said he was running for the position of District Attorney and that if elected, he would back me all the way on cleaning up the County.

Both of us won, but Jeff and I had no idea about the inner workings of politics. From our very first days in office, there was harassment action against us after I'd closed all the whore houses and run the gamblers out of the County. This harassment never let up.

I received a call from the man who was handling all the slot machines in the County. He said that if I would just be reasonable, I could close a lot of the money makers in the County and still do all right for myself. They offered me $150,000 a year if I'd let slot machines run in four clubs in Yuma: the VFW, the American Legion, the Elks and the Eagles.

From then on, the workings of the people who didn't want my kind of County were so tough that I believe few people could have survived them. I made it, though, and we arrested and successfully prosecuted the perpetrators of every crime of violence during the two years of my tenure as Sheriff. A great deal of this success could be laid at the doors of Jeff Richards and my newly-acquired Under Sheriff, George Ferguson, who retired in time to get to Yuma and help me pick my deputies.

The defense attorneys in Yuma had been having an easy time of it for many years. The sheriffs before me were so busy collecting from the different prostitution and gambling houses, that they had little time to investigate a felony case. Accordingly, when one was brought to court, it was so poorly investigated and prosecuted that the defense attorneys were winning most of them.

The first crime of any consequence that we got our teeth into was a case concerning the disappearance of Ward Junior Kenoyer, a Montebello, California, man who had come to Yuma to sell produce space on the Southern Pacific Railroad to the lettuce shippers. He had rented a motel room on March 2 and worked the Somerton area that first day. He then went across the border to San Luis, Sonora, came back with a couple of bottles of tequila and returned to his motel.

He was never seen alive again. He had been driving a new, gold-colored Biscayne Chevrolet and it also disappeared. We were advised by the Montebello Police Department that he had been a very active homosexual and had been arrested in Phoenix for this offense.

About two weeks after Kenoyer disappeared, his gold-colored Chevrolet was driven over the curb and into the side of a house in Sun City, Arizona. The occupants of the automobile fled before deputies arrived and the Maricopa

HILARIOUS HIGH JINKS

County Sheriff's Office in Phoenix impounded the car.

Two weeks later a citrus grower six miles south of Yuma made a "grissly discovery," as the detective magazines would say. It was Kenoyer's body, badly decomposed but clearly showing his throat had been so viciously cut that the head was almost severed from the body.

The citrus grower notified my office and I departed with my Under Sheriff and two of our technicians. We had the dispatcher notify Jeff Richards and he, too, drove out to the scene.

When Jeff arrived, the photographer was busy taking pictures and another technician was taking measurements. "Now let's do this right," Jeff said, and his tone indicated he knew what he was talking about. "Measure from the road to the body first. Then measure from the ditch to the body."

We called the Maricopa County Sheriff's Office in Phoenix and learned that when the car was driven into the side of the house and abandoned, the trunk contained a pair of laborer's pants, made in Mexico, a lettuce-cutting knife and a few dried lettuce leaves.

I then called the Produce Growers Association in Phoenix and learned that although there had been more than 70,000 Mexicans working in the Valley of the Sun at the time the automobile was wrecked, there were only 16 lettuce sheds functioning. All the other laborers were pulling carrots and onions. This eliminated them as suspects as there had only been dried lettuce leaves in the trunk of the car.

I asked the sheriff's office to prepare photos of the wrecked automobile and told them that some of my men would pick up the photos the next day. The following day I sent two of them, armed with the photographs, to Maricopa County to begin a systematic check of the 16 lettuce sheds that were operating the day the Kenoyer automobile was abandoned. We felt that the sight of a Mexican laborer driving a new, gold-colored Chevrolet to work would be fresh on many people's memory.

At the third shed they hit pay dirt. The shed manager told

them that a big, tough, Mexican national named Rafael Moreno Guerrero had been employed by him as a lettuce cutter and that Moreno invariably drove the new, gold-colored Chevrolet to work until he and the automobile disappeared. The date of his disappearance, according to the shed records, jibed with the date the car had been abandoned in Sun City. The foreman's records also showed that Moreno Guerrero had been living in Tolleson, Arizona, a small town near Phoenix.

The deputies drove there and found that Moreno Guerrero had a girlfriend living in Tolleson whose name was Ramona Arredondo. The deputies went to her house to talk with her.

Ramona said that she had been intimate with Moreno for some time and that he appeared in Tolleson the morning after the death of Kenoyer, driving the gold-colored Chevrolet that he said he was buying from a grape picker in the San Joaquin Valley of California. She said that Moreno had left Tolleson mysteriously some weeks before, but that he had returned and she had seen him in the pool hall that very morning. The deputies went down to the pool hall, where they found Moreno and arrested him.

Moreno's story was that he had been working in the Somerton area, near Yuma, as an assistant cook in a labor camp with some Filipinos and that on the night of March 2 he decided to quit and return to the Phoenix area. He said that he hitched a ride to Highway 80, where he caught a Greyhound bus for Phoenix. He said he knew nothing of Kenoyer. When they questioned him about the gold-colored Chevrolet he had been driving immediately after Kenoyer's death, he said that it belonged to another lettuce cutter named Luis Garcia who had no driver's license and who had asked Moreno to chauffeur him around. He said they were both employed at the same lettuce shed.

The foreman stated that there had been no one named Garcia working at the shed when Moreno was driving the gold-colored Chevrolet.

About this time a young Mexican boy was walking along the

road about half a mile from where Kenoyer's body had been found. Under a culvert in the road, he found all of Kenoyer's identification papers, his order forms and a large kitchen knife with blood on it.

One thing led to another and we finally had to go to trial with Moreno Guerrero, although we felt we had a weak case. Jeff Richards did an outstanding job in the prosecution, but we got a hung jury.

"Let's do it again," Jeff told me. "Let's find out where those Filipinos are where he was working when he killed Kenoyer. They'll be able to help us."

The Filipinos had left Yuma when the lettuce was harvested and, like most produce laborers, left no forwarding address.

I talked with Henry Adonis, head man of the Filipino colony in Yuma County. I told him we had to find the cook, Joe Magasai, who had been Moreno Guerrero's boss. Henry called San Francisco and learned that the cook had gone to Las Cruces, New Mexico, from Yuma County, so I called the sheriff in Las Cruces. He reported that Magasai had been there, but had left some three weeks before for Alamoso, Colorado.

A call to the sheriff's office in Alamoso got results. The cook and his entire crew, minus Moreno Guerrero, were working at a lettuce camp 12 miles out of Alamoso.

I advised Jeff Richards. "Let's drive to Alamoso, Colorado and see them," Jeff said. "We'll take pictures of Moreno Guerrero, the gold-colored Chevrolet and also of the knife Moreno used to murder Kenoyer."

We left the next morning in my official automobile. We drove through New Mexico and turned north at Gallup toward the Colorado border. Having nothing else to occupy my mind, I checked the distance between telephone poles with my speedometer. Being an old race horse man, it surprised me to, learn that they were a furling apart. That is, it was exactly 220 yards between poles. I thought of the dastardly trick Hank Adams had pulled on me as we drove to Los Angeles from Las Vegas years ago, and I quickly dreamed up a situation in which I could relieve Jeff Richards of some of his pocket money.

"Jeff," I said in my sly but honest-appearing fashion, "in order to alleviate the monotony of driving across this relentless expanse of high pasture land, let us make a few bets on the distance between objects on the road. For instance, let's start at the next telephone pole and I'll bet you $10 I can come closer than you can to the distance between it and that small hill up ahead."

Jeff was always suspicious of me. I've never learned why, but he apparently decided I couldn't possibly have an edge on him with this proposition, so he agreed.

"I think it's a mile and a half," he said confidently, but it seemed overdone to me.

I quickly counted the poles. There were eight of them, which made it a dead mortal cinch to be one mile away.

"It isn't near that far, Jeff," I told him sagely. "I say it's a flat mile."

The speedometer clicked it off and I missed by less than a tenth of a mile.

Jeff paid off. "Play you again," he said. "Take that windmill up ahead of us. How far do you say that is?"

I could see that he figured if I'd go first, he'd have a little better break.

I quickly counted the poles. There were nine of them. Nine furlongs is a mile and an eighth, or a mile and 220 yards.

"That windmill is a mile and two tenths from this next pole," I told him, as though that settled it.

"Now I've got you!" Jeff said, "It's exactly a mile!"

When I beat him that time, he waited about 10 minutes before he went again. He spotted a watering tank alongside the road and it was less than a mile away.

"Quick!" he yelled, "I'll guess that's half a mile! That water tank there!"

The telephone poles showed that it was less than four poles away, so I guessed four tenths of a mile and got him by about

HILARIOUS HIGH JINKS

100 yards. We kept this up until I'd relieved him of most of his walkabout money.

We began to get up into the high country of Colorado, and started seeing clear, white trout streams flashing by us. "When we get to Alamoso, Jeff, I'll spring for trout dinner. Just imagine eating a great big fresh one apiece, right out of these cold streams!"

We checked into a motel which seemed to have one of the finest restaurants in town, and after a quick tidying up, sat down for dinner.

"We want the two largest and freshest trout the cook can come up with," Jeff told the waitress.

When she brought them, they actually hung over the sides of the plates. We devoured them like the hungry gluttons we were, washing them down with liebfraumilch from the Rhineland of Germany.

"Let's go back to the kitchen and congratulate the cook," Jeff said as he finished off the last of the wine.

We went back and told the cook how we enjoyed the excellent trout, cooked to perfection, and how much more palatable they were when fresh.

"Where were they caught?" Jeff asked. "Which one of these cascading streams produced such examples of culinary grandeur?" The liebfraumilch had started making him garrulous.

"Don't know," the cook said, "le'me see."

He went over to the garbage can and brought out a couple of food packages. Jeff and I looked at them and went reeling off to bed. Our deliciously fresh Colorado trout had come frozen from Japan.

The next morning we met the sheriff. He told us where we could find the Filipinos and Jeff and I drove out there. The cook, Joe Magasai, had been told of our coming. We showed him the picture of Rafael Moreno Guerrero.

"He was my assistant," he said, "he left without saying goodbye."

We showed him a picture of the butcher knife, found with Kenoyer's identification papers in the culvert near the death scene. "That's my butcher knife!" he said, "I'd know it anywhere!"

He looked at the picture of Ward Junior Kenoyer, but shook his head. "Maybe the man who came by and picked Guerrero up," he said. "Guerrero say to us when he come from Somerton, he has a date with a beautiful American girl, we all watch to see. When come to pick him up, it's a man. We make fun of Moreno Guerrero when he leave and some of the boys say, 'Yeah! American girl friend, eh?'"

We showed Joe Magasai the picture of the gold-colored Chevrolet. "That's exactly like car that man picked up Moreno Guerrero in when he leave labor camp in Somerton."

We took statements from Joe Magasai and three other Filipinos, all of whom remembered the gold-colored Chevrolet picking up Moreno Guerrero on March 2. Also, one of them said he could positively identify the knife found in the culvert as being part of the culinary equipment of Joe Magasai.

Jeff, George Ferguson and I held a council of war when we got back to Yuma. George, as I have said, was a retired Master Sergeant in the Army and had killed with knives in combat.

George said, "Damn it, boys, when Moreno Guerrero sliced across Kenoyer's neck with that big sharp knife and severed his jugular, blood must have gushed out for a couple of feet. There's no way Moreno could have dodged it. When he drove Kenoyer's car over to Phoenix, he must have been saturated with blood."

I remembered that the Mexican girl, Ramona Arredondo, was the first person he contacted when he arrived there. I went up to see her and Jeff Richards went along.

We found Ramona and the first thing Jeff asked her was, "Where's Rafael Moreno's jacket? We've come for it."

"I've got it back here in a trunk," she said.

"Was it very bloody when he gave it to you?"

"I'll say it was!" she replied. "Said he'd been in a fist fight in

203

Bakersfield. I ran it through my washing machine, though. Think I took it all out."

She found it and gave it to us. We had her write her initials in it so she'd know it in court. It was a suede jacket and I sent it to the FBI laboratory in Washington, D.C.

We got a report quickly. "It's saturated in blood," it said. "Further analysis shows it's human blood."

We went to trial again. Jeff brought out all the things we'd introduced in the first trial and then he went to bat with the Filipino cook. When he identified the knife, the defense lawyer ridiculed this, saying no one could tell their kitchen knife from someone else's. We knew we had him there. There were eight women on the jury and any woman can identify her butcher knife if it was placed among 50 others.

The cook remembered Moreno being picked up in a gold-colored Chevrolet and he remembered March 2 as being the date Moreno Guerrero disappeared. This testimony was corroborated by his associates.

And then we brought on Ramona Arrendondo and she testified that when Moreno appeared at her home on the third of March (which date she could remember because it was the day the rodeo started), he was wearing a suede jacket and it was covered with blood. She said Moreno told her it was from a fight he'd had in Bakersfield. She said he gave it to her and she ran it through her washing machine and stored it in her trunk. She identified the jacket Jeff showed her as being the one she was talking about.

Then Jeff put an FBI laboratory technician on the stand. He qualified him quickly, then showed him the suede jacket.

"Do you recognize this jacket?" Jeff asked quietly.

"I do. That jacket was sent to me from the Sheriff's Office in Yuma for chemical analysis. Here are my initials on it," he replied.

"And did you give this jacket your usual analysis?" Jeff asked innocently, "and if so, what did it reveal?"

When he asked this last question, Jeff turned his back on the witness and started strolling away.

"It showed that the front of the jacket was saturated with blood," the witness said, quietly.

There was nothing quiet about Jeff Richards, however. He stopped walking away, whirled around to face the witness, threw his arms in the air and squawked, "Blood? Did you say blood on that jacket? Dripping out of the seams, all over the front of it?"

By this time the defense lawyers were on their feet, screaming at the judge to stop it. The judge was pounding on his desk with his gavel and yelling at Jeff to desist.

"Blood, was it?" Jeff was shrieking by now. "Matted up and curdled all over the front of that suede jacket?"

The judge finally got him to shut up, but the jury was sitting on the edges of their chairs and their eyes were bugged out like marbles. Big raw marbles.

Jeff Richards was the most apologetic and contrite man I've ever seen in a court of law. He apologized to the court, the defense lawyers and the jury, but it was mighty easy to see he'd struck a hard, solid blow for justice.

Then he quietly, but cannily, asked the witness if his analysis showed what kind of blood was in the texture of this suede jacket.

"Why, yes," the witness confidently replied, "it was human blood."

Jeff rose again. He stood on his tiptoes with his arms high in the air.

"Human blood!" he screeched, "human blood dripping down out of that suede jacket...coming out of the seams?" He took a quick breath and began again. "All matted up and..."

By this time the venerable judge banged so hard on his desk and the defense lawyers yelled so loudly that they finally quieted Jeff down again.

And again, he went through his ritual. He apologized to the judge, the defense lawyers and the jury. I began to think he was going to turn and apologize to the audience and the two stiff-backed bailiffs.

The judge said, "Just one more outburst like that, Mr. Prosecutor, and you'll be back in my chambers. Just one more!"

Jeff apologized again.

We rested the case. The defense tried to counteract the testimony of the Filipino cook, the Tolleson girl, Ramona Arrendondo, and the laboratory technician from the Federal Bureau of Investigation. However, we could see that they were beat. Jeff Richards rose in his courtly manner and dramatically closed with a sincere and devastating appeal. It only took the jury a few minutes to come trooping back with a conviction.

CHAPTER TWENTY-EIGHT
CRIME AND POLITICS IN YUMA

The hardest job for me as Sheriff of Yuma County was getting good men as deputies. When I took office my 1961 salary was $800 a month. That, along with my $600 a month pension from the Government, allowed me to get by. My big problem was salaries for my deputies. Regular deputies were paid $400 per month. This meant I had a choice of three types of employees: an incompetent, a thief, or a young deputy who wanted to learn the trade. The third type could cross the Colorado River into California and double his salary.

I went for the young men and started a training program with the help of the local Customs special agents, the FBI and other agencies. I lost many of our trained deputies to law enforcement units in Southern California, but we managed to keep many well trained and dedicated boys. We dressed them in good looking, western uniforms. My predecessor had allowed them to come to work in bedroom slippers and pajama tops if they so desired. The *esprit de corps* was high and with George Ferguson giving them the old pep drive, they solved everything that came along in the way of felonious crimes.

One of the criminal cases that hit us occasionally was hitchhiker murders. Three interstate highways ran through

HILARIOUS HIGH JINKS

Yuma County and it seemed every couple of months someone would pick up a hitchhiker who would murder the good samaritan, take his automobile, money and credit cards, then leave for greener pastures. A hitchhiker murder seems hard to solve, but actually that is not the case. An all-points bulletin on the automobile, after the body had been found, and a lookout for the illegal use of the victim's credit cards would usually lead us right to the murderer.

There hadn't been a bank robbery in Yuma in about 15 years, but we had three within two months after I became Sheriff. We caught the robbers with well planned road blocks since, when leaving Yuma in any direction, a robber must go a long way before branching off onto several different roads that offer concealment.

We had one armed robbery that got mighty hairy. A young giant of about 260 pounds and standing some six feet, six inches, drove up to a big motel in Yuma, pulled a pistol on the manager and walked away with $2,600.

The manager gave a good description of the getaway car and within an hour we found it in a grocery store parking lot. We jimmied the trunk and found a good picture of the robber hugging a beautiful Mexican girl. We also found his size 13 shoe tracks leading away from the car.

There was a Border Patrol officer in Yuma who was one of the best trackers since Geronimo and I asked him to help. I showed him the huge shoe tracks leading into the desert and with his nose to the ground, he started following them. The tracks led in a big circle, back onto Fourth Avenue, next to a taxi stand.

About three hours had passed since the motel robbery. I went up to the taxi driver, showed him the photo and asked him if this big booger had hired his taxi.

"Yep," he said. "He sure did. I just got back from taking him to Calexico, where I let him out right at the Customs house, going into Mexicali, Mexico. He gave me a magnificent tip, too!" he said.

"I imagine he did," I told him. "He sure had both front pockets full of money!"

I drove over to Calexico and then to Mexicali where I went to the police station and showed them the photo of the culprit. I asked if they would furnish me a couple of detectives to check all the hotels in town. By then, it was about 8:00 p.m. and if he wasn't bedded down, he'd have at least registered.

We covered the entire city. I'd forgotten how it had grown since I worked there in the early 30's. It was a city of at least a half million people and it seemed there was a hotel for every 10. Finally about 10:00 p.m., we went to a ratty, little Chinese hotel, down on the banks of New River, and I showed the photo to the night clerk.

"Yep," he said, "that big man is sleeping in room number 18, right down the hallway."

It was summertime, and the weather was mighty warm. None of the wooden doors were shut, but each room had a screen door with a little steel catch to hold it shut. We got to number 18, I could see the big man in the room. He was bunched up in the bed with his right arm under the pillow and sound asleep. I figured his gun was under the pillow and I told the Mexicans I would jerk the lock off the door, dive for him, and grab the gun before he woke up. I told them to have their 28 inch billy clubs ready in case I had any hard luck with him and needed help.

I jerked the door open and as I dove for him, he came up with the pistol and jumped out of bed. I grabbed onto the barrel and he began throwing me around the room as though I was a little feisty dog. Finally, he turned the gun loose with his right hand, still holding onto it with his left, and let go with a Sunday punch. By the time it hit the top of my belly, I could hear the wind whistling from the power of his blow. I was lifted about six inches off the floor, but managed to hold onto the pistol.

The Mexicans had been admiring our maneuvers around the floor and I fully expected them to start clapping to the rhythm of our impromptu dance. When I came down, I yelled at them to get busy with those damned billy clubs. They finally got into action and beat him to the floor while I still had hold of the gun which I managed to pull away from him.

"I won't agree to extradition from Mexico!" he said, as I put the handcuffs on him.

"You won't have to," I told him. "These boys are declaring you *persona non grata* and will put you over the border into Calexico."

"Then I won't agree to extradition from California into Arizona," he said.

"Fine," I told him. The top of my belly felt like it was on fire. "We'll haul you over to San Luis, Sonora, and they'll dump you across the border into Arizona."

He then agreed to go back to Yuma without any trouble. Jeff Richards got him 10 years on an armed robbery charge, but he damned near ruined me. He broke all five of my stomach linings. A couple of years later, a hernia developed that required an operation. They were able to put sutures in three of the linings, but the two next to my stomach were torn so badly from the robber's mighty blow that they couldn't get them back together.

The robber got 10 years, but I was filled with 154 stainless steel sutures and to this day the two bottom linings still don't mesh. Whenever I go through an airport metal detector, it lights up like I hit three plums on a Las Vegas slot machine. I explain to security that I'm full of stainless steel sutures, but they usually haul me off to a little room and peel me down to my drawers for the search. Only then am I allowed to put my clothes back on and board the plane.

When it came time to run for reelection, the defense lawyers (who hadn't won a case since Jeff Richards and I got elected) started a fund in order to beat the two of us. The gamblers and pimps joined the foray and we could see they were determined to make a run at us.

About this time, I received a telephone call from Senator

Thomas Dodd of Connecticut, the Chairman of the Senate Subcommittee on Juvenile Delinquency. He had learned of my many years in Mexico where I had attempted to stop the growth of opium in the Badiraguato Mountains northeast of Culiacan. He desired to send two investigators there to determine if opium was still available and in what quantities. He also wanted to learn about the heroin-producing plants in the Culiacan. He asked if I could get away from my duties as Yuma County Sheriff for two weeks to accompany the investigators on this slightly hazardous trip.

The county supervisors agreed to the trip and stated it would help our country to find out what was going on down there, and maybe even get it stopped. I secretly laughed at this. To my knowledge, opium has been grown in the Badiraguato Mountains since 1928 and undoubtedly many years prior to that time.

I met the two investigators from Washington in Tucson and we proceeded by plane to Culiacan. I had asked Senator Dodd if I could contact my informant in the Santoro-Petrelli case. He agreed and I contacted my old accomplice, Bert Farnsworth, in Panama where he was working in a mahogany lumber plant. He agreed to meet us in Culiacan and arrived the same day. I had a good reunion with Bert and consider him one of the bravest men I've known.

Bert got busy immediately. He found lots of crude opium and several heroin-producing plants. We could purchase up to six kilos immediately and we were told that in a couple of weeks they would have 20 kilos available for delivery anywhere in Mexico.

I bid goodbye to Bert Farnsworth and he went back to Panama. It was our last time together as he died shortly after that. The two Senate investigators went back to Washington and I returned to Yuma to await a subpoena from the Senate subcommittee.

In the meantime, a former deputy under the Sheriff I beat in the 1960 election decided to run against me. He had only been

HILARIOUS HIGH JINKS

in Yuma a couple of years and a lawyer friend of mine advised me to return from Washington via the deputy's home town in Ohio to see what I could learn of his background.

I received the subpoena and flew to Washington where I testified for an entire day before the subcommittee. I told them of my work in Mexico during the early 40's, the huge poppy fields in the Badiraguato Mountains northeast of Culiacan, and of a little town in those mountains called San Pedro de Macoris where crude opium was used as a medium of exchange. The growers would go into the store, purchase meat and *garbanzos*, and hand the grocer a big ball of opium. He would break off enough to pay for the purchase and give the remainder back to them.

The opium itself was harvested by young children who were armed with razor blades set in wood. A quarter of an inch of the blade was outside the wooden container. This was to keep the blades from going into the pod of the poppy and injuring the seeds that were used the following year to grow a new crop. The children would go down the rows of poppies slashing the pods. Within a few minutes, a big drop of white liquid would form from the cut and other children would then come along behind and knock the white drops off into beer cans. When the cans were full, they would pour them out on a newspaper in the sun and, as the liquid dried, it turned brown and became crude opium.

I explained to the subcommittee about my work with the director of Public Health, who was also in charge of all the narcotics investigators in Mexico. His monthly salary was the equivalent of $400 in Mexican pesos. However, he lived in a huge home in Chapultepec Heights and had a Rolls Royce and two Mercedes Benz in his garage.

I told them that I worked as a Treasury Attache, under Ambassador Josephus Daniels, who had been Secretary of the Navy in World War I. He put a lot of pressure on the director to furnish me with two buses fully loaded with soldiers and a Mexican colonel for a trip into the Badiraguato Mountains to destroy the poppy crop in March, before the opium was bled from them in early April.

I met the colonel in Culiacan and, with the two buses of soldiers, we proceeded to the mountains. In the foothills, we spotted 10 hectares of poppies growing about half a mile off the road. The soldiers quickly disembarked from the buses. While some surrounded the fields with guns at the ready, others moved in with machetes and rapidly cut down the entire growth as a cameraman took movies of the operation.

In testimony to the subcommittee, I told of my suggestion that we proceed into the mountains to destroy the big fields. The colonel, however, shook his head. He showed me his orders and they only allowed him to go to the foothills. He said he'd hurry back to Mexico City, get his orders changed and come back as soon as possible. He came back with new orders in late April, about two weeks after the last of the poppies had been bled. He moved into the Badiraguato Mountains with his cameraman and cut down all the poppies, taking movies as he went. The opium, by then, was safely in the warehouses in Culiacan.

I testified about our latest journey to Culiacan and what we found regarding crude opium availability and the ability to buy heroin with delivery anywhere in Mexico. The townspeople of Culiacan told of a section of the city called Rio Blanco, where all the big narcotics traffickers had beautiful homes, rivalling those in Beverly Hills. They also told us that the traffickers were known as *Los Valientes*, the valiant ones, and were highly respected by most of the people.

The testimony was covered by the media and went to newspapers all over the United States and Mexico. The newspapers in Mexico lost no time in ridiculing my testimony, saying there was no opium grown in Mexico and, in fact, there were no narcotics of any kind available there.

One newspaper in Mazatlan stated, "This Sheriff of Yuma, Arizona, must have been reading the works of Sir Arthur Conan Doyle to have dreamed up such a fantasy. He comes

HILARIOUS HIGH JINKS

from a town in the United States where they have the ugliest girls in the world, and if you cross the river into California, they'll take your oranges away from you!"

On my way back to Yuma, I stopped off in Ohio where I talked with the sheriff in the hometown of my proposed opponent. He told me the man had been fired from his job, abandoned his wife and children and married the woman he ran off with somewhere in Mexico without benefit of a divorce. His lawful wife had been desperately trying to find him.

I had only been back in Yuma three days when my opponent went on the radio to announce his candidacy. He said, "The present Sheriff hasn't explained to my satisfaction why he made a trip to Washington or who paid for it. Did the Sheriff pay for it himself? Did the U.S. Government pay for it? Did Yuma County pay for it? I would like to have answers to these questions!"

A couple of days later a lawyer called him from Ohio. I don't know what he told him, but the ex-deputy left town that night with his second wife and was never heard of again in Yuma.

By then, the opposition was beginning to roll. They put together a bankroll of over $80,000 to beat Jeff Richards and me. In lieu of the man who had left town, they ran a man for sheriff who had worked on the Yuma Police Department as a patrolman for 10 years. It was a dirty campaign and I was completely lost in it. They beat me further than Wild Bill went into the mountains and they'd have beaten Jeff Richards, too, but his sweet little wife, Janice, a registered nurse, had gone up to the Indian reservation near Parker to work among the Indians and she got a big bunch of them to vote for Jeff, which barely put him back in office.

I was sitting around the house a few days later, feeling like somebody had broken an egg in me, when I got a call from Byron Engle in Washington. Jeri Jelsch, whom he had married by then, was on another phone.

"Hear you got your butt beat," Byron said.

"Further than Ghengis Khan went into Asia Minor," I told him, "but don't sit around back there in Washington and make fun of me! I feel bad enough already."

I could hear them both laughing. "No, Lee," Byron said, "come on back here, we've got a good job for you."

"Where is it?" I asked, getting highly interested, as I'd been contemplating having to live on my $600 a month pension.

"Now, Lee," Jeri said, laughing again, "You're too smart to ask that over the telephone. You get on back here!"

The job was in the Dominican Republic. I was to get more salary than both my ex-sheriff's job and pension, a $4,500 yearly house allowance, 15% hazardous duty pay, 15% cost of living increase, $1,500 for little Juanita's school, and I was to get back on the Government payroll the day after my Yuma County paychecks stopped. Financially, this turned out to be the best thing that ever happened.

I flew back to Yuma and told Helen about it. We put our house on the market and sold it quickly. From there we went to Washington where I attended several schools preparing for my new job in Santo Domingo.

CHAPTER TWENTY-NINE

SANTO DOMINGO AND THE BIG REVOLUTION

Prior to my assignment in the Dominican Republic, I studied all I could about the history of this turbulent country. The chaos got so bad in 1916 that the United States Marines waded ashore to try to salvage something out of the terrible disorder.

The Marines left in 1924 and four years later a military man with purpose and know-how moved in. He was Rafael Leonidas Trujillo Molina and he ruled as an absolute dictator until his luck ran out in 1961. He was gunned down on his way from Santo Domingo to his old home in San Cristobal.

During the 31 years of his reign, Trujillo allowed little freedom. He killed people who opposed him, or put them in prison. But along with the bad things, he rebuilt the capital city and he made a model of cleanliness of the country. He built hospitals, roads, markets and bridges. He built piers and he dug out channels. He took care of the poor with free medical care and food...and, while at it, he skimmed off $800,000,000 for himself.

A man doesn't do all these things without gaining enemies and it brings up the old axiom that when thieves are in the

HILARIOUS HIGH JINKS

market place, honest men will join with revolutionaries to throw them out.

Several attempts were made to kill him and overthrow his Government, but the early ones were half-hearted and amateurish. Finally, a group began training in the Sierra Maestra Mountains in the northern part of Cuba's Oriente Province. Although all the training and inspiration for this cadre of revolutionaries came from Fidel Castro, he sold out to Trujillo as he was desperately in need of American dollars at the time.

From information furnished Trujillo by Castro, two Dominican tanks with 75 mm cannons were awaiting the arrival of the first contingent of 80 men who arrived at Constanza Airport on June 14, 1959. The tanks, aided by two crack infantry companies, killed or captured these men and the following day, a ship landed on the north coast in Samana Bay. Trujillo's Air Force decimated the landing party and they, too, were killed or captured. And by the time Trujillo's bully boys got through with the survivors, they would have been much better off perishing in the ill-fated onslaught.

Finally, in late May, 1961, a group of highly dedicated Dominicans who had enough of "The Great Benefactor" ambushed him on George Washington Boulevard. There were three carloads and they dispatched him quickly. However, one of them who was unfamiliar with the Thompson submachine gun shot himself through the foot. Trujillo's chauffeur, although shot several times, got to a telephone and reported the deed to Trujillo's Secret Intelligence officers. The driver told them Trujillo may have wounded one or more of the assassins, therefore, all hospitals were immediately staked out.

When the wounded conspirator checked into a hospital, the bullyboys grabbed him and tortured him until he gave the names of the men who participated in the assassination. The conspirators were rounded up, tortured and slain, except for two who escaped, Antonio Imbert Barerra and Luis Amiami Tio who went into hiding. It quickly became evident that

Ramfis, the young playboy son of Trujillo, couldn't hold the country and Government together. Therefore, the entire family got out of Santo Domingo on the great four-masted family yacht, carrying his body and, among other things, a famous young race horse which Trujillo had purchased from the old Aga Khan. Dominican gun boats overtook the escaping party, put them ashore in Martinique, and brought the beautiful yacht, *Estrellita*, back to the Dominican Republic as property of the Government. Antonio Imbert Barerra and Luis Amiami Tio returned and were made Generals for life. The country began to recover and the people made demands for a free election.

With the procedures for a free election established, Juan Bosch, a man who had been in exile for 26 years, returned to the Dominican Republic and announced himself as a candidate for President. He had lived in Cuba for several years and then moved to Mexico where he remained until his return for election. Bosch was a poetic dreamer with Marxist leanings who had no prior administrative training. The populace, disgusted with 31 years of complete dominance by a military dictator, voted him into office by a sizeable majority.

Juan Bosch took office as President on January 1, 1963. He had only been in office a few months when I arrived in the country to start working in my new position. I soon learned that Bosch had four well-known Communists in his 12-man cabinet.

My job in the Dominican Republic was working with the Secret Police and other investigative groups to aid in setting up a modern criminal laboratory. On my arrival, the Chief of Police, Belisario Peguero, held a dinner party at the Police Officers' Club for my wife and me and two other public safety advisors and their wives. They were "Tony" Ruiz, a retired Captain of Detectives from the Los Angeles Police Department, and "Jake" Jackson of the Indiana State Police.

At that dinner, I met several men who would play a big part in my life in the next few years. One of them was Colonel Francisco Caamano Deno. He was a tough, entertaining young officer who could speak English. This doesn't seem to be too much of an accomplishment, but in the Dominican Republic, a person who could speak English was rare indeed. Trujillo had been extremely reluctant to allow Dominicans to leave the country and, as a result, the great majority of them could only communicate in their native language of Spanish.

Francisco's father had been one of the meanest and most arrogant of the Secret Intelligence officers and had killed many people. There was a saying that he had his own graveyard. Francisco went through the Dominican Naval Academy, but the professors had such a fear of his father that he was allowed to appear for Monday morning muster in need of a shave and, at times, even barefoot. Because of his father's influence with Trujillo, he was allowed to go to Quantico, Virginia, for an additional two years' training, and learned English while there.

On his return to Santo Domingo, Francisco chose to go into the Police Department instead of following his Navy training. His intelligence and administrative and managerial abilities enabled him to rise quickly and, at 29 years of age, he was a full colonel in charge of the Cascos Blancos.

Now, the Cascos Blancos, so named because of their white helmets, were an elite corps of 500 young riot control officers who had been trained by two Los Angeles police officers. They were a unit to be reckoned with given their 26-inch riot sticks and their knowledge of how to use them. Their various V-shaped attack formations could break up a riot quickly without too much physical harm to the rioters. They were stationed in the old Fortaleza Ozama at the mouth of the Ozama River and their director was Francisco Caamano.

I also met Colonel Manuel Despradel Brache who was administrator of the Radio Patrol Section. He was an excellent, dedicated young officer and, at that time, a close personal friend of Francisco Caamano.

Probably the most interesting man I met at this dinner was Antonio Imbert Barerra, the man who reportedly killed Trujillo. He was there in his well-tailored General's uniform, but with no troops under him, quite a frustrated man.

There were some fairly good pistol shooters in the National Police. Every Saturday morning they would hold 50 yard slow-fire matches at the pistol range in back of the Police Horse Patrol. They would each put up a peso, equivalent to an American dollar, and the winner would get the entire pot.

One of their best shooters was Lieutenant Colonel Luis Arzeno Regalado, Chief of the Records Section, and another, Captain Viriato Brito Pilier who was tough as whitleather and completely fearless. In fact, when I first met him, he was in jail at the Fortaleza Ozama awaiting trial for holding a police colonel at gun point and making him march back and forth in the reception room of the Police Headquarters at Moca, 40 miles north of the capital. He was released unconditionally after the court martial.

It was brought out at the hearing that the colonel, drunk at the time, was marching Captain Brito back and forth at gun point teaching him "some discipline." Brito kept getting a little closer to the big gun case at the end of the room. He finally grabbed a loaded BAR gun and put the barrel right in the surprised colonel's face. Then it became the colonel's turn to march. As it turned out, Captain Brito was completely exonerated and the colonel was fired.

I was invited to join this group at the range every Saturday and confident that I would win the pot most of the time. Therefore, I would bring along a couple of cases of Tuborg beer and two or three barbecued chickens for good relations, hoping to pay for the spread with my winnings.

I could usually do it! Colonel Caamano was probably the best shot on the Police Force and when he lost, he would hustle to his car and go roaring off, mad as a bee-stung bear. That's when I learned that along with his affability, he had an enormous temper.

The boys in the Secret Police had informants who had infiltrated the three Communist parties in the country. The 14th of June was the largest party with an estimated 4,000 members. Their strength was among students and workers and Castro's influence was considerable. Next, the Partido Socialista Popular Dominicano, with about 1,000 members, closely followed the aggressive Communist Russian line. The third Communist party was the potent Movimiento Popular Dominicano with only about 500 members. When these groups all joined forces in the Spring of 1965 they were a force to be reckoned with.

The infiltration of these parties by the Secret Police revealed that many of the Communists had gone to Cuba, Czechoslovakia and Red China for training, using false documents. They learned that a big revolution was planned for the future, provided the Communists didn't take over the country first through riots and with the assistance of the President, Juan Bosch.

After nine months in office, President Juan Bosch had increased the number of Communists in his cabinet to eight, making it an eight to four majority. Further, huge riots were beginning to take place all over town with the crowds turning over automobiles, starting fires with used automobile tires, breaking into stores and looting. And while all this was going on, President Bosch refused to allow the Cascos Blancos to leave the barracks in the Fortaleza Ozama.

The Secret Police had devised an ingenious scheme to get photographs of most of the ring leaders of the Communist parties. They had recruited three young men who looked even younger than they actually were. They outfitted them with ragged clothing and shoe-shine boxes. Inside the shoe-shine boxes were expensive cameras with the lenses pointing out of small holes in the front of the boxes. The shoe-shine boys became very adept at obtaining excellent photos, unbeknown to the subjects.

By that time, Colonel Despradel Brache had replaced Caamano as Director of the Cascos Blancos, while Francisco Caamano took over the Radio Patrol.

Despradel told me he was completely frustrated by the

President's order, but Bosch told him the riot control group would only further antagonize the rioters and disallowed his request to move in on them.

Finally, at midnight on September 25, 1963, I got a telephone call from Police Colonel Jose Morillo stating that at daylight, members of the Army, Navy, Air Force and National Police would arrive at President Bosch's home, overthrow him, put him and his wife on a plane and send them out of the country. They would appoint a three-man civilian triumvirate until they could hold another free election.

This was accomplished and Bosch and his wife were flown to a small French island, and returned later to Puerto Rico, across the Mona Passage from Santa Domingo.

A triumvirate was appointed, headed by an honest, young automobile dealer named Donald Reid Cabral. However, the top military people decided they had inherited the right to steal from Trujillo and they began all sorts of skullduggery. A couple of them opened their own pharmacies, bringing in huge loads of merchandise from Miami in military planes without paying the import duties. Others were bringing in new automobiles with high Customs duties unpaid, and it wasn't long until many people who had no Communist leanings at all were joining with the revolutionaries to "get the thieves out of the market place."

The Secret Police people told me they had learned through their infiltrators that a huge revolution was planned for May 1965. This intelligence was furnished to Donald Reid Cabral, but apparently not to Francisco Caamano.

About this time, Francisco Caamano learned from a garage owner that the chief of police had bought 50 automobiles from a dealer in Puerto Rico, ostensibly for the Radio Patrol, of which Caamano was Director. Instead, the chief had the garage owner file off the motor numbers, put new ones in their place and put them on the open market.

Caamano got an affidavit from the garage owner to this effect and told Donald Reid Cabral about it on April 24, 1965.

HILARIOUS HIGH JINKS

He demanded that Reid fire the chief immediately. However, Reid knew of the impending revolution. He feared that if he fired the chief of police, the revolutionaries would feel that the Government had weakened and they might begin the revolution immediately. Reid knew that the Army had not built itself up sufficiently to crush a revolution at this time. Therefore, he told Caamano that he was making him Consul General to Jamaica and that he was to leave immediately.

Caamano said he wouldn't accept it and, literally fuming with rage, roared out to the San Ysidro Airport in his car where he knew his old rightist friend, General Wessin y Wessin, would save him from the assignment in Jamaica.

The revolutionaries planned to start the war by taking over a huge arsenal across the river from Santo Domingo, bringing the armaments into Pueblo Nuevo by trucks, distributing them to their cohorts and moving in on the various installations. They would then set up strongholds, and lead mobs to the anti-Communist newspapers, radio stations and the one television station in Santo Domingo, thus taking over all communications. They would then move in on the Government Palace, the power company, the telephone company, the post office and other installations in order to completely paralyze the city of Santo Domingo.

Some of the conspirators who were working at the arsenal were discussing this plan on April 24, when the commanding officer overheard them. He attempted to arrest them but they killed him. With the aid of a Communist prostitute, Belkis Maldonado, they then lured three of the arsenal guards into a room where they, too, were killed, thus starting the revolution a month earlier than anticipated.

They loaded three big trucks with small arms and ammunition, quickly crossed the bridge that spanned the Ozama River and began passing out the guns and ammo. At first, they asked to see a person's Communist Party card but, later, they gave weapons to any taker.

They got a French-made tank equipped with a 75 mm gun

across the river. They called the police headquarters and told them to send a truckload of officers to the rebel zone as there were people breaking into stores. The police sent 23 men and, as they arrived, the tank went into action with the cannon and two machine guns blazing and quickly killed all the police. Another truckload of police was requested for reinforcement but the police began to realize what was going on and didn't send the second group.

The Communists (51 hardliners) who had been trained overseas set up commando posts in the rebel zone and began running the revolution. They moved in on all communication and Government installations. The Palace was taken with little opposition.

About this time, Francisco Caamano made one of the biggest mistakes of his young life. He drove down into the rebel zone and joined the revolutionaries.

The Communists realized what a windfall this was, since they would be able to hide their true colors behind this son of one of Trujillo's strongest supporters and they quickly elected him "President of the Dominican Republic." Although this great "honor" only made him president of about 20 square blocks in the downtown Santo Domingo area, it was a great boost for the morale of the revolutionaries and it also drew many unsuspecting people to their cause.

I telephoned Caamano the evening of his defection and asked, "What in God's name has come over you, Francisco? You have joined the group that is furnishing guns to every Communist in the Republic! You have set your country back at least 50 years!"

"No, Lee," he told me, "We have to do it this way to win the revolution. When we do, I have a plan to get all the guns back."

"Oh, you dreamer boy!" I told him. "You'll never get any of them back, and furthermore, you can't win this revolution with that gang of bums at your back. Our Country wouldn't let you!"

HILARIOUS HIGH JINKS

"Well," he replied, "we'll either win it or I'll die in the Dominican Republic!"

It took him almost eight years to live up to this prediction, but he finally made it.

Meantime, he surrounded the Fortaleza Ozama with 20 mm cannons, 50-caliber machine guns and mortars and began trying to shoot down the huge mahogany doors to get at his old friend Despradel and the dreaded Cascos Blancos.

On April 26, eight more truckloads of guns and ammunition crossed the big bridge on the Ozama River and then the revolutionaries, fearing that General Wessin y Wessin would move in with the 50 French tanks from San Ysidro Airport, put two huge trucks laden with sugar cane crossways on the bridge. The formidable tanks arrived and one of them moved up to the edge of the bridge for a little exploration. It was quickly put out of commission by rocket-firing guns concealed in a newly-built, high-rise apartment building on the Santo Domingo side of the river.

General Wessin y Wessin then decided he would blast the trucks off the bridge with his Air Force bombs. This was stopped quickly, however, when the rebels dragged out relatives of the bomber pilots from their homes in Santo Domingo and tied them to the trucks.

By this time, the revolutionaries had taken nearly all of the capital city and had begun a strong attack against the American Embassy. Many people throughout the city were being killed. American Ambassador J. Tapley Bennett phoned President Lyndon Johnson and asked that all American women and children be evacuated immediately.

Coincidentally, a group of U.S. warships was passing the island of Hispaniola on its way to Culebra Island for a war games training exercise. They were headed by Vice Admiral John McCain on the amphibious assault ship *USS Boxer*. President Johnson ordered the ships to hold off the coast of Santo Domingo and evacuate the American dependents by helicopter.

It was arranged for the dependents to meet outside the Hotel Embajador, located about a quarter of a mile from the main road, and go by caravan to San Cristobal where helicopters would fly them to the *USS Boxer* and other ships in the convoy.

As I was driving to the hotel with Helen and little Juanita, the radio was blasting away for all the revolutionaries to proceed to the Hotel Embajador and find and kill Communist hater and baiter, Rafael Bonillo Aybar. It was said that Bonillo, who had owned an anti-Communist newspaper and radio station, was trying to escape with the American women and children.

As we drove along in my Oldsmobile 98, grim-looking rebels were passing us in all sorts of vehicles. They were armed with various types of pistols and rifles and as we drove into the complex, there were hundreds of them milling around among the American dependents. I decided to drive back out to the main road until the situation resolved itself, but in the middle of the street, a rebel armed with a Belgian BAR gun stopped me.

"Open your trunk!" he ordered in Spanish. "Have you got Bonilla Aybar in there?"

As I got out to open the trunk, Bonilla Aybar and two or three of his compatriots opened fire from the fourth floor of the hotel with Thompson submachine guns. This brought immediate fire from the BAR of my inquisitor and Bonillo trained his fire on my car. I pulled Helen and Juanita out of the car as the bullets hit the concrete beneath the Olds. I had them lay on the street alongside the car.

My next move was to get my inquisitive friend away from my car and I told him in Spanish, "Get away from here quickly before you get my wife and daughter killed!"

As I pulled Juanita from the back seat, I saw a huge screwdriver on the floor of the car. I grabbed it and began forcefully goosing the revolutionary.

This got results and he moved in back of another car about

HILARIOUS HIGH JINKS

20 feet away. He began firing again and Bonillo and his group moved their fire toward him. Quickly loading my little family in the car, I broke the unofficial quarter mile record getting them back out to the main street. Bonillo Aybar and his friends managed to get down the back way of the hotel and escape down a cliff.

The caravan finally got started to San Cristobal and a quick survey showed that the only person killed in the melee was a Frenchman. I never did figure out how he got in the act.

The women and children were safely evacuated by helicopter. On the way back, I listened on the car radio as the revolutionaries ordered their people to capture all Americans and bring them downtown to rebel headquarters.

I was driving down Teniente Guerrero Street when I saw a road block ahead. I quickly counted nine men and only one was armed. He had a British Lancaster machine-pistol. This gun loads from the left side. The magazine holds 50 mm bullets and can be held by the shooter, thus cutting down tremendously on the recoil.

I had a .45 Colt semi-automatic pistol in my glove compartment, loaded with hollow-point bullets. I brought it out quickly and put it in my lap. The Communist rebels were waving me down and the man with the machine pistol had it aimed at my car.

I thought, "Now, if he's smart, he'll stand away from my car door, with the pistol aimed at me, and order me out of the car. If he isn't smart, he'll cradle the gun in the crook of his left arm, stick his head in the door and then order me out."

I held the .45 in my right hand, although I'm left handed, and placed it right at the bottom of the rolled down window.

He wasn't smart! He cradled the gun and stuck his head in.

"Venga aca," he said, "con sus manos arriba!" ("Come here with your hands up!")

I raised the .45 about four inches and shot him. As he fell, he hurled the Lancaster gun in front of my car. I saw one of the revolutionaries running for it and I put the gas pedal to the floor hoping to get to the next corner before he could retrieve the gun. Realizing he would get to the gun first, I aimed the car right at him, threw him up on the hood, over the top and back onto the trunk and he fell off the back end.

I made it to and around the first corner on two wheels and reached the American Embassy to find it under heavy attack. A couple of bullets hit the body of the car, but I got around behind the Embassy for concealment.

I told several of the Foreign Service people about my encounter at the road block and they advised me not to tell the Ambassador. "He'll have you out of here on the first plane," they told me. I took their advice.

CHAPTER THIRTY

HELP FROM THE 82ND AIRBORNE AND THE U.S. MARINES

With most of our Marine guards dead, our classified material burned and our Embassy full of employees who hadn't had their clothes off for six or seven days, Ambassador Bennett again called the President. He thought troops should be sent in, not only to save our Embassy and all its employees, but to save the little democracy of the Dominican Republic from going Communist.

President Johnson complied. He ordered the 82nd Airborne to leave their base in North Carolina immediately and for Admiral McCain to return to the area and put his Marines ashore by helicopter as quickly as possible. This meant an additional few days on the ships for our women and children, but they didn't seem to mind.

The 82nd Airborne arrived some 15 hours later in their huge C130 Hercules planes. They began their trek to the Ozama River bridge enroute to their objective, the embattled American Embassy. They arrived at the bridge and observed the two sugar cane trucks and the weapons protruding from the high-rise apartment building across the river. They moved up two, 106 mm recoilless rifles and completely destroyed the guns and the defenders in the apartment house. They then moved up an armor-plated bulldozer that pushed the trucks into the Ozama River and in about 15 minutes the entire 82nd was crossing the river and moving toward the American Embassy. They encountered a few snipers enroute, but quickly disposed of them and came marching down the street to the Embassy with their band out in front playing, "The Stars and Stripes Forever." They were joyously greeted by the most wretched, woebegone, patriotic group of Americans I have ever seen.

The Marines came the other way and met the 82nd at the Embassy. The plan was to move through the rebel zone to the sea wall. Had this been accomplished, the revolution would have been over in half a day with minimal loss of life.

However, when the 82nd came down from North Carolina, a group of East Coast newspaper reporters and television people were permitted to come in as well. Apparently they had already made up their minds who we should be backing in the revolution. Also, the Communists, through their "President," Francisco Caamano, explained to the media that they were trying to win the revolution in order to get Juan Bosch, a freely-elected President, back in as the legal head of the Government.

As a result, the banner headlines and copy in the Eastern papers stated that our Government was backing the wrong group in the Dominican Republic.

For whatever reason, the Johnson Administration changed the plan. The 82nd and the Marines were ordered to form a corridor across the city, thus blocking the revolutionaries in the Pueblo Nuevo section from the remainder of the city. This wasn't a very good operation as there were as many Communists on one side of the corridor as the other and the slaughter went on. The rebels had killed most of the police throughout the city, but they hadn't been able to get to Colonel Despradel Brache and his 500 Cascos Blancos.

Caamano kept up a solid barrage against the huge mahogany doors with all the weapons he could bring up. He finally telephoned Despradel.

"Manuel, come out of there with all your men or I'll send a group of rebels out to your newly-built home and blow it to pieces."

"Go ahead," Despradel told him. "When I get out of here, I'll blow yours up."

A few hours later, Caamano called him again. "I have blown up your house. Now I have your wife and if you don't come out now, I'll hurl her from the top of the cathedral."

Manuel told me later that this called for a very hard decision, but he thought of the fate of his 500 men if he agreed and he finally told Caamano, "Well, Francisco, go ahead. When I get out of here I will see to it personally that not only your wife but your children will be killed, too."

Caamano then laughed and told Despradel he was only joking, "But you'd better come out of there right now with all your people or we'll kill them all."

Finally, Colonel Despradel called me at the American Embassy. (It was an odd thing, the phones seemed to work well throughout the revolution...they never had before!) He stated that they had plenty of water to last for a long time, but that they had been completely out of food for four days. He said that if we could hustle up some C-rations from the Marines or the 82nd, he had a Dominican Air Force flyer who would make a pick-up, fly over the fortress, drop it off to the beleaguered Cascos Blancos and then skedaddle out of there before they could get the anti-aircraft guns on him.

I talked with a Marine colonel and he agreed to furnish the food. We were getting it together when Despradel called again. I could hear heavy gun fire and he told me it was too late; that the rebels had finally shot down the huge doors and were in their midst. He said most of the Cascos Blancos were dead and that a few of them were going out the back way and try to swim across the Ozama River. He said he was shot through the groin and that most of the men who were left alive were also wounded, but that they were going to try the swim, rather than surrender and face certain death.

That was the last we heard from Despradel until about 10 days later when he called from the hospital at the San Ysidro Air Base. He said that only a handful of his men had made the swim as the sharks, smelling the blood from the wounded men, had attacked and killed most of them before they could reach the banks of the river. Within a few days, Despradel was back in action against the Communists.

Captain Viriato Brito Pilier of the Dominican Secret Police was extremely busy all this time. He had several informants with whom he would meet late at night in the rebel zone and advise of all sorts of goings-on among the Communists. He was walking near the rebel headquarters about 2:00 a.m. when a Jeep, taken from two 82nd Airborne soldiers who were unlucky enough to get lost and stray down into the rebel zone, rolled up on him.

"That's him! Let's get him!" one of the two rebels said.

Captain Brito pulled a Browning automatic pistol from his belt and killed them both before they could get out of the car. He put one of the dead rebels in the passenger seat of the Jeep and the other he laid across the hood. About 2:30 a.m., the Marine guard on duty at the American Embassy summoned me saying I was wanted at the front of the Embassy. When I arrived, Captain Brito was standing there with his two dead rebels and the 82nd Airborne Jeep.

"What am I going to do with all this?" he asked with a big grin on his face.

I suggested he take the entire caboodle next door where the 82nd was headquartered and give it to them. "It's their Jeep," I reasoned. He promptly got in the Jeep and left.

Meanwhile, people of great importance began flying down to Santo Domingo with all sorts of plans to stop the revolution. McGeorge Bundy arrived, as did Cyrus Vance, ex-Ambassador John Bartlow Martin and even the local Papal Nuncio got in the act. None of their plans worked, however, and the killing went on. A 48-hour truce was called at one point in order to clear the dead bodies from the street and buildings. It was estimated that as many as 23,000 people were killed during the bloody six- to eight-week war.

Meantime, Antonio Imbert Barerra was the most frustrated man in the Dominican Republic. There he was, a General, but he did not have any troops under his command. He saw his way clear to change this situation. He began getting together all the police and army personnel available and wandered aimlessly around in the holocaust. He dressed them in fatigue uniforms, had them wear their caps backwards so they wouldn't shoot one another by mistake, and began a sweep from the Perla de Antilles Race Track toward the corridor, killing Communist rebels who were attempting to shoot their way through the 82nd Airborne and back to safety in Pueblo Nuevo.

About this time, Ambassador Bennett asked if my car still ran. I told him I thought it did and he said he'd like for Tony Ruize and me to take a couple of VIP's to the airport. We agreed and started down the corridor to the Ozama River bridge. On the way to the river, the fighting had become hot and heavy as homemade bread, what with the Communists trying to fight their way ahead of Imbert's terrible assault and through the 82nd's corridor. When we crossed the river and looked up the corridor, there wasn't a car moving. The street was filled with Jeeps and carryalls with Marines and soldiers under them, fighting for their lives.

We got out of the car and began surveying the situation when some rebels in the shot-out high-rise apartments began shooting at us. One of the bullets hit the side of my car.

"Holy cow! Any place else would be an improvement on this!" Tony said.

"I'm with you!" I told him. "Let's get the hell out of here!" We jumped in the car and began moving up the street.

As we moved along, we could see bullets throwing up

sparks where they were hitting the pavement and soon we got them through the side of the car. They sounded like sledge hammer blows.

I looked over at Tony and he had slipped down in the front seat to where he was practically sitting on his backbone with his eyes barely high enough to see over the bottom of the windshield.

"Get up, Tony!" I told him, "Raise up like a man!"

"Why should I?" he asked.

"There's nothing between me and those bullets at all," I told him, "with you all hunkered down like that!"

"To hell with you, Lee Boy!" he said, and as he grinned he got down a little lower.

When we finally made it to the American Embassy we had picked up eight bullets. As we entered the front door, Ambassador Bennett was walking up and down and we could see he had learned of General Imbert's move and was somewhat worried about us. He got a big grin on his face when he saw us.

"How did it go, Lee?" he asked.

"All right," I told him. "At least we made it back, but if you ever send me down that bloody corridor again, Mr. Ambassador, there are three things I want first."

"What are they?"

"First," I said, "I want a flak-jacket. Then I want a bottle of George Dickel whiskey. And thirdly, I want a hell of a lot more money!"

The newly-arrived Marines had taken over the Marine guard duty at the Embassy. They dug a lot of fox holes in the front yard and put a Marine in each of them. They had a big Marine gunnery sergeant and he'd walk among them, smacking them on the rump with a little stick to keep them down because of sniper fire.

On one occasion the gunnery sergeant and I were standing at the foot of the Embassy steps, watching a fire fight between a group of rebels and the Marines about two blocks away.

Suddenly, the Marine gunner grabbed his belly, bent over and looked at me.

"I got one!" he told me, And started unbuttoning his shirt.

I felt down inside his shirt and found a spent .45 bullet laying between his shirt and his belt. I showed it to him and he began squeezing his belly with both hands.

"What are you up to?" I asked him.

"I'm trying to get it to bleed," he said. "I'm going to get a Purple Heart out of this or die trying."

About this time, Ellsworth Bunker arrived. He was a sort of American roving ambassador and most of us felt he'd have no more success at stopping the war than the others, but he turned out to be a horse trader of a different stripe.

First, he began by telling General Wessin y Wessin that if he'd leave the country on a very important government assignment, that he would get Caamano to leave, too. He also told Wessin y Wessin that if this could be effected, he would set up an interim government suitable to both sides until a free election could be carried out. Wessin y Wessin agreed to this if the interim president was Garcia Godoy, whom he respected as an honorable man.

Then Bunker took his information to Francisco Caamano and his Communist advisors. They agreed and their plan would be to run Juan Bosch as President. With his victory, they would achieve their goal of taking over the country.

With both sides in agreement, General Wessin y Wessin went to the United Nations and Caamano to the Court of St. James in London as Military Attache. Other leaders on each side were also put out of the country on various diplomatic missions.

Garcia Godoy, as expected, held the Government together until the election. Juan Bosch returned from Puerto Rico to run for the presidency again. And Juan Balaguer, who had been the last President under Trujillo, returned from New York to run against him. Balaguer defeated Juan Bosch further than the Ostrogoths went into the Thuringian Forest, as the saying goes.

HILARIOUS HIGH JINKS

Meantime, Francisco Caamano apparently had been completely tarred with the Communist brush. He was tailed into Spain where he met with Communist leaders who had left Santo Domingo. The day after Che Guevara was killed by Army troops in the Bolivian mountains, Caamano disappeared from London and it was learned later he was flown to Cuba to train for the replacement of the dedicated revolutionary, Che Guevara.

This seemed rather amazing to me. A revolutionary such as Che Guevara had to be a man who could practically live off the land. Francisco Caamano couldn't fill that pattern. He was what is known among gourmands as one of their leaders. One time I had a party at my house for a group of high-ranking police officers and their wives. I had cooked up a huge pot of a local dish called *paella*. The ingredients, among other things, were rice, chicken, fish and pork. It had a helatious amount of spices and sauces and actually, even though it doesn't sound like it, it is pretty good fare.

I had it cooling off a little out in the kitchen while most of the guests were out on the patio dancing to a local merengue band. Caamano got to snooping in the kitchen and found it. I'll be damned if he didn't eat the whole thing and it was enough for about 12 guests, who were getting hungrier by the minute. Luckily, a chicken barbecue stand wasn't too far away, so I tore off down there and recouped my edibles.

I've often wondered how Castro could possibly expect an eater like Francisco Caamano to head up an insurgency unit that had to live off the land until they finally struck their blow.

When the terrible conflict finally settled down, Helen and Juanita came back. They'd been living on the beach at Santurce, Puerto Rico, with a real good girlfriend of Helen's and her little boy. While they were gone, I had our house filled with Dominican women and children. Some of them were widows and orphans of Dominican Secret Police who had been killed by the revolutionaries and some had their houses burned down because of their husbands' association with the police.

They were eventually able to find homes with relatives outside the capital.

Meanwhile, as most of the Cascos Blancos were killed, we began forming a new group within the Police Department. With the aid of a couple of experienced people from Washington, augmented by some Green Berets from Panama, we set up a counterinsurgency unit comprised of about 500 young, intelligent police officers. Within six months, they had accosted and killed three Cuban insurgency groups that had hidden in the mountains and begun recruiting men for another assault against the Government.

The Communists, as I had warned Caamano, didn't turn in any of the guns they had been supplied with when the revolution began. They buried them in various parts of the city, but the Police Department, using metal detectors borrowed from the 82nd Airborne, located most of the weapons.

The Agency for International Development went about the job of rebuilding the country. They brought in agricultural advisors who taught the farmers that they could grow a variety of winter vegetables and fruits for shipment to market in New York and not be dependent on a single crop of sugar cane. American money and know-how set up various commercial ventures that hired local help and soon the country was looking to many years of prosperity.

I remained in the Dominican Republic and worked with the police until the Spring of 1968, when I transferred to Washington, D.C. as a faculty member of the International Police Academy.

When Helen, Juanita and I flew out of Santo Domingo, there were more than 100 Dominicans from all walks of life out to see us off. There were laborers, housemaids, gardeners, police officers, lawyers, politicians...even the vice president was there to wish us well in our new venture.

At a going away party, a group of Foreign Service people presented me with a plaque. It was of native wood and had an

HILARIOUS HIGH JINKS

outline in a different colored wood of the Dominican Republic. There was a brass plate on the bottom of it that read:

"Wrestle a bear, tackle a puma...All else can be expected, from the Sheriff of Yuma!" I still have it in a prominent place in my den.

CHAPTER THIRTY-ONE
WIN, LOSE OR DRAW

We flew into Washington in March, 1968 and after getting ensconced in a hotel, began looking for a home. We were sure we didn't want to live in or near Washington. With my usual good luck, we met a CIA officer who had a beautiful split-level home in McLean, Virginia. He was being transferred to London within 10 days and we were able to lease his fine home for a two-year period.

We went around Virginia after we moved in looking for a horse for Juanita and we found a big grey gelding. He was a thoroughbred race horse, four years old, and he had run as both a two and three year old. He had won the unbelievable sum of $64 for his two years of racing and I believe he probably got most of that for pulling the water wagon around the track.

He could jump over a wooden fence about four feet high like a goosed milkmaid so we bought him for $300. We contacted a woman who agreed to teach Juanita the intricacies of English-style riding as practiced in the hunt country of Virginia and Maryland. This would keep Juanita busy for the next couple of years.

My job turned out to be exciting and interesting. Most of it was on the weapons range at the International Police Academy. The man I worked with was Ellis Lea, whom I had known and shot with for several years prior to World War II.

HILARIOUS HIGH JINKS

He had been a member of the West Virginia State Police Team. He enlisted in the Army when the War started and came out a Colonel. He had been running the weapons range at the Academy since it began in the mid 60's.

My other job at the Academy was lecturing to the various classes that had come for training from all over the free world. My lectures concerned counterinsurgency and how to form units to keep revolutionaries from taking over their countries.

This was fine as long as I lectured in English. But, when I tackled a class from Latin America and spoke to them in Spanish, it usually wound up with me being a prime subject for the loony bin since there were invariably five or six Brazilians who spoke Portuguese instead of Spanish. Somehow, a man who speaks Portuguese can understand Spanish quite well, but a Spanish speaking person can't understand a damn thing said in Portuguese. When I'd finish my talk, a Brazilian would always raise his hand and ask me a long question in Portuguese, all of which went over me like a mesquite bush over an undocumented alien.

I said earlier that there were very few Dominicans who could speak English. Francisco Caamano was one. Xavier Montez was another. He had gone to many schools in the United States and spoke English fluently. Xavier Montez was now going through the International Police Academy with a group of Dominican Police.

When a very interested Brazilian raised his hand at the end of one of my talks and went into a long harangue in Portuguese, I turned to Montez and asked, "What is he saying, Xavier?"

Montez looked at me a long time. "Echols," he finally said, "I don't have any idea what language he is speaking, let alone what the hell he is saying!"

I learned that when I finished a lecture in Spanish, my next move was to quietly, but quickly, step out the side door and disappear.

About a year after we'd lived in McLean, Virginia, Juanita

and her big gray horse graduated from riding school and she began entering competitions all over Virginia and Maryland. She won many trophies and medals and was invited on many fox hunts in Maryland.

The first one she attended got to be mighty funny. The big gray gelding, whose name was "Gay" something-or-other, somehow got the idea he was back on the race track again. The hounds started off, baying and yowling. Then came the master of the hunt in his bright red jacket. The fox hunters on their horses were to stay a defined distance behind as they careened through the Maryland countryside, jumping fences and creeks.

Gay didn't go for this at all. With Juanita trying to slow him down, he easily passed the other fox hunters. Then he lowered his head, closed his mouth on the bit so Juanita couldn't jerk him up, and took dead aim at the master of the hunt. He closed in and passed him, lengthened his stride and overtook the hounds. He was about to trample the fox to death by the time Juanita finally got him pulled up. He snorted and pawed as he waited for the other horsemen to appear, thinking that he had at least outrun the field and won the race.

Our two-year tour with the International Police Academy drew to a close and I began to look forward to one more assignment overseas, before I recomputed my retirement and went out with 38 years' service with the Government.

CHAPTER THIRTY-TWO

A MIGHTY ROUGH ASSIGNMENT IN URUGUAY

My good friend, Byron Engle, answered my overseas assignment wish by telling me he had a vacancy in the office of Public Safety in Montevideo, Uruguay. He wanted me to go but the AID Director didn't want any more public safety advisors. He wanted an agricultural advisor.

Byron resisted and the State Department backed him up. When Byron suggested me, the AID Director said I was too damned old. I was 62 years old at the time so Byron had me go through a complete physical check-up. The State Department doctors gave me an okay for a foreign assignment so the Director in Montevideo had to accept me.

I began reading up on the new assignment. Luckily, the Chief Public Safety Advisor in Uruguay was Dan Mitrione. He had been a member of the faculty of the International Police Academy and he was undoubtedly the best liked man on the staff. He was born in Italy and his parents brought him to Richmond, Indiana when he was two years old. He joined the Navy in World War II and served on a destroyer in the Pacific.

HILARIOUS HIGH JINKS

After the War, he joined the Richmond Police Force. He moved up through the ranks and became Chief of Police.

Dan went through the FBI Academy and, upon completion, applied to the Office of Public Safety. Byron hired him and, after a crash course in the Portuguese language, he went to Belo Horizonte and later to Rio de Janeiro, prior to returning as a faculty member of the International Police Academy.

Mitrione had gone down to Montevideo as Chief Police Advisor in 1969. He had two top advisors, Richard Biava, formerly of the Berkeley Police Department in California, and Richard Martinez, a fine officer from the San Antonio Police Department. I had known them both for several years. Things looked good for an enjoyable two years in Montevideo, Uruguay.

I had about two weeks to study the situation in Montevideo and it didn't look good. A gang of young Uruguayan revolutionaries who were university- educated anarchists and called themselves "Tupamaros" had decided to start taking over the country. There were about as many girls in the organization as men and they resorted to kidnappings, assassinations, bank robberies, assaults on Government installations and bombings.

Their organizer was a fiery-tongued young revolutionary named Raul Sendic, half Spanish, half Yugoslav. They were almost impossible to infiltrate since they used the Communist cell system. Whenever a young man or woman met up with a member of one of the small cells and expressed a desire to join them, he or she would be given a pistol and told to go kill a brother, uncle, or some close relative who was working for the Government. If the prospect refused to do this, chances were that person would be killed. They were completely dedicated, and loss of life, even their own, was of little consequence if the cause was furthered by death.

Aiding them in their mindless assaults was the fact that Uruguay was the most democratic and open society in Latin America at that time. The parliament was elected by popular vote. The Communist Party was recognized by the Government and had sufficient members in parliament to hinder the Government in its efforts to declare a state of emergency whereby police could search without warrants and interrogate prisoners without an attorney present.

In other words, the Tupamaros could violate every statute in the books but the Government had to proceed strictly by the law.

These were some of the things I was thinking about as Helen, Juanita and I flew out of Washington on July 4, 1970 for Montevideo, Uruguay.

CHAPTER THIRTY-THREE

THE DEADLY TUPAMARO TERRORISTS

When we arrived at the Montevideo Airport, Dan Mitrione, Dick Biava and Richard Martinez and their families were out to greet us. They put us in a hotel until we could find quarters.

I met with the public safety advisors in Dan's office the following day. One of my assignments would be to advise the investigative unit of the police on ways of stopping a wave of bank robberies. The Tupamaros were executing four or five each week, making off with between $50,000 and $80,000 in Uruguayan pesos at each bank.

All four of us were in accord that bank robberies by gangs are perpetrated in the same manner all over the world. Stolen cars are used, the bank is "cased" and the robbers dress in clothing that matches the customers'. They drive up to the front door and the "wheelman" awaits the robbers with the car engine running. The robbers enter the bank and the "tiger" moves to the middle of the bank and yells the orders. He usually has a shotgun or a submachine gun. The "bagmen" go behind the cages, scoop up the money into bags and flee. The "wheelman" takes off rapidly to the next stolen car located four or five blocks from the bank, where they jump into it with loot and weapons. Then they go to a third stolen car and drive it for about a mile. Finally, seeing no pursuit, they transfer to a "clean" car and leisurely drive to their rendezvous.

We dreamed up a plan to thwart the bank robbers. We wanted the chief of police to meet with all the bank managers in the city. If they would agree to foot the bill, he would have electronic devices installed in every bank, with alarm buttons on the floor that the employees could reach with their feet. When the employee steps on a button, a tape would start in the radio patrol room of the nearest police station, saying, "bank robbery in progress" and furnishing the address of the bank. The rest of our planning had to do with advising the police on detailed procedures for apprehending the robbers.

On the night of July 30th, we stayed late at the American Embassy discussing another police problem in Dan's office. Tupamaros and their sympathizers were sniping police officers from the tops of downtown buildings. Dan said he thought we should recommend that the officers get .22 caliber rifles with telescopic sights. I was all for shotguns using one-ounce slugs. I told Dan that a telescope on a shotgun made it the deadliest weapon in the world for knocking snipers off buildings.

"What if they are juveniles?" he asked. "A shotgun slug would kill them and a .22 bullet would only wound them, aimed properly."

"Well, Dan," I told him, "the way I look at it, if a juvenile is old enough to kill policemen from rooftops, he's surely old enough to get knocked off the roof with a ball that will do something to him besides make him mad!"

Dan didn't like it, though. We sat around the office with Dan smoking his inevitable pipe, his feet on his desk.

"We're a bunch of professionals, boys, and one thing for us all to remember is that we've had it if the Tupamaros ever grab any of us. The Uruguayan Government won't deal with them for a ransom demand and neither will our Government. The Department of State has issued a worldwide proclamation that our Government pays no ransom for the release of our people from kidnappers. And it's a good rule, too."

Dan refilled his pipe and got his feet into a more comfortable position on his desk. "If the U.S. Government ever paid a ransom one time, we'd have people kidnapped every few days all over the world!"

It's ironic that Dan talked like that. The following morning, Richard Martinez and his police driver arrived to pick me up at my apartment.

"They just got Dan," Richard said.

They had rammed him with a stolen truck about two blocks from his home and six to eight Tupamaros got out of two more cars parked nearby. They pistol-whipped his police driver and hustled Dan to a covered pick-up, beating him over the head with guns and cursing him in Spanish. They threw Dan into the bed of the pick-up and drove away.

We arrived at the Embassy to learn that in addition to the kidnapping of Dan Mitrione, the Tupamaros had also grabbed the Brazilian Consul General from his home and a Third Secretary of the American Embassy as he was getting ready to drive to the Embassy from his garage. They tied the Secretary in a blanket and threw him into the back of another stolen pick-up, but he was able to roll out of it onto the street, uninjured and free.

We set up a command post in the Embassy and manned it 24 hours a day. We telephoned Byron Engle in Washington, advised him of Dan's kidnapping and requested that he send two top public safety advisors immediately to give us a hand. Dave Arroyo and Pete Elena arrived late the following day.

Dave was a retired Lieutenant of Detectives from the Los Angeles Police Department and Pete was retired from the Pasadena Police Department. Both of them were well trained and experienced police officers who had many years in Latin America as public safety advisors.

A few days later, three Tupamaros walked into an Agriculture Extension Office and drove away with Dr. Claude Fly, an American agronomist.

HILARIOUS HIGH JINKS

Meantime, Uruguayan Police had located a meeting place for important members of the Tupamaros and had staked it out. They saw two men and a girl enter and went in with guns drawn. They arrested these three and identified them as high echelon members. One of them was the high cockalorum himself, Raul Sendic. The police held them in a back room and waited. Within a few minutes, two more men arrived and they were placed under arrest. One of them was Luis Greysing, known to have murdered five policemen. They captured eight Tupamaros at this meeting place and possibly could have caught more. However, one of the Tupamaros drew a pistol and the police had to shoot him. After this, they had to abandon the Tupamaros' hiding place.

Police found Dan Mitrione's watch on one of these prisoners and his passport in the coat pocket of one of the women.

Because of Uruguayan law, interrogation of these prisoners was impossible as police could not ask their names without an attorney and a doctor present—the lawyer to tell the prisoner that he didn't have to answer questions and the doctor to see that the prisoner was not harmed physically.

The following day the Tupamaros released a short note from Dan to his wife stating that although he had been shot, Tupamaro doctors were taking good care of his wound. He asked her not to worry and said that he loved her and the children and hoped to see them soon.

Two days later, the Tupamaros released a tape recording of an interrogation wherein one of their members who spoke English questioned Dan extensively. He accused Dan of training Brazilian police officers in torture methods to be used on prisoners, which, of course, Dan denied. He asked Dan about the Central Intelligence Agency and if Dan was a member of it. Dan said he wasn't and then he asked Dan to give him the names of CIA agents in Uruguay. Dan replied that he didn't believe there were any, and if there were, he didn't know them.

He then asked Dan what he knew about the FBI.

"Oh, I know a lot about them," Dan replied. "I went through their Academy near Washington a few years back and I belong to the FBI Academy Graduates Association."

Most revolutionary groups in Latin America believe that the Federal Bureau of Investigation sends investigators all over the Western Hemisphere to work against leftist movements. Nothing could be further from the truth. There are a few FBI agents in Latin America but they have strict orders not to engage in any investigations of a political nature. They operate solely as legal advisors to the embassies under the title of legal attaches and assist in such things as getting fugitives extradited to the U.S. for trial.

This interrogator, however, really thought he'd found something when Dan said he knew a lot about the FBI and that he'd graduated from their Academy. He questioned Dan at great length about this and it is believed that the Tupamaros thought they could show the world that Dan was, in truth, in Uruguay investigating them in his capacity as an FBI agent. This is undoubtedly the reason they released the tape, thinking they had an important secret agent in their net.

Dan was allowed to send another note to his wife and children and then on August 9, the Tupamaros released a demand to President Pacheco Areco that he either release 62 Tupamaros being held in prison or they would execute Dan Mitrione. As Dan had predicted, the President tersely dismissed the demand by stating publicly over radio and television that his regime didn't deal with outlaws. He said that every Tupamaro in prison was there because they were common criminals and not because of political beliefs.

So on the morning of August 10, Dan's 50th birthday, they bandaged his eyes, drugged him, tied his hands behind his back and took him out in a stolen Buick convertible. He was shot twice through the head and once through the back.

The horror of this cold-blooded deed covered the world and even the Communist Party of Uruguay denounced the Tupamaros as "insane fanatics." Moscow's *Pravda* described them as "petty bourgeois pseudo-revolutionaries" and "tollocking, loud-mouthed thugs, using gangster tactics."

After they'd murdered him, the Tupamaros tried to build up Dan Mitrione as a ruthless, calculating, deceitful man. They described him as an FBI super agent whose life work was that of installing repressive, semi-fascist regimes throughout Latin America, teaching advanced torture techniques and organizing a campaign of repression against "revolutionary" leaders.

Nobody believed it, though, and our Government immediately augmented the patrol of the Montevideo Police with 60 new radio cars. This almost doubled the patrol force and the Montevideo Police lost no time in getting the bank managers to install the electronic equipment to notify precinct police stations when a bank robbery was in progress. We also worked out inner and outer perimeter road block possibilities and it wasn't long before it was all prepared and ready.

Meantime, the Tupamaros released the Brazilian Consul General when his wife raised the $250,000 ransom demand.

When the next bank was hit by the Tupamaros gang, the robbery-in-progress message went to the precinct station. The first patrol car to arrive at the bank shot out the engine of the getaway car. They ordered the "wheelman" out and he complied quickly. They then barricaded themselves behind cars and awaited the robbers. There were six of them, four men and two women, and they came out shooting. The police killed two men and a woman and captured the rest.

Three days later another bank was attacked. Police cars were on it immediately and they captured the "wheelman" and four Tupamaros coming out of the bank.

Two weeks elapsed before the gang attempted another robbery. They needed about $40,000 a week to support their underground people, so the police knew it was about time for a hit. They tried a branch bank in the outskirts of Montevideo, but it didn't work, either. Four killed, three captured.

Meantime, Dan Mitrione had been replaced by Roy Driggers, a huge ex-Captain of the New Mexico State

Police. He came from Colombia, where he'd been stationed for several years.

We set up an intricate system of driving to the American Embassy from our homes. We never travelled the same route twice in succession, nor would we leave for work at the same time.

In addition, our official and personal automobiles were armor-plated with bullet proof windows. When Helen and I went to the market, she would drive and I would sit in the front seat armed with a riot shotgun. A trusted Montevideo police officer rode in the back seat with a 9 mm machine pistol.

After watching my wife do all the driving, he finally asked me if I could drive a car. I told him I was a fair driver, but that my wife was the world's worst shotgun shooter and that she'd probably shoot one of us if the Tupamaros attacked.

The Tupamaros had a vexatious habit of driving by a precinct police station in a stolen automobile and raking the front of it with machine gun fire, killing as many policemen as they could who were in front of the station.

Most of the police who guarded the front of these stations were armed with submachine guns. We talked them into changing to riot shotguns, loaded with number four buckshot. We advised them to build little cement houses called *garritas* at each precinct station, with a long slit where a shotgun barrel could emerge. Then when the Tupamaros came driving by and shooting, the man in the *garrita* could let them get within about 70 yards and with one shot, he could put everybody in the vehicle out of business. The Tupamaros had to quit this form of harassment quickly.

About this time, Dr. Claude Fly was dumped out of a stolen car near the British Hospital. He had suffered a heart attack in their so-called "people's prison."

After I'd been in Montevideo 20 months, the Tupamaros finally sighted in on me. Apparently they decided to build me up first. Their initial salvo in a leftist newspaper covered two full pages. They said that I directed all police investigations

HILARIOUS HIGH JINKS

against them and that I'd taken over where Dan Mitrione left off in teaching torture methods to the Montevideo Police.

This was followed a few days later by a more scathing article. This one stated that I had spent many years in Santiago, Chile, ostensibly as Chief of the U.S. Information Service, but actually, as a super spy, operating against the leftist movement. It stated that when I foresaw the defeat of the two rightist parties in Chile and the rise to power of the Frente Amplio and the Communist Salvador Allende, I was spirited out of Chile and sent to Vietnam from where I sent long reports to Latin America, trying to justify the U.S. presence in Southeast Asia. It went on to say that when Dan Mitrione was killed, I was brought to Uruguay to replace him, although I had no previous police experience. My main business in Uruguay was teaching rightist youths how to make gelatine dynamite bombs to kill little babies.

Actually, I had been in Santiago, Chile, three days in my entire life. That was in 1958 when I flew there from La Paz, Bolivia, where I was Chief Public Safety Advisor. And as far as Vietnam was concerned, the closest I'd been to that troubled country was Catalina Island off the coast of California, when I was working with Carl Eifler in OSS.

The American Ambassador, however, decided it might be better for me to go to the States for a while. The Chief of Police of Montevideo was being sent on a VIP tour of the larger police facilities in the United States and it was decided to send me along as interpreter and companion. The tour took three weeks and one of the places we visited was Richmond, Indiana, the home town of Dan Mitrione.

There we met his two brothers, his oldest daughter and the Richmond chief of police. We went to Dan's grave where the Montevideo Chief placed a large wreath in the name of his Uruguayan Police.

When we returned to Washington, I learned that the Department had decided to cancel the three months left on my Uruguay assignment. I was to be counsellor for a class of Latin

Americans who were arriving that week for three months' training at the International Police Academy.

I recomputed my retirement following that assignment. I had 22 years as a Special Agent with Customs, four years as a Naval Officer in World War II and 12 years with the Department of State. I went out with 38 years in the service of the United States Government.

CHAPTER THIRTY-FOUR

RETIREMENT? HARDLY!

The State Department gave Helen and me a big retirement party and a lot of people were there with whom I had worked all over the western world. The Dominican Ambassador was there and he gave us a case of Old Granddad whiskey. He made quite a presentation speech and told of the fine job I'd done during the 1965 revolution. In accepting it, I said that I didn't deserve such an approbation, but I'd had arthritis for 15 years and I damn sure didn't deserve that either, so this sort of evened things up.

We bought a new Cadillac in Washington and drove straight through to Chula Vista, California, where we intended to settle down. Settle down? I believe I've been as active since retirement, sometimes even more so, than ever before.

In the first place, we purchased a three bedroom condominium. When our household effects arrived from Montevideo, one of the men who was unpacking asked what I had been doing in Uruguay. I told him about my duty there.

"I'm a Lieutenant Commander in the Naval Reserve," he said. "We hold a school every two weeks on subversion at the Naval Headquarters in Coronado for Reserve Army colonels and Reserve Navy captains. Could we recruit you to talk to them about your Latin American experiences?"

And the next thing I knew, I was giving talks to the Navy.

HILARIOUS HIGH JINKS

The Navy captain who ran the school seemed to like my presentation and he told the director of a similar school at Eglin Air Force Base, Florida, about me. I began flying there once a month to lecture to the Air Force officers in the school at Eglin. When the Carter Administration took over, all the money for anti-subversion terrorist activity training was cut out and my work at Eglin and Coronado abruptly stopped.

Helen and I kept active. We went to Europe for six weeks with Jeff and Janice Richards. Switzerland was first and, as we explored that beautiful country, I couldn't help but think how fortunate I was that the Manhattan Project cracked the atom before that bedlamite of a Carl Eifler led me and my 10 men through Switzerland into Bavaria to kidnap the German scientist.

We proceeded to Bavaria on the railroad along beautiful Lake Constance and visited the castles built by such people as Mad King Ludwig. We flew to West Berlin and then to Vienna, where we saw everything from the Opera House to the beautiful white Lipizan horses at the Spanish Riding School.

Back in the States and I got busy writing articles for national magazines. Most of these were gun articles, western historical articles and even race horse articles. I had only been in the race horse business in a small way, but I had learned blood lines and could write about them well enough to have sold one article to *Sports Illustrated.*

About that time, my old friend Dave Phillips, who had been Chief of Station with the CIA in Santo Domingo, retired as Chief of the Western Hemisphere Section of the Central Intelligence Agency and formed the Association of Former Intelligence Officers.

Dave contacted Carl Eifler and me and told us he was forming this association to get before the public the dire necessity of having covert operations all over the world and the absolute necessity of keeping them secret.

By then, I had acquired another fine friend in the San Diego area, Don Perry, a retired Navy Commander who had been both a fighter-pilot and also an intelligence officer. Don, Carl Eifler and I got together and decided to form the first U.S. chapter of AFIO in San Diego.

We rounded up 19 people with intelligence background and held our first meeting. It didn't take long before we had a San Diego membership of over 150. By then, Dave and others were recruiting members throughout the country.

Naturally, most of the prospective members lived in the immediate vicinity of Washington, D.C. This was a help to the organization as so many of our top people were able to assist Congress in their difficult task of making decisions on matters of intelligence.

We were able to hold the 1978 national convention in the San Diego area at the old Hotel del Coronado. Don Perry was President of the local chapter and it turned out to be an excellent convention. They elected Perry as a member of the National Board of Directors and me the California State Chairman.

Don Perry introduced me to a young Coronado lawyer, Duncan Hunter, who was running for Congress in the 80th California District. He was running against a man who had been in office for 18 years, but Duncan didn't let that bother him. He frequented the shipyards and talked with the workers, met folks at the various big shopping centers and held fundraising barbecues. And that's where I fit in with his plans. He recruited me to put on exhibition pistol demonstrations before the huge crowds at these fundraisers. I had a portable backstop built and went through the typical set of pistol shooting acts.

I found that as I got older, I couldn't hold as true as when I was in my 30's, but I remedied that by shooting a little closer to the point of impact, which seemed to go unnoticed by the spectators. I would start off by breaking a few poker chips, then pieces of chalk and then I would split playing cards edgewise.

For my next little gem, I would ask for a watch from the

HILARIOUS HIGH JINKS

audience. This one had to be handled with care and required the help of at least three compatriots. We would pick out the victim well in advance and manage to get a good look at his watch. Then I would frequent jewelry stores in Chula Vista until I found an old clunker that looked very much like the watch of the intended victim. When I called for a watch from the audience, my compatriots would go after our pre-selected victim, snake the watch off his wrist and bring it up to me. He would usually accompany them, squawking like a limb-whipped victim, trying to get his watch back.

As they escorted him back to his seat, I would switch watches and fasten the old clunker to the backstop. Then I would explain over the microphone how we call shots according to the hour on the clock.

"For instance," I would say, "here's a one o'clock shot," and I'd fire one into that clock position.

Then I'd tell them, "Here's a nine o'clock one," and I'd shoot it at nine.

Then my third cohort would call out from the audience, "Lee, give us a *close* six o'clock shot!"

I'd get a fiendish grin on my face and reply, "Why, all right!"

I'd hit the damn thing right smack in the middle and the wheels, fulcrums and things would fly all over the audience.

Then I'd give a double-take and say, "I've done that shot about 50 times and this is the first time I've ever hit a man's watch. I feel that I should make restitution for it."

Then one of my plants would say, "Now we all know Lee didn't hit the man's watch on purpose and I feel the club (or in this case, the candidate) should pay for it."

The other man who had helped drag the victim up to me would say, "The way I look at it, if a man doesn't have any more sense than to let Lee Echols shoot at his watch, then let him pay for it himself."

I would study this logic, but not for long, and then I'd say, "Well, that suits me," and I'd go on with the exhibition, leaving the victim on the hook for about 10 minutes before I'd call him up and give him his watch back.

In the case of Duncan Hunter's fundraiser, we picked his father, R.O. Hunter, for the victim. He'd just bought a beautiful gold wristwatch with an alligator skin band. I found a worn-out watch that looked a great deal like it and I purchased an alligator skin band to go with it. Don Perry and the old, world-famous bronco rider, Casey Tibbs, were the men to skin the watch off his wrist and he fought them like a Punjab tiger. I fastened the worn out watch to the backstop and sighted in on it and we went through our act.

Following our quick talkfest about who would pay for it, the elder Hunter finally told me, "I've a good mind to go home, get my pistol and shoot *your* damned watch!"

I told him, "Now, that makes a lot of sense, R.O., but it has one terrible flaw in it."

"What's that?" he wanted to know.

"Why!" I told him, "I'm entirely too smart to let you shoot at my watch!"

Then I put an axe blade on the backstop with the blade toward me, and a clay pigeon on each side of the blade and fired a flat-nosed wadcutter bullet at the blade, splitting the bullet and breaking both the clay pigeons. This is a spectacular-looking shot, but it's like splitting playing cards edgewise. You're not shooting at something the width of the axe blade, but at something twice the width of a .38 bullet. And after the "Oh's" and "Ah's" were over, I ceremoniously gave Mr. Hunter his watch back, in excellent condition!

But to get back to our AFIO operations, Don Perry and I finally formed five chapters between San Diego and San Francisco. We also formed one in Arizona and another in New Mexico. We got a lot of help with the Arizona and New Mexico chapters from George Wiggins in Yuma and Adolf Saenz of Albuquerque. In 1982 I was elected to the National Board of Directors of AFIO. That year the National Convention was held in San Diego.

HILARIOUS HIGH JINKS

The next two conventions were held in the beautiful Crown Plaza Hotel in Rockville, Maryland. Don Perry and I attended them both. Along with getting a lot accomplished at these conventions, we always had a great time meeting friends known through the long years of service.

As usual, I would live up to my reputation of throwing the long loop, as my cow-country ancestors used to say. At the 1985 convention, a group of us gathered in the hospitality room after a day of speeches and briefings. I started telling them about my activities as western Field Manager for the National Rifle Association.

"I spent quite a bit of my time at the Los Angeles Police pistol range in the late 40's," I told them. "There were quite a few Class B movie actors and aspirants there, all of whom were either playing in or trying to get a part in western movies. They were anxious to improve themselves in handling handguns in order to look good on film.

"There was one man there who introduced himself to me. 'I am Ronald Reagan,' he said with a big smile, 'and as I hear you were the National Individual Pistol Champion back in 1941 I sure would like your help and some pointers on pistol handling and shooting so I won't look like they just handed me my first gun when I'm in the movie!'

"Well, I did indeed give him some advice and instruction on handling pistols and the rudiments of shooting them," I said.

I could see there were some skeptics in the group, but I went right on with my story.

"Then a few years ago I began putting on exhibition shoots for Congressman Duncan Hunter at his fundraising barbecues. At a breakfast given by President Reagan, Duncan related my exploits with a pistol. The President said, 'My God, Duncan! He taught me how to shoot back in 1947! Is there any way you could get him to come up to the ranch when Nancy and I are there and put on a demonstration for our guests and the Secret Service?'

"Well," I continued, "it was arranged and I spent a weekend

with the Reagans and just had the time of my life. They all enjoyed the exhibition very much."

I could see that a few of the listeners were about ready to start throwing lemons and olives at me from the bar and that's when I played my trump card.

"By the way," I said, with a look on my face like a hoptoad full of mint julep worms, "here's a picture I got from the White House a couple of days before I left California."

I passed around a photo of President Reagan and me standing in a yard with a big red barn behind us. He had one arm around my shoulder and was waving the other one. Around the edges of the picture was written, "To Lee Boy...come back to the ranch! Bring your pistols!" It was signed, "Ronald Reagan."

Well, that put a stop to the doubting Thomases. I didn't get around to telling them about the camera shop in Seaport Village on San Diego Bay where there is a life-size photo of Ronald Reagan. For $5, you get your picture taken with the President that looks so authentic you almost begin believing it yourself.

Actually, I've never been closer to Ronald Reagan than I have to Muammar Qaddafi.

In the Rio Grande Valley of Texas, about 80 miles down the Rio Grande River from Laredo, there used to be a night club with a huge, red neon sign that ran clear across the roof. You could see it from miles away and it read:

"YOU CAN'T BEAT FUN"

I have been an adamant follower of that philosophy my entire, active life while pursuing *HILARIOUS HIGH JINKS AND DANGEROUS ASSIGNMENTS.*